# Lecture Notes in Artificial Intel

Subseries of Lecture Notes in Computer Sci
Edited by J. G. Carbonell and J. Siekmann

# Lecture Notes in Computer Science

Edited by G. Goos, J. Hartmanis and J. van Leeuwen

**Springer**
*Berlin*
*Heidelberg*
*New York*
*Barcelona*
*Hong Kong*
*London*
*Milan*
*Paris*
*Singapore*
*Tokyo*

Jürgen Lind

# Iterative
# Software Engineering
# for Multiagent Systems

## The MASSIVE Method

Springer

Series Editors

Jaime G. Carbonell,Carnegie Mellon University, Pittsburgh, PA, USA
Jörg Siekmann, University of Saarland, Saarbrücken, Germany

Author

Jürgen Lind
iteratec GmbH
Inselkammerstr. 4, 82008 Unterhaching, Germany
E-mail: Juergen.Lind@iteratec.de

Cataloging-in-Publication Data applied for

Die Deutsche Bibliothek - CIP-Einheitsaufnahme

Lind, Jürgen:
Iterative software engineering for multiagent systems : the MASSIVE
method / Jürgen Lind. - Berlin ; Heidelberg ; New York ; Barcelona ;
Hong Kong ; London ; Milan ; Paris ; Singapore ; Tokyo : Springer, 2001
(Lecture notes in computer science ; 1994 : Lecture notes in
    artificial intelligence)
    ISBN 3-540-42166-1

CR Subject Classification (1998): I.2.11, D.2, I.2, C.2.4, D.1

ISBN 3-540-42166-1 Springer-Verlag Berlin Heidelberg New York

Springer-Verlag Berlin Heidelberg New York
a member of BertelsmannSpringer Science+Business Media GmbH

http://www.springer.de

© Springer-Verlag Berlin Heidelberg 2001
Printed in Germany

Typesetting: Camera-ready by author, data conversion by Boller Mediendesign
Printed on acid-free paper     SPIN 10782125     06/3142     5 4 3 2 1 0

# Foreword

Agent-based techniques are beginning to be used to develop a wide range of commercial and industrial applications. This take up is occurring because the agent-based approach offers a natural and powerful means of conceptualising, designing and building complex, distributed systems. The key conceptual components from which this new approach to software engineering derives its power are: (i) the autonomous components (agents) that can achieve their objectives in flexible ways; (ii) the high-level interactions (e.g., cooperation, coordination and negotiation) in which these agents can engage; and (iii) the organisational structures (e.g., teams, coalitions and various forms of hierarchy) into which the agents can arrange themselves. When taken together, the agents represent the application's basic units of computation, the interactions represent the inter-connections between these units and the organisational structures define the way the components relate to one another.

Although the agent-based approach appears to offer a promising new paradigm for building complex distributed systems, to date, the majority of the agent-based applications that have been developed have been built by researchers who specialise in agent-based computing. However, if agent-based computing is to become anything more than a niche technology practised by the few, then the base of people who can successfully use the approach needs to be broadened. A crucial step in this broadening endeavour is to find mechanisms by which professional software engineers can gain access to the philosophy, the concepts and the methods of agent-based computing without having to immerse themselves in the research community. Perhaps the key mechanism for achieving this is to develop methodologies for agent-oriented software engineering. Such methodologies should assist developers in the analysis, design and development of their application; particularly, they should identify the key steps that are involved, the key models that need to be built at the various steps, and how the different models and stages relate to one another.

Against this background, this book, *The MASSIVE Method: Software Engineering for Multiagent Systems*, presents one of the first coherent attempts to develop such a methodology for a broad class of agent-based systems. In particular, it provides a clear introduction to the key issues in the field of agent-oriented software engineering and provides a comprehensive overview of the state of the art. It then describes and illustrates the application of the MASSIVE methodology to a number of real-world applications. When taken together, these components make the book an important contribution to the fledgling field of agent-oriented software engineering and, as such, essential reading for both researchers and practitioners alike.

August 2000                                                    Nick Jennings

# Contents

# List of Figures

# List of Process Models

*Our ability to imagine complex applications will always exceed our ability to develop them.*

*Grady Booch*

# 1. ntroduction

Although agents and agent-based computing have been an active research area for many years, it is only until now that these topics begin to gain industrial relevance: agent technology is beeing recognized as a powerful tool for the development of large and complex systems. These days, typical software architectures contain many dynamically interacting components, each with their own thread of control and engage in complex coordination protocols [Ciancarini and Wooldridge, 2000]. Therefore, a new programming metaphor that captures these systems is needed. Although the basic structural elements of the agent-based approach as well as their connections are not yet fully understood, it nonetheless seems to be a promising means for dealing with these highly complex systems.

However, although the agent-oriented view is likely to become a major tool to describe complex software systems, development methods, i.e. methods that provide guidelines how to build actual agent-based applications or multiagent systems, are still in their infancy and must be more advanced in order to establish the technology in an industrial context. [Parunak, 1999b], for example, claims that "Relatively less attention has been paid to the important question of the process that designers go through. Industrial users will use agents more readily if basic principles and guidelines are available ...". The strong need for agent and agent systems development methods in industry is exemplified by the major European telecommunication companies that have launched a joint research project to foster the definition of a development method for agent applications [EURESCOM, 1999]. Furthermore, the engineering topic of agents and multiagent systems is not only a technical matter that has been picked up by industry, it is also an interesting research field that can provide new methods and techniques for a better understanding and modeling of highly complex systems [Wooldridge, 1997], [Jennings et al., 1998], [Jennings, 1999].

It has long been recognized in the Software Engineering community that a software development method for a particular application domain must be tailored towards the characteristic needs of this domain [Basili, 1989], [Basili et al., 1994] as there is no "silver bullet" [Brooks, 1986], i.e. a method that can be used for all types of problems. To illustrate the idea, consider the following scenario from the home improvement domain: any of us has at

J. Lind: The MASSIVE Method, LNAI 1994, pp. 1-7, 2001.

one time or another used a screwdriver to drill a hole – either because there was no other tool available or, more likely, because we were to lazy to get a drill machine. However, whereas using a screwdriver will work for materials such as wood, it is likely to fail for, e.g. concrete. Even worse, the outcome of the process with an inadequate tool will normally be worse then using the better tool right away. Hence, returning to the topic of this volume, what we need is a software development method that is specifically designed for multiagent applications in order to achieve the best possible outcome of a software project using this technology.

It is the goal of this volume to provide such a development method that allows for a better understanding and modeling of multiagent systems and that is a step towards industrial needs for clearly specified product and process models that can be readily used by software engineers. Software Engineering methods, however, are often a very individual matter that vary greatly over people, organizations and projects. Hence, this book is not trying to define the silver bullet for multiagent applications (as this is likely not to exists as stated above) but it is rather a collection of practices that have shown to be working in real software development projects and from which the readers can choose those that fit their personal needs and requirements.

Probably the hardest problem in designing a development method for multiagent systems is to define its scope. Neither should it be too specific in that it covers only a small fraction of multiagent applications, nor should it be too general because unrelated details make the method less useful in the specific context. Although there is no generally agreed definition for the term "multiagent system" the different characterizations that have been proposed, e.g. [Gasser, 1995], [O'Hare and Jennings, 1996] [Goodwin, 1993], [Fulbright and Stephens, 1994]      [Franklin and Graesser, 1997]      and [Wooldridge and Jennings, 1998] share the basic ideas and assumptions. The smallest common denominator is that multiagent systems are systems with a variable number of interacting, autonomous entities that communicate with each other using flexible, complex protocols. The agents within a multiagent system usually have complex individual components and act concurrently in a distributed environment. This characterization of the term "multiagent system" suggests that applications that are built on this concept are far from being easy to design. More specifically, multiagent systems are usually complex, decentralized systems that are often ill-structured but on the other hand have the desirable properties of being modular and changeable [Parunak, 1999b]. Thus we want a general software development method that supports the development of systems with these specific properties.

According to [Booch, 1996], a software development method encompasses a *notation*, whose purpose is to provide a common means of expressing strategic and tactical decisions, ultimately manifesting themselves in a variety of artifacts and a *process*, responsible for specifying how and when certain artifacts should be produced. The notation serves as the language for communicating decisions that are not obvious or cannot be inferred from the code itself. It provides rich enough semantics sufficient to capture all important strategic and tactical decisions and it offers a concrete form for humans to reason about decisions. Besides this general characterization, an ideal development method should exhibit some additional properties such that it can be used for a broad range of multiagent application projects. Now, what does this mean?

First, the method should not be committed to a particular technology, e.g. to a specific platform, agent technology or agent architecture such as BDI agents [Rao and Georgeff, 1995] or to a certain software development process model. Also, it should be possible to adapt the method to the particular needs of the organization that is using it and to the specific project in which it is applied. Thus, it should be possible to selectively pick parts of the method that are considered useful in a particular situation without having to use potentially unnecessary parts as well. This kind of modularity is probably one of the most important features of a method that can be widely accepted. Furthermore, the method should be simple in that it is straightforward to use and does not require extensive training for the user of the method. The simpler it is, the better it will be accepted in the multiagent systems community. A good means to achieve this goal is to provide a set of core ideas that can be used directly and to reserve more complicated features of the method to the experienced user. However, there is a thin border line between "simple" and "trivial" and thus it must be the goal to make the method "as simple as possible, but not simpler" (Albert Einstein).

Another important property is that the method must be applicable in a wide variety of development environments. For example, it should not be limited to a particular programming paradigm (e.g. object-oriented programming) or even a particular programming language (e.g. Java). Instead, the method must allow the user to maintain his or her development environment as far as possible and it must be changeable according to specific user requirements.

Furthermore, the method should be scalable in order to be applicable to development problems of almost any size, ranging from small, single person projects up to large, industrial projects. An important aspect that must be considered in the development of a design method is that it should enable the designer or – even better – the organization as a whole to represent and preserve any kind of knowledge that was obtained during the project execution and to transfer this knowledge over project boundaries in order to support knowledge reuse. An overemphasis on originality can easily lead to the re-invention of the wheel and this is likely to repeat mistakes that were already made by other designers and could be avoided [Parnas, 1996]. Ideally, the institutional framework that is needed to establish such a project framework should be small and allow the organization to introduce the scheme with as few impact on the ongoing business processes as possible. The last requirement, finally, is that the design method for multiagent system should be clearly related to existing Software Engineering approaches. Thus, we do not want a method that operates in "free space" without making use of the benefits of software engineering research. Instead, we want a method that operates within a standard software engineering context.

The approach presented in this book has evolved over several years and it has been successfully applied and refined in different types of multiagent systems: The multiagent solution for the Train Coupling- and Sharing (TCS) approach [Voges and Mierau, 1997], [Lind and Fischer, 1998], [Lind and Böcker, 1999], [Lind et al., 1999b], [Lind et al., 1999a] is a system for scheduling and cost optimization of a large number of railroad transportation tasks using novel railroad technologies. The re-organization of the traditional freight transport would require some major investments by the railroad companies and thus the potential of this idea must be carefully investigated in a simulation. The TCS project was funded by the Deutsche Bahn AG in order to evaluate the potential savings that could result from the novel approach. Multiagent systems are particularly well suited for the transportation domain because of its inherent complexity and natural degree of distribution [Fischer et al., 1993] and there is active research in this area [Fischer et al., 1994], [Fischer and Müller, 1995], [Kuhn et al., 1994].

The TEAMWORK LIBRARY [Denzinger, 1994], [Lind, 1996a], [Denzinger and Lind, 1996] is a framework for distributed search that was originally developed for equational theorem proving but that was also used in other application fields [Kögl, 1995], [Leopold, 1995].

The MoTi / T project was initiated by the Bavarian local government as part of AYERNIN O [Bayrische Landesregierung, 1996] and is concerned with the design of a **P**ersonal **T**rip **A**ssitant (PTA) for individual travelers. One of the services required in the PTA domain is intermodal route planning for which a multiagent solution has been implemented [Siemens AG, 1997] according to the FIPA [FIPA, 1997] [FIPA, 1998] standards.

In the course of this book, I will frequently use the TCS project to illustrate the proposed method and how it is applied in a real-world application; the other projects are reviewed in an separate chapter at the end of the book. This book is organized as follows.

**Chapter 2** In this chapter, I will outline the basic characteristics of intelligent agents and multiagent systems (MAS) and their relation to Software Engineering issues. I will start with an introduction to intelligent agents from a very general point-of-view and then extend the single-agent case to systems with several intelligent agents. After the general introduction, I will then briefly discuss some related research fields and provide a personal view on various topics of a relatively new research field called "agent-oriented software engineering".

**Chapter 3** The software development method that is presented in this book is built upon a number of standard Software Engineering concepts and combines them effectively into a single, coherent model. In this chapter, I will introduce these basic concepts and their relationships by starting with an investigation of a cognitive model of design in general. From this general model, I will derive some basic skills that are essential for a successful software engineer and I will outline some requirements for software engineering tools and methods that follow from these considerations.
After these general remarks, I shall then introduce a general model of software engineering and explain the individual parts of this model. The rest of this chapter is dedicated to an extensive discussion of software engineering process models.

**Chapter 4** The ideas and concepts of Chapter 3 constitute the basis of general Software Engineering methods which will be refined for the particular case of multiagent system development in this chapter. To this end, I will explain how the basic concepts and ideas of the MASSIVE[1] method are derived from them and how the resulting building blocks are assembled into a coherent method that can be used to develop multiagent applications.

**Chapter 5** The product model of MASSIVE is the core of the entire method. It allows the system designer to break the target system down into several views that concentrate on particular aspects of the system and abstract away from others. In Chapter 5, we will at first discuss the general nature and the intended scope of a view as well as a number of features and design patterns that belong to a view. The general considerations are applied to a case study in order to demonstrate how the theoretical concepts are used in a practical situation.

**Chapter 6** A development method will never be accepted in an industrial context if it cannot prove its validity in practice. The MASSIVE method is not a method that was developed in the laboratory and then transfered to actual projects. Rather it is derived from projects that were successfully carried out at the DFKI and elsewhere and that were analyzed after completion in order to find similarities in the product and process models. The advantage of this approach is that it provides further case studies that show how the method works and that demonstrate that the method can be used for a broad range of multiagent applications.

---

[1] Multi**A**gent **S**ystem**S** **I**terative **V**iew **E**ngineering

## Acknowledgments

Writing a book about Software Engineering is tough as I have rarely experienced the difference between academia and industry more sharply then in this field of Computer Science. While scientific researchers somtimes try to solve problems of the "real world" that do not exist there, industrial software engineers on the other hand mechanically reject results from academia as beeing only useful in the "ivory tower" they have been developed in. Therefore, I am thankful to all people that have contributed to this book and tried to help me to bridge this gap.

First of all, I thank the head of the Department for Deduction and Multi-agent Systems, Jörg Siekmann, for stimulating my interest in Artificial Intelligence and for guiding me through the rough ways of writing this book. His immense knowledge and experience were a steady source of inspiration and our fruitful discussions helped my to bring my ideas into the present form.

I am also grateful to Nick Jennings who contributed more to this book then he may be aware of. Not only that he is one of leading researchers in the field of multiagent technology but he is also the scientific advisor of the Multiagent Systems group of the DFKI. Therefore, I often asked myself while working on particular parts of MASSIVE how I could present these idea to him at the next meeting of the scientific advisory board. This helped me greatly to improve the structure and the quality of this book.

Furthermore, I thank the people at the Multiagent systems research group of the DFKI: Steve Allen, Thorsten Bohnenberger, Hans-JürgenBürckert, Alastair Burt, Klaus Fischer, Petra Funk, Andreas Gerber, Christian Gerber, Christoph Jung, Matthias Klusch, Michael Rovatsos, Christian Russ, Michael Schillo, Gero Vierke, and Ingo Zinnikus. I also thank the Omegas, the VSE people and the staff at the AGS for the pleasant working atmosphere during the last four years. Also from DFKI, Christian Schulte and Ralf Scheidhauer from the Programming Systems Lab deserve some special acknowledgments for teaching me the bright sides of Oz. During a short term research fellowship at BT's Adastral Park Labs, I had the opportunity to discuss aspects of my work with the people of the Intelligent Business Systems Research group. Paul Kearney, Divine Ndumu, Brian Odgers, Simon Thompson, Matt Sullivan and Paul O'Brien helped my a great deal by pointing out matters that needed further clarification.

Also, I thank Joachim Hertel from SAP Retail for teaching me a more practical view onto the software development process and the problems within an industrial environment. These hints and tips are becoming more and more useful to me as I am now working as a full-time software architect in an industrially productive environment at iteratec. I would like to thank all the people there for broadening my horizon during the past few months.

In the industrial and research projects within the last four years, I worked with many people from different areas. In the TCS project, these were Jörg Böckers from the IVE and Bernd Zirkler, Wolfgang Voges and Ulrich Mierau from the Deutsche Bahn AG. The MoTiV-PTA project was a collaboration between the DFKI and Siemens AG where I worked with Donald Steiner, Hartmut Dieterich, Berhard Bauer and Gerd Völksen. The Teamwork library, finally, was built at the University of Kaiserslautern in collaboration with Jörg Denzinger and others at the department for Rewriting Systems. I am also indebted to my friend and colleague Alexander Knecht for the countless discussions during that time, especially about "agents vs. objects" but also for the philosophical explorations of the essence of programming.

Finally, I thank my family and my friends for their support throughout my entire carreer.

# 2. Agents, Multi gent S stems  nd Softw re Engineering

In this chapter, I will outline the basic characteristics of intelligent agents and multiagent systems (MAS) and their relation to Software Engineering issues. I will start with an introduction to intelligent agents and then extend the single-agent case to systems with several intelligent agents. The basic concepts are still presented from a very general point-of-view and will be refined in subsequent chapters; the reader already familiar with MAS may safely skip this chapter and continue with chapter 3; a more thorough introduction to the field for the unfamiliar reader can be found in [Weiss, 1999]. After the general introduction, I will then briefly discuss some related research fields and finally provide a personal view on various topics of the relatively new research field of "agent-oriented software engineering" [Jennings et al., 1998].

## 2.1  ntelligent Agents

In this section, I will introduce the basic ideas of intelligent agents at a rather high level of abstraction. The main aspect of this introduction is its use of a very general notation scheme for the description of agents in order to be independent of any particular agent school.

### 2.1.1 What's an Agent, anyway?

Answering this question, which was first asked in [Foner, 1993], is far beyond of the scope of this book as there exist roughly as many definitions of the term as there exist researchers in the field — or perhaps even more. Therefore, I will use a notion of agency that is widely accepted because it covers almost any of the more specific definitions and is therefore not suspicious of being too much biased. Basically, an agent is a software system that is situated in an environment and that operates in a continuous *Perceive-Reason-Act (PRA)* cycle as depicted in Figure 2.1. Thus, the agent receives some stimulus from the environment and processes this stimulus with its perceptual apparatus. Next the agent starts a reasoning process that combines the newly incorporated information and the agents existing knowledge and goals and this then determines possible actions of the agent. One of these possible actions is then

J. Lind: The MASSIVE Method, LNAI 1994, pp. 9-33, 2001.

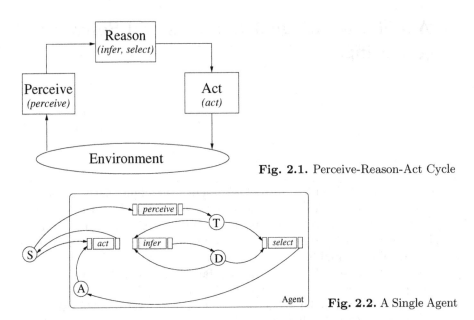

**Fig. 2.1.** Perceive-Reason-Act Cycle

**Fig. 2.2.** A Single Agent

selected and executed by the agent. The action activation changes the state of the environment which in turn generates new perceptions for the next cycle.

This cycle was already introduced in [Genesereth and Nilsson, 1987] and it is also used in [Russell and Norvig, 1995]. To capture the basic PRA cycle more concisely and formally, we introduce the following notation that is oriented at the formalism used in [Genesereth and Nilsson, 1987]. One of the basic assumptions in the above description about agents is that they are situated in some environment. Let us denote this environment by $\mathbf{S}$ as a set of external states without imposing any constraints on the structure of the elements in the set. Then, we can describe an agent as a 7-tuple $\langle \mathbf{D}, \mathbf{T}, \mathbf{A}, \mathit{perceive}, \mathit{infer}, \mathit{select}, \mathit{act} \rangle$ where $\mathbf{D}$ is a database that contains the agent's acquired knowledge, a set $\mathbf{T}$ of partitions of the environment $\mathbf{S}$ which constitute the possible perceptions of the agent and a set $\mathbf{A}$ of possible actions of the agent. An agent is then defined by the following four functions. The $\mathit{perceive} : \mathbf{S} \to \mathbf{T}$ function determines how the state of the environment is perceived by the agent, i.e. it limits the amount of information that is provided to a partial view on the complete state. The $\mathit{infer} : \mathbf{D} \times \mathbf{T} \to \mathbf{D}$ function is used by the agent to update its internal knowledge base according to the newly received perceptions. The $\mathit{select} : \mathbf{D} \times \mathbf{T} \to \mathbf{A}$ function is then used to determine the best action for the current cycle and the $\mathit{act} : \mathbf{A} \times \mathbf{S} \to \mathbf{S}$ function, finally, changes the state of the environment accordingly. In Figure 2.2, I have depicted an agent that consists of these components and the information flow between them.

To illustrate the ideas that are captured in this rather simple model, consider an automated container terminal where a robot has the task to

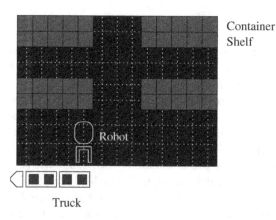

Container
Shelf

**Fig. 2.3.** A Container Stock Area

Truck

unload incoming containers from trucks and to store them on shelves in the storage area. Figure 2.3 shows such a facility with several shelves, one robot and a truck that has just delivered some containers that must be unloaded.

Using the abstract description scheme given above, the scenario is modeled as follows. The environment **S** of the agent (robot) is a grid world with labeled objects on grid locations, the possible actions **A** of the agent are pick_container, drive_to_location and drop_container, the robot's perception **T** is the content of the field in front of the robot and the knowledge base **D** of the agent, finally, contains the destination of each container that is delivered by a truck container.

The Perceive-Reason-Act cycle of the agent is started when the *perceive* function of the agent determines the presence of newly arrived containers in front of the robot (assuming that the default waiting position of the robot is at the container ramp of the terminal). Then, the *infer* function decides that the only possible action is to pick up a container which is consequently scheduled for execution by the *select* function and finally executed by the *act* function of the robot. As a result of this action, the state of the environment changes (because the robot is now holding a container) and thus the next PRS cycle is started in which the robot will determine the destination of the container and bring it into the storage area.

In this example, the problem solving capabilities that are necessary in the problem domain are directly associated with the agent. This concept, however, has sometimes shown to be too restrictive and it is becoming more accepted now that an intermediate concept that de-couples the agent from its associated problem solving capabilities adds clarity to the modeling process [Kendall, 1998a]. This intermediate concept is called a "role" and it is discussed in the next section.

## 2.1.2 Roles

What is a role? Unfortunately, this question has no straightforward answer as there exist several definitions of the "role" concept in the agent research community that differ mainly in their focus on generic properties.

A very general definition is given in [Sundermeyer, 1993] where a role is seen as a primary sociological concept that must be operationalized for the context of agent systems. Thus the question of what is a role cannot be defined in a general fashion but needs the context in which it is to be used. A more specific definition for a role is presented in [Weiss, 1999] where a role is "The functional or social part which an agent, embedded in a multi-agent environment, plays in a (joint) process like problem solving, planning or learning. ...". [Werner, 1989], on the other hand, limits the concept of a role to purely cognitive states that are defined by the knowledge, the permissions, the responsibilities and the assessment of the agents current situative context.

Probably the best idea to work on a broad definition that is still useful is to start in the field of sociology as suggested in [Sundermeyer, 1993]. In [Bahrdt, 1994], the major characteristics of a role are given as follows:

- A role is a collection of expectations towards the behavior of the inhibitor of a particular position that allows the members of the society to predict the inhibitors behavior and to plan according to their expectations.
- There exist mutual dependencies between roles, some roles can only exist if other roles do exist as well, for example the role of a "teacher" only makes sense if the corresponding role of (at least one) "pupil" exists as well.
- A member of a society can play several roles even at the same time. This property is called *role multiplicity* and can lead to so-called *role conflicts*.

A major problem in the field of sociology is the delimitation of roles that occur within a society. Not every set of coherent behavior can be regarded as a role, there must exist some special properties that make such a set a role. In developing agent applications, the system designer is faced with a similar problem in identifying coherent sets of behaviors that can be grouped together to form the roles that occur in the problem domain. However, I will postpone this problem to Section 5.4 where I will discuss my approach to solving it and instead continue with the more abstract view on agents that we begun with earlier in this chapter.

Formally speaking, the concept of a role is modeled as an extension of the agents current knowledge, the possible actions and the *perceive, infer, select* and *act* functions. Thus, agents that can play several roles from a set of roles $\mathbf{R}$ are described by the 7-tuple $\langle \mathbf{D} \cup \mathbf{D}_r, \mathbf{T}, \mathbf{A} \cup \mathbf{A}_r, \textit{perceive} \cup \textit{perceive}_r, \textit{infer} \cup \textit{infer}_r, \textit{select} \cup \textit{select}_r, \textit{act} \cup \textit{act}_r \rangle$ with $r \in \mathbf{R}$.

To illustrate these ideas, we add a second role of the robot within the container terminal scenario by extending the original perception function of the agent by the possibility to receive external commands. The (human) area operator can now direct the robot to search for a particular container in the stock and to report the status and position of the container. Thus, we now have two possible roles for the agent, i.e. "carrier" or "verifier".

I have already said in the introduction of this chapter that the concepts that will be discussed operate on a rather high level of abstraction. Now, I will become slightly more technical and explain how these theoretical concepts can be mapped into executable machinery.

### 2.1.3 Architectures

In order to show how the theoretical concepts are actually implemented into computer hard- and software we need an intermediate layer of abstraction that is provided by agent architectures. In [Sloman, 1996] an agent architecture is defined "as the portion of a system that provides and manages the primitive resources of an agent". This definition, however, is still to general to be directly applicable and therefore, a two step process is used to bring the conceptual abstractions down to an actual implementation.

The first level of abstraction is given by cognitive models that refine the basic abstractions into more specific concepts. One of the most prominent examples for a cognitive model are BDI architectures [Rao and Georgeff, 1995] that have gained much attention in the agent community in recent years. In the BDI theory, an agent is described by its *Beliefs* that determine the agents current world knowledge, its *Desires* that determine the goals of the agent and finally, the *Intentions* that are generated from reasoning about the current beliefs and goals and therewith determine the best possible actions.

But even these more concrete specifications of agents are still difficult to break down into operational concepts. Therefore, a second level of abstraction is necessary that describes how the abstract concepts of the first level are made executable on computer hardware. [Wooldridge, 1997] suggests three possible means to achieve this goal. The first possibility is functional refinement as it is common in most standard Software Engineering environments, the second one is direct execution of the specifications which implies powerful description languages and runtime environments and the third possibility, finally, is compilation of the abstract specification into executable code. All three of this methods are currently used and none of these has proven to be better then any other.

Because of the huge impact of the decision for a particular agent architecture, Section 5.7.3 will provide the reader with a characterization scheme that structures the requirements of the problem domain and that supports the decision for or against a particular architecture. In this section, I will therefore not go into further details but instead discuss the connection between agents, roles and architectures in the next section.

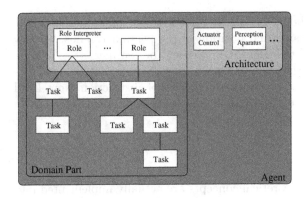

**Fig. 2.4.** Agents and Roles

### 2.1.4 Agents, Roles and Architectures

In the previous sections, I have introduced three fundamental aspects of intelligent agents. But how do these concepts relate to each other? Basically, the relation between agents, roles and architectures can be reduced to the following equation.

$$agent = roles + architecture$$

Thus, an "agent" is an abstract concept that is filled with a particular content by defining the possible roles of the agent and by providing a runtime environment that is capable of executing the given role models. In Figure 2.4, the above relation is interpreted graphically. The concept of an agent encloses the *architecture* that contains the perception and actuation subsystem as well as the *role interpreter*. The role interpreter links the domain-independent architecture to the domain specific aspects of the different roles by associating each role with a particular task tree.

In the example of the container terminal, the hardware of the robot corresponds to the agent architecture that implements the runtime environment for the possible roles. The roles itself are modeled as task trees, e.g. the "carrier" role has the subtasks of checking for incoming containers, determining the destination of each container and then taking each container to the indicated destination.

The above relation between the basic entities in an agent application has some implications on the development of agent (and later multiagent) applications because it determines the basic structure of each application in this class. A possible generic application architecture is depicted in Figure 2.5 where I have shown a conceptual model that consists of three layers. Still, other generic architectures [Horn and Reinke, 1999] are possible but beyond the scope of this introduction.

The basic layer is of course the *Platform Layer* that hosts the target application. Figure 2.5 shows the rather simple case where the entire applications runs on the same hardware platform. In the case of more complicated applications, it may spread over several platforms and therefore may require an

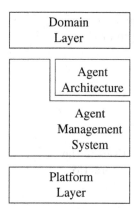

**Fig. 2.5.** A Generic Agent Application Architecture

additional layer that provides an abstract interface to the individual platforms. However for the sake of simplicity, I have not included this additional
layer.

The *Agent Layer* of the generic application architecture contains two major elements. The *Agent Management System* provides the interface between
the agent architecture and the hardware platform and the *Agent Architecture*
implements the runtime environment for the domain dependent roles of the
agent.

The roles themselves are subject to the *Domain Layer* that covers the
domain specific aspects. Note the interface between the agent management
system and the domain layer which is necessary whenever the systems functionality is not entirely covered by agents.

In the next section, I will extend the single-agent case and lift the view
one step further onto systems of intelligent agents.

## 2.2 S stems of Agents

In a multiagent system, several intelligent agents exist within the same environment. The term "environment" is hereby used is a very broad sense and
covers physical environments for robotic agents as well as runtime environments for software agents, virtual reality environments etc. To express the
fact of a shared environment, a system of multiple agents is described by a
set structure $\{\mathbf{S}, \langle\mathbf{D}, \mathbf{T}, \mathbf{A}, perceive, infer, select, act\rangle_i\}$ where $\mathbf{S}$ denotes the
environment just like before and each of the different agents that share the
environment has a unique identifier $i$ that distinguishes it from the other
agents.

In [Fulbright and Stephens, 1994], other forms of agent coupling have
been discussed. However, I will limit the focus to this particular form a
coupling via the environment because it is predominant in the multiagent
research community and none of the other forms presented there has gained

general acceptance. The main feature of a system that is comprised of several intelligent entities is that a major part of the systems functionality is not explicitly and globally specified, but that it *emerges from the interaction* between these individual entities. Therefore, interaction is the main aspect of multiagent systems.

### 2.2.1 Interaction

Coordinated interaction among several autonomous entities is the core concept of multiagent technology. But first of all, what is interaction? To be as general as possible, let us define the concept as follows.

**Definition 2.2.1 (Interaction).** *Interaction is the mutual adaption of the behavior of agents while preserving individual constraints.*

This very general definition has some interesting properties that need further clarification. First of all, interaction is not limited to explicit communication or even more specific to the case of message exchange as, of course, the predominant means in the multiagent literature. Interaction is defined as any kind of behavior that is related to other agents [Weiss, 1999]. The example of an ant hill illustrates the basic idea where the single ant does not reflect about the existence of other ants but it still adapts its behavior to the behavior of other ants in a way such that the entire society shows coordinated interaction. The communication between the ants is carried out by several means e.g. physical tactile behavior, chemical substances, vision and others.

The second important property of Definition 2.2.1 is the focus on *mutual* adaption, i.e. the requirement that the participating agents co-ordinate their behavior. For example, a pedestrian, who jumps out of the way of an approaching car and the driver of the respective car do not have any kind of interaction according to our definition. The pedestrian has unilaterally adapted his behavior in order to avoid a situation that would have yielded a worse payoff to him then to the driver of the car.

The third major focus of the above definition is the aspect of *balancing* between social behavior that is manifested in the mutual adaption and the self-interest of the agent. Neither egoism nor altruism are the best means to achieve globally optimal system states, but a good combination of these two aspects of interaction can yield the best global results [Axelrod, 1984]. It is therefore important to equip the agents within a multiagent systems with a mix of self-interest and social consciousness that allows them to value the performance of the entire society over their individual performance.

Especially the second and third of the above properties of Definition 2.2.1 contain the potential for conflicts within the agent society that must be resolved in one way or the other.

Coordination in a (natural or artificial) society is the process of conflict resolution within the society and can be achieved in a number of ways. The most natural conflict resolution strategy that can be found in a physical environment is simply to do nothing. The laws of physics clearly define the outcome of actions that include more than one agent. For example, two robots that approach the same location will be coordinated by the physical law that only one of them can occupy the particular location. Thus, either the first robot to reach the location or the stronger of the two robots will finally occupy it. Obviously, this is a somewhat artificial example for a coordination strategy and it far away from being reasonable. Although it is straightforward and therefore easy to implement, it is usually a better idea to implement some sort of collision avoidance strategy except for the case when you have extremely robust robots.

The second conflict resolution strategy uses external mediation to solve the conflict [Georgeff, 1983], [Cammarata et al., 1983]. Mediation means that the conflicting parties apply to a third, neutral party that decides what should be done. The most important prerequisite for this sort of conflict resolution is the mutual agreement of the agents to obey the decision of the mediator. The advantage of the mediation solution is that the decision about what to do is not based on local preferences of the agents but on a more global view (depending on the knowledge of the mediator). However, this sort of conflict resolution is often not seen as "real" multiagent technology because the agents loose some of their autonomy by relying on an external mediator.

The third way of conflict resolution, finally, is negotiation. This approach is mostly used in multiagent systems and it has shown to be a powerful tool to solve all kinds of conflict situations. In a conflict resolution process based on negotiation mechanisms, the agents exchange messages until they have reached a agreement on how the conflict is settled to their mutual benefit.

Besides its ability to solve conflicts among agents, negotiation mechanisms are a good means to attack complex optimization problems by simulation a market situation where the agents negotiate in order to find a solution that optimizes the local performance of the agents as well as the global performance of the entire agent society.

Coordinated interaction is the core concept of multiagent systems and the most common form of coordinated interaction that is used in multiagent systems is negotiation. Generic forms of interaction will be discussed in Section 5.5 and so I will not go into further details here. Instead, we will now turn to structural aspects of an agent society.

## 2.2.2 The Social Dimension

The social structure of a society determines how the entities within the society relate to each other. Thus, the major questions that occur in conjunction with the social structure of an artificial society are clearly related to sociology and to organizational theory and therefore, I will use some definitions from the field of sociology [Bahrdt, 1994] to explain the basic ideas of agent societies.

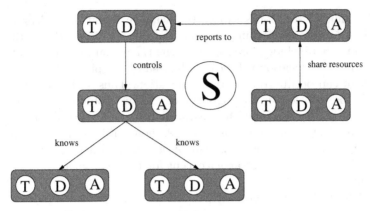

**Fig. 2.6.** Sociogram

**Definition 2.2.2 (Structure).** *A* **structure** *is a collection of entities that are connected in a non-random manner.*

This definition prescribes two important properties for an agent society that is built upon the definition. First, it requires the agents to be able to perceive existence of other agents, otherwise the term "connected" would not make sense. Second, it requires that the agents are arranged towards a particular intention, i.e. any structure must have a purpose. The structural description of the agent society can serve two purposes. A *descriptive society model* is used to model a society that already exists and which should either be modeled by a multiagent system or that constitutes the organizational context of the system, whereas a *prescriptive society model* captures the developers intention of how the agent society should look like. Regardless of the purpose of the characterization, however, a sociogram as it is shown in Figure 2.6 can be used to express the structural connections between the agents in an agent society. Each link in the figure has an associated characterization of its meaning that describes the nature of the connection between the entities.

However, having a non-random structure alone does not make an agent society [Gerber, 1997] and thus we must find additional properties that refine the intuitive concept.

**Definition 2.2.3 (Society).** *A* **society** *is a structured set of agents that agree on a minimal set of acceptable behaviors.*

This is a very general definition of the concept that leaves sufficient freedom for the system designer to model a wide variety of agent societies. The term "acceptable behavior", however, needs some additional clarification. The definition of what is acceptable behavior can be implemented into the agents themselves by the agent designer. The agents then do not have a chance to show non-acceptable behavior. In this case, it is straightforward to achieve acceptable behavior of all agents within the agent society. Unfortunately, this method is only applicable in closed agent societies. In an open agent society such as the Internet, no central definition of acceptable behavior exists. Each agent may have a different view on the topic and the first difficulty is for the agents to agree on a common definition. Furthermore, the agent society must be equipped with punishment mechanisms that can be used against agents that violate the commonly agreed definition. This case is difficult to handle and up to now, no satisfactory solution (especially for punishment mechanisms) has been proposed.

However, having defined the concept of an agent society is still not sufficient. An agent society, just like a structure, does not exist for its own right, instead it must have a purpose. Hence the next definition.

**Definition 2.2.4 (Social System).** *A* **social system** *is a society that implements a closed functional context with respect to a common goal.*

This definition adds the teleological component to the agent society in that it puts the society into a well defined functional context. Thus the agents within a social system must have a common goal that they pursue as long as they are part of the society.

It is one of the most difficult parts of the development process to find the society structure that is suited best for a particular functional specification because the quality of the solution is usually determined by several, sometimes contradicting, aspects. In Section 5.6, I will outline some of this influential factors and present a micro process model that supports the developer in finding the best society structure for a given problem.

## 2.3 Rel ted Fields in Com uter Science

In the previous section, I have outlined the basic characteristics of intelligent agents and multiagent systems. Now, I will briefly render some related research fields as shown Figure 2.7 where the connections between multiagent applications and applications in other fields of computer science are depicted.

Multiagent applications basically have two roots: distributed systems and agent-based computing . Distributed systems [Fox, 1981], [Mullender, 1993] [Tanenbaum, 1988] is the sub-field of computer science that is concerned with the design and implementation of computer applications where several computers or processors cooperate in some way [Tel, 1994]. Distributed systems are often systems where the participating entities have little or no autonomy in what they do. The designer specifies the entire system behavior and the only purpose for the distribution is usually performance enhancement through the exploitation of parallelism. Agent-based computing [Shoham, 1993], [Bradshaw, 1997], [Huhns and Singh, 1998] [Jennings and Wooldridge, 1998], on the other hand, is concerned with the design and implementation of flexible, autonomous entities [Jennings et al., 1998]. These entities – the agents – are

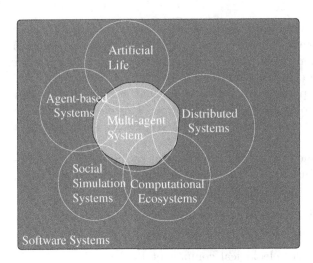

**Fig. 2.7.** MAS-Related fields in Computer Science

situated in an environment that they perceive with their sensor apparatus and on which they can act upon using their effectors. The agents are equipped with reasoning capabilities that allow them to deliberate upon their next actions in order to fulfill their goals.

Multiagent systems are also related to computational ecosystems [Kephart et al., 1989], [Parunak et al., 1997] where the designer tries to imitate the situation within a natural ecosystem. The entities within such a system are not necessarily cooperative and they may have strong interdependencies that can have positive or negative effects. Thus the entities usually compete for scare resources if it is necessary for them to improve their performance.

There are two other related fields that have only minor connections to multiagent systems, one is artificial life and the other are social simulation systems. Research in artificial life [Langton, 1989], [Boden, 1996], [Adami, 1998] is concerned with the formal basis of life and the mechanisms that produce lifelike behavior [Franklin, 1997]. These mechanisms are then implemented in computer programs that synthesize the behaviors and allow for the analysis of the emergent functionality. Social simulation systems [Heise, 1992], [Epstein and Axtell, 1996], finally, were introduced by sociologists to simulate the behavior of large groups of individuals. These systems are useful because they allow the researcher to abstract away from individual characteristics of humans and to focus on particular properties of the system. However, these systems only play a minor role in the field of computer science.

The computer science research fields that have been briefly discussed in this section are all recognized and accepted research fields in their own right. However none of them has lead to a similar hype as currently about agents and agent-based computing. Therefore, we will now investigate the flesh and bones of agent-oriented software engineering and try to find out whether it is justified to call it a new programming paradigm at all.

## 2.4 Agent-Oriented Softw re Engineering

It was already mentioned in the introduction that agents and multi-agent systems are currently one of the most interesting research fields in the computer science community. But is this enough to make agent oriented software engineering (AOSE) a new software paradigm? What makes the idea distinctive from other approaches? How does it fit in a more general picture of software engineering?

In this section, I will present my personal viewpoint on agent-oriented software engineering by relating it to other programming paradigms. Especially the relation between object-oriented and agent-oriented methods is particularly interesting because they seem to be closely related. In order to clarify their relationship, I will describe the levels of abstraction that make up programming paradigms in general and demonstrate the instantiation of the general case for object-orientation and agent-orientation in particular. Furthermore, I will point out what could be the major contributions of the agent oriented paradigm to software engineering and provide an outlook on how the new paradigm can change the way we think about software systems.

### 2.4.1 Aspects of Programming Paradigms

The term "programming paradigm" is extremely fuzzy because it is often used to capture a set of different software-related aspects under a particular catch-phrase. These different aspects are often located on different levels of abstraction and their interrelationships are seldom explicitly formulated. In this section, I will use the triangle shown in Figure 2.8 to describe the different levels of abstraction that in my view make up a programming paradigm. The form a triangle was chosen to express the fact that the number of concepts (and therewith the complexity) on a particular level of abstraction increases on higher levels. Furthermore, a layered approach is quite common in computer science theories to clearly separate the concepts on different levels of abstraction. The main advantage of a layered approach is that no knowledge of lower levels is necessary to understand and to work with higher level concepts because ideally, each level of abstraction represents a conceptually closed framework. In reality, unfortunately, the higher level theories are not only much more complex then lower level ones, but they are often incomplete [McCarthy, 1979]. Therefore, it often becomes necessary to combine several higher level theories to obtain a full coverage of the intended part of the world that should be modeled.

Note furthermore, that the distinctions between the different levels are not too sharp. Because of the fact that most programming models are assumed to be essentially equal in their computational power (Church's thesis), any programming model can be implemented in terms of any other model. Thus, it is possible to write object-oriented software in a purely imperative programming language or to implement a deductive database in an object-oriented

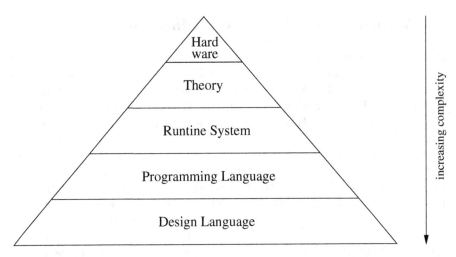

**Fig. 2.8.** Levels of Abstraction

framework. In the following sections, I have therefore tried to produce a break-down of concepts that clearly separates intra-model aspects and that allows for an inter-model comparison of these concepts. I am well aware that some concepts can be shifted along the abstraction hierarchy, but I think that the current assignment to a particular level is adequate.

**Hardware.** The first level of abstraction encapsulates the architecture that is implemented in the computer hardware. Today, most computers still have the von Neumann architecture that was introduced in the late 1940s [Hennessy and Patterson, 1990]. The architecture consists of a *processor* that is subdivided into units for computation and control and a *memory* store that holds the instructions and the data of the program.

This architecture is still common in modern computers although it has been greatly optimized by using techniques such as pipelining, caching or parallelism to speed up computation. A recent trend in the hardware community is to turn away from integrated, large-scale systems and towards networks of normal personal computers that jointly work on a computationally demanding task. These virtual supercomputers combine the advantage of lower costs through the use of standard hardware with an extreme scalability that allows to add more computational resources whenever this is necessary. In one vision on the future of the Internet [McNealy, 1996], the entire net becomes a virtual supercomputer that makes individual computational power obsolete.

However, whether sequential, parallel or distributed, from the point of view of a programming paradigm, all hardware looks the same. There have been attempts to build hardware architectures that implement a particular programming paradigm directly into the hardware device, but none of these attempts has been successful. Therefore, we can safely assume that all programming paradigms share the same ground.

**Theories.** On the next higher level of abstraction, however, things are different. Theories are conceptualizations of a particular computational model that abstracts away from the characteristics of the hardware. The first theories were aimed at capturing the in-principle capability of a computational device in order to allow for general statements about what can be automatically computed and what cannot [Turing, 1937]. Turing's theory, for example, is a radical mathematical conceptualization of the von Neuman architecture that enables us to formally analyze all possible programs that can be executed on such an architecture. Other computational theories are intended as tools to help the programmer to express the ideas of what a program is supposed to do more naturally. An early computational theory that was meant as the foundation of a "natural" way of programming is declarative programming [Kowalski, 1979] but it has been demonstrated by empirical investigations in cognitive psychology that this claim does not necessarily hold true [Ormerod, 1990].

Let's start the comparison of the object-oriented and agent-oriented issues with the entities that are handled on this level of abstraction. In the object-oriented world, these entities are the *objects*. An object can be anything ranging from a concrete entity from the real world to a conceptual entity that only exists in the designers head. Each object within the system is associated with a particular *class* that determines the objects basic properties. Classes can be linked with each other in several ways. Probably the best known relation between two classes is *inheritance* that models a conceptual extension of a common base specification. During their lifetime, objects communicate by sending *messages* to each other. These messages can be used to request services from the receiving object such as to provide internal information or to change the current state. Although there are several additional concepts in the object-oriented paradigm I will restrict myself to this brief introduction and refer the reader unfamiliar with object-oriented concepts to the available literature, e.g. [Booch, 1994]. In summary, the collection of object-oriented concepts is clear and manageable in size and does not vary greatly in different object-oriented approaches.

In the agent-oriented universe, on the other hand, we are faced with the first serious problem as there is no single agreed definition of the entities that are dealt with. The existing *agent theories* are more or less built upon one out of two widely accepted notions of agency [Wooldridge and Jennings, 1995]. In the *strong notion* of agency, an agent is modeled in terms of mentalistic notions such as beliefs, desires and intentions. Furthermore, the strong notion requires that these mental concepts have an explicit representation within the implementation of the agent. Thus, this notion forces a *white-box* on the agent. The *weak notion* of agency, on the other hand, requires only a *black-box* view on the agent in that it defines an agent only in terms of its observable properties. According to this definition, an agent is anything that exhibits autonomy, reactivity, pro-activity, social ability [Wooldridge and Jennings, 1995].

In my opinion, these two notions of agency are both too strict. I would argue for a more pragmatic definition of agency that allows the designer to decide what should be an agent regardless of a particular implementation or a minimal degree of external properties. I call this the *very weak notion* of agency. To explain why this absence of formal aspects still makes sense, I have to fall back upon a famous article from the early days of Artificial Intelligence.

In [McCarthy, 1979], the author argues that it is useful to ascribe mental qualities such as beliefs, goals, desires, wishes etc. to machines (or computer programs) whenever it helps us to understand the structure of a machine or a program or to explain or predict the behavior of the machine or the program. McCarthy does not impose any constraints such as a minimal required complexity onto the entities that we want to ascribe mental categories or onto the mental categories that we would like to use. In his view, ascribing mental qualities is a means of understanding and of communication between humans, i.e. it is a purely conceptual tool that serves the purpose of expressing existing knowledge about a particular program or its current state:

> "All the [ ... ] reasons for ascribing belief's are epistemological; i.e. ascribing beliefs is needed to adapt to limitations on our ability to acquire knowledge, use it for prediction, and establish generalizations in terms of the elementary structure of the program. Perhaps this is the general reason for ascribing higher levels of organization to systems."

To illustrate why this point of view is reasonable, McCarthy uses the example of a program that is given in source code form. It is possible to completely determine the programs behavior by simulating the given code, i.e. no mental categories are necessary to describe this behavior. Why would we still want to use mental categories to talk and reason about the program? In the original paper, McCarthy discusses several reasons for this. In the following list, I have selected those reasons that seem to be most relevant to me:

1. The programs state at a particular point in time is usually not directly observable. Therefore, the observable information is better expressed in mental categories.
2. A complete simulation may be too slow, but a prediction about the behavior on the basis of the ascribed mental qualities may be feasible.
3. Ascribing mental qualities can lead to more general hypothesis about the programs behavior then a finite number of simulations.
4. The mental categories (e.g. goals) that are ascribed are likely to correspond to the programmers intentions when designing the program. Thus, the program can be understood and changed more easily.
5. The structure of the program is more easily accessible then in the source code form.

Especially the fourth point in the above enumeration is extremely important for AOSE because the task of understanding existing software becomes
increasingly important in the software industry and is likely to outrange the
development of new software [Balzert, 1998a]. Thus, if it becomes easier to
access the original developers idea (that is eventually manifested in the design) it becomes easier to understand the design and this leads to higher cost
efficiency in software maintenance.

A more general conclusion from McCarthy's approach is the idea that
*anything can be an agent*. This view has been discussed from controversial
points of view [Wooldridge and Jennings, 1995] and it has been argued that
it does not buy us anything whenever the system is so simple that it can be
perfectly understood. I do not agree with this. In my view, the conceptual
integrity that is achieved by viewing every intentional entity – be it as simple
as it may – in the system as an agent leads to a much clearer system design
and it circumvents the problem to decide whether a particular entity is an
agent or not. In my personal experience, this problem can be quite annoying
during the design phase whenever two software designers have different views.

In the above paragraphs, I have identified the basic structural elements
of object-orientation and agent-orientation, respectively. Now I will outline
some of the basic concepts of describing and arranging these elements and
point out some fundamental similarities that can be identified.

As I have already said above, the basic descriptional element is object-
oriented programming is the class. A class definition specifies the class variables of an object and the methods the object accepts. Classes can be linked
with each other via several forms: one class inherit from another class such
that the new class is an extension of the existing class, instances of two
classes can collaborate with each other by exchanging messages, and finally
they can have a structural connection in that one instance of a class contains
an instance of the class.

These concepts correspond to the agent-oriented world by replacing class
with *role*, state variable with *belief/knowledge* and method with *message*.
Thus a role definition describes the agent's capabilities, the data that is
needed to produce the desired results and the requests that trigger a particular service. Besides this fundamental relation, there are many other conceptual similarities between object-orientation and agent-orientation that can be
mapped onto each other. Due to the limited space, however, these are briefly
summarized in Table 2.1.

Turning away from the conceptual issues and similarities of the two programming approaches, we will now come to more technical aspects of the
runtime environment and discuss the general structure for object-oriented
and agent-oriented systems, respectively.

**Runtime System.** The runtime system of a particular programming
paradigm provides the environment for the program interpretation and these
environments can be radically different. In the more simple forms, they

**Table 2.1.** Mapping OOP to AOP

|  | OOP | AOP |
|---|---|---|
| Structural Elements |  |  |
|  | abstract class | generic role |
|  | class | domain specific role |
|  | class variables | knowledge, belief |
|  | methods | capabilities |
| Relations |  |  |
|  | collaboration (uses) | negotiation |
|  | composition (has) | holonic agents |
|  | inheritance (is) | role multiplicity |
|  | instantiation | domain-specific role + individual knowledge |
|  | polymorphism | service matchmaking |

are restricted to administrative tasks such as managing the heap or they provide slightly more elaborate services such as garbage collection. However, there also exist very complex runtime environment that provide complete reasoning engines for logic programming [Kowalski, 1979] that are for example used in declarative programming languages such as Prolog [Clocksin and Mellish, 1994].

Objects and agents and the various relationships that exist between them within their respective programming model are conceptual abstractions that require an implementation such that they can be used by higher levels of abstraction. In the following paragraphs, I will divide the implementation of the theoretical concepts into the implementation of the entities themselves and an implementation of a meta-level that manipulates the basic entities.

In an object-oriented runtime system, the objects are statically represented by the *object architecture*. This architecture is usually quite simple as it only contains the current state of the object and the relation to the objects class (which determines the operations that can be performed on the object). An object is usually represented as arbitrary collection of data elements with associated functions and the granularity of objects is potentially not limited. However, efficiency issues dictate that not every entity is modeled as an object and so in reality this conceptual benefit is slightly weakened. The *object management system* is responsible for representing the relations such as inheritance between the defined classes and object manipulation such as creating or destroying objects. Furthermore, the object management system is also responsible for dynamic aspects such as method selection of polymorphous objects, exception handling or garbage collection.

In an agent-oriented runtime system, things are distinctly more complicated although similar in their general structure. The basic entities are the agents that are implemented by their agent architecture as it was introduced in Section 2.1.4. However, agent architectures are far more complex then the object architecture, especially because of the dynamic aspects that must be dealt with. Because of the richness of the agent-oriented world, there exists a large number of different agent architectures [Müller, 1996a], [Müller, 1998], [Jung, 1999]. Due to the vast number of approaches, it is impossible to identify *the* best or most general architecture. However, the smallest common denominator seems to be the basic *perceive – reason – act* cycle discussed earlier where in each iteration, the agent perceives the state of its environment, integrates the perception in its knowledge base that is used to derive the next action which is then executed. This generic cycle is a useful abstraction as it provides a black-box view on the agent architecture and encapsulates specific aspects.

The task of the *agent management system* as the meta-level of an agent based runtime environment is to provide a "life-space" for the agents, i.e. a collection of mechanisms that enables the agents to get in contact with each other. To enable agents of different designers to interact with each other, it is necessary to standardize the basic services that are provided by agent management system. One such standard is defined in [FIPA, 1998].

**Programming Language.** In this level of abstraction, the syntactical framework for the manipulation of the entities on the runtime level is defined. The programs that are written in a particular programming language are either directly interpreted by the runtime system or they are compiled into an intermediate format that is understood by the runtime system or directly to assembler code.

The syntactical constructs that are provided by the programming language should allow the programmer to use the underlying semantic concepts efficiently and to express the intended functionality of the program elegantly. For example, it is generally possible to implement a particular conceptual model with any general purpose language, e.g. it is possible to write object-oriented programs in C, but in general, it is much easier and more comfortable for the programmer if the terms of the conceptual framework can be used directly. Even an integration of several conceptual models into a single high level programming language can be problematic as is often difficult to find a good combination of concepts that is not overwhelming for the average user and then to find a concise syntactical representation for these different concepts.

I think that object-orientation as well as agent-orientation are such general concepts that can be attached to almost any other programming language. In the case of object orientation, this approached work for languages such C, leading to C++ [Stroustrup, 1987], Cobol (ObjectCobol [Doke and Hardgrave, 1998]), perl [Wall et al., 1996] and numerous other languages. But not only imperative languages have been enhanced with objects. The Mozart programming system [Programming Systems Lab, 1999], for example, provides a very elegant combination of constraint-logic programming with object-oriented concepts.

In the context of agent-oriented software engineering, these trends are not so clear until now. Currently, there is no – at least to my knowledge – widely accepted agent-oriented programming language that goes beyond the experimental state. However, some approaches are designed as an extension of established languages, e.g. JAMagents [Intelligent Reasoning Systems, 2000] that combine agent-oriented concepts with Java [Sun Microsystems, 1999].

**Design Language.** Design languages are further abstractions from a particular programming language that aim at the conceptual modeling of a system at a more coarse grained level. Design languages often use graphical notations that make it easier fro the designer to access the overall system structure. Probably the currently best known design language is the *Unified Modeling Language (UML)* [Booch et al., 1999] discussed in Section 3.4.2 that tries to integrate several, until then separated design notations under a common hat. Due to the general nature of the core UML, it is not always suited for all problem areas, and therefore, extensions that cover special aspect have already been proposed [France and Rumpe, 1999].

In a more general sense, however, design languages should not necessarily be constraint to modeling aspects of the system. In my personal view, I would count general software architecture frameworks or frameworks for a particular application area to design languages as well. The reason for this view is, that these frameworks provide their own set of structural abstractions that represent a "language" on this particular level of abstraction.

In the object oriented community, examples for such frameworks include Java Beans [Sun Microsystems, 2000] as a means of providing off-the-shelf components together with flexible interconnection mechanisms between the basic structural elements or software development environments such as Visual C++ [Microsoft Corporation, 2000] that focus on a support for the development of graphical user interfaces. In the latter case, the structural elements of the design language are graphical elements that are combined according to a given grammar that regulates how different elements can be put together.

In the agent-based world – although a relatively new area –, a large number of different frameworks already exists. This may be due to the fact, that the increasing complexity can only be dealt with by using adequate tool support. Examples for agent-based design languages range from source-level frameworks such as SIF [Schillo et al., 1999] [Lind et al., 2000] and Swarm [Minar et al., 1996] up to complex and powerful tools such as the ZEUS toolkit [Nwana et al., 1999] from British Telecom that provides drag-and-drop mechanisms for putting together multi-agent applications. A more detailed description of these tool-kits is provided in Appendix A.

### 2.4.2 A Historic Perspective

In this section, I will discuss a few historic aspects in the development of programming paradigms that can be helpful in understanding why the agent-oriented approach is a natural successor to the prior development.

**Table 2.2.** Historic development of programming paradigms

|  | Machine Language | Structured Programming | Object-Oriented Programming | Agent-Oriented Programming |
|---|---|---|---|---|
| Structural Unit | Program | Subroutine | Object | Agent |
| Relation to Previous level |  | Bounded unit of Program | Subroutine + persistent local state | Object + independent thread of execution + Initiative |

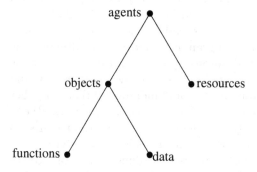

**Fig. 2.9.** Programming Concepts

In [Parunak, 1999a], Table 2.2 is used to capture the historic development from machine language to agent-oriented programming. In the early days of programming, a program was thus seem as a monolithic block without any inherent structure. This view was subsequently changed in that it was recognized that a program is made up from several smaller structural units, i.e. subroutines. However, the concept of subroutines alone was not powerful enough as it emphasized the control flow aspect of programming and neglects the data that is involved. Consequently, the view changed a second time, this time grouping data and computation together in a single structural unit called an "object". Currently, we are faced with the third change of perspective, leading away from merely passive objects and facing towards active structural units which we call "agents".

I like the above presentation of the historic development because I think that it captures the main ideas in a concise form. However, I am not completely satisfied with the characterization of agents in the above table. While the requirement of an independent thread of execution sounds very technical, the term "initiative" is to fuzzy to be operationalized.

To draw on the basic ideas of [Parunak, 1999a] but to develop a more coherent structure, I suggest the three-step characterization shown in Figure 2.9.

In the first step, programs are seen as a collection of *functions* that establish a well-defined goal. These functions can be described as an sequence of statements (*imperative programming*), as a collection of mathematical expressions that are linked together (*functional programming*) or as a set of goals without imposing a particular way of achieving the goal onto the interpreter (*declarative programming*).

In the next development step, a program is interpreted in terms of the *data* that is manipulated and the *functions* that operate on that data. This leads to structured programming where semantically related aspects of the program are spatially related. An even stronger and explicit relation between data and functions is introduced by abstract data types, eventually leading to object-oriented programming.

In the final step of the characterization, the objects are augmented with *resources* such as computation time, that can be freely used. This freedom in the (internal) resource allocation process lead to the concept that I find most fundamental for agent-oriented programming: *autonomy*. Although the weak notion of agency has identified autonomy as a central concept of the agent-oriented viewpoint, it was only credited as one among others. I would argue, on the other hand, that autonomy is more fundamental then the other aspects of the weak notion and that it is even a prerequisite for the others. For example, pro-activeness can only be achieved when the agent is free to decide when to become active; the same argument holds for reactivity.

The idea of agents as autonomous agents is so striking and revolutionary because it leads to a new way of thinking about software systems. Such a system is no longer a collection of passive objects. Rather, these objects have a "life of their own", i.e. they are perceived and modeled by the designer as active entities. This view on complex systems is completely different from traditional approaches in that it explicitly accepts the fact that the software designer is not responsible for specifying the systems dynamics down to the least bit. Instead, the designer sets out the initial state and specifies the initial goals of the autonomous agents and then the system takes over. In such a system, there is no such thing as the "central scrutinizer" [Zappa, 1979] that controls everything. Rather, the ongoing interactions determine the overall system behavior.

Another major advantage of the agent-oriented view is that it supports the principle of locality even better then the object-oriented view does. In object-oriented systems, the control-flow specification is spread all over the entire program code. The agent-oriented view introduces a further tool for conceptual grouping that comes with the agents well defined bounds [Lander, 1997]. All elements that make up the control-flow of a particular agent are grouped under the common concept, making it easier to identify larger units of the program that belong together semantically.

### 2.4.3 The Bottom Line

After the sobering remarks about the basic similarities of the agent- and object-oriented approaches one may be tempted to conclude that agent-

orientation are just the emperor's new clothes. But that is not what I was trying to say. Even if the technical contributions or agent-oriented software engineering are not really revolutionary the conceptual contribution is nonetheless huge. Agent-oriented software engineering provides an epistemological
framework for effective communication and reasoning about complex software system on the basis of mental qualities. It provides a consistent new
set of terms and relations that adequately capture complex systems and that
support easier and more natural development of these systems.

As an example for the importance of a clear terminological framework, consider abstract data types (ADTs) and objects. It is argued in
[Wirth, 1995], that objects are essentially the same thing then ADTs that
were introduced years earlier. But: why do programmers prefer objects over
ADTs? I think because the terminological framework provided by object-
oriented approaches allows the programmer a more natural way of modeling because it allows for thinking in terms of the real world that should be
modeled by a software system. Furthermore, I think that it will be a major
reason for the success of the agent-oriented view that programmers already
use some sort of mentalistic notion to develop their object-oriented systems
that is subsequently translated into object-oriented terms. This additional
transformation can be dropped as soon as the adequate tools for expressing
the ideas directly in the already used terminology become available.

As a second point that I have explained above, I think that adding autonomy as an accepted property of formerly passive objects is the main contribution of the agent-oriented view. It leads to a completely different modeling
approach that stimulates a system design built upon the desirable properties
[Conte et al., 1996] of loose coupling between system components with a high
cohesion of these components.

I shall now return to the initial question of the section that was whether
agent-oriented software engineering is really a new programming paradigm or
not. To answer this question, consider the following quote from the Webster
On-line Dictionary [Merriam-Webster, 2000]

Main Entry: par·a·digm
Pronunciation: 'par-&-"dIm also -"dim
Function: *noun*
Etymology: Late Latin *paradigma*, from Greek *paradeigma*, from
*paradeiknynai* to show side by side
Date: 15th century
**1: example, pattern**; *especially*: an outstandingly clear or typical
example or archetype
**2:** an example of a conjugation or declension showing a word in all
its inflectional forms

**3:** a philosophical and theoretical framework of a scientific school or
discipline within which theories, laws, and generalizations and the
experiments performed in support of them are formulated

According to this definition, the answer to the above question is clearly "yes" because agent-oriented software engineering provides us with the required new framework, built upon the basic property of autonomy, that allows for the modeling and understanding of agent-based applications. Furthermore, I think that the agent oriented view is a necessary prerequisite for accepting artificial intelligence at all because I think that we must get used to ascribing basic qualities such as goal, beliefs, desires before we can ascribe "intelligence" to a machine.

### 2.4.4 Where Next?

It must be the goal for the agent community to broaden the acceptance of the new paradigm among the people who really develop software, i.e. software engineers. But just as it was the case with object-oriented technology, I do not believe that this acceptance will develop quickly. Object-oriented technology was around for about 10-15 years before it became a widely accepted and naturally used software engineering discipline. So the question one may ask in this respect is why it takes so long for a new paradigm to become state of the art? An interesting answer to this question is provided in Kuhn's theory about the *Structure of Scientific Revolutions* [Kuhn, 1975]. According to Kuhn's theory, scientific development is not a continuous flow, but rather a sequence of disjoint revolutions. Every such a revolution is preceded by a phase of normal scientific activities in which the researches use the current state of the art (the current paradigm) as the general background of their daily work and the research questions are draw from yet unsolved problems of the current paradigm and can in principle be solved within the existing framework. From time to time, however, a question is raised or a phenomenon is observed that cannot be answered or explained within the current paradigm. These anomalies require a radical change of perspective, i.e. a new general research paradigm that can deal with the newly observed phenomena. This is then called a revolution. Ideally, the new paradigm should also capture the past experiences although this is not always possible. As an example for this sort of scientific development, consider Newton's theory on mechanics. Newton's mechanics was the research framework for several hundred years until several observations on the atomic level could not be explained in Newton's theory. This lead to the development of quantum mechanics that were able explain the observations on the atomic level.

The major point in Kuhn's theory is, that the new research paradigm is not introduced into the research by established researchers that "convert" to the new paradigm. Rather, it is introduced by the upcoming generation of young researchers that grow up in the spirit of the new paradigm and that they naturally accept as the general framework. Scientific history is full of examples for this process. The above mentioned theory of quantum mechanics is such an examples, as is Darwin's theory on the origin of species [Desmond and Moore, 1994]. On a much more specific level, this observation is also true for object-oriented software development. While established researches neglected the novelty in the concepts [Wirth, 1995], it was readily accepted by the younger generation and it is now a widely accepted programming paradigm.

In the near future of agent-oriented software engineering, however, it is necessary to make the main contributions accessible to the people that should use it. Therefore, we need conceptual frameworks such as described in this book that support the development of agent-oriented applications.

## 2.5 Summ r

In this section, I have outlined the basic ideas of intelligent agents and multi-agent systems. Starting from a very general formalization of an agent, I have discussed the concept of different roles and introduced agent architectures as the runtime environment for role models. The single-agent case was then lifted to systems with several agents and the fundamental aspects such as interaction and the social dimension of an artificial society have been discussed. In the last part of the section, I have presented my personal view on the idea of agent-oriented software engineering as a general software engineering paradigm.

# 3.    sic Conce ts in Softw re Engineering

The software development method that is presented in this book is built upon a number of standard Software Engineering concepts and combines them effectively into a single, coherent model. In this chapter, I will introduce these basic concepts and their relationships by starting with an investigation of a cognitive model of design in general. From this general model, I will derive some basic skills that are essential for a successful software engineer and I will outline some requirements for software engineering tools and methods that follow from these considerations.

After these general remarks, I shall then introduce a general model of software engineering and explain the individual parts of this model. The rest of this chapter is dedicated to an extensive discussion of software engineering process models.

## 3.1 Cognitive As ects of Softw re Engineering

The literature on cognitive aspects of software engineering is sparse. The existing investigations stem mostly from cognitive science or Human-Computer interaction research and deal with psychological theories on the nature of programming. Unfortunately, not much of the available results has been used by software engineers to understand their very own task or to improve their tools. Why is this the case?

First, software engineering is often identified with the task of developing *software*. However, this is only one side of the medal. Actually, software engineering is a very general design task [Grenno and Simon, 1988] and the existing results for these tasks can be applied. Furthermore, software engineering is a very broad subject that is made up from several, sometimes independent, activities that deal with many different products besides the code of the respective software system. Figure 3.1 shows a non-exhaustive list of activities that occur with a software engineering task and that deal with various (intermediate) products on different levels of abstraction. Before the interdependencies between these different activities can be structured into process models, it is necessary to *understand* these interdependencies on a cognitive level.

J. Lind: The MASSIVE Method, LNAI 1994, pp. 35-95, 2001.
© Springer-Verlag Berlin Heidelberg 2001

**Table 3.1.** Software engineering activities

| domain analysis | testing | extension |
|---|---|---|
| code analysis | validation | code documentation |
| architecture design | reuse | user documentation |
| component design | simulation | $\vdots$ |
| coding | refinement | |

Second, software engineering is often identified with *developing* software. However, a major task of todays software engineers is to *comprehend* either software that was developed by other team members or existing, third party software. This topic will become more and more important in the future because software is used in almost any part of nowadays life and the effort to maintain this existing software already exceeds the effort to develop new software [Balzert, 1998b], p.34. Thus, it must be a goal to todays software engineers to develop tools and techniques that ease the understanding of newly developed software for future use.

### 3.1.1 Basic Human Information Processing

The way in which human beings handle data about their environment and the internal processes that are performed during information processing are subject of research in cognitive psychology. In this section, I will briefly introduce some concepts and models that are needed later when the cognitive model of software engineering is presented.

The model of cognitive processes that is assumed in this chapter is based on the so-called Single-Store model of memory [Spada, 1990]. This model views the human memory as single, coherent structure that consists of a collection of *cognitive units* [Anderson, 1983], [Anderson, 1996] that are linked in network-like manner. The network is organized as hierarchically ordered levels where the elements of one level are abstractions of the elements on lower levels. For example, on the lowest level of abstraction, the sensory information that are associated with a particular item are stored whereas on a higher level, a symbolic representation for that same item is used.

The Single-Store model distinguishes between two activation levels for each cognitive unit. The units with a low level of activation are kept in the *long-term memory (LTM)* that is used as a passive, permanent knowledge store with a potentially unlimited capacity. Every cognitive unit can enter the LTM, but no unit can leave it afterwards. However, some cognitive units may become irretrievable in the course of time which is commonly referred to as "forgetting".

Some of the units in the LTM may have a higher level of activation then the rest. These cognitive units are said to reside in the *short-term memory*

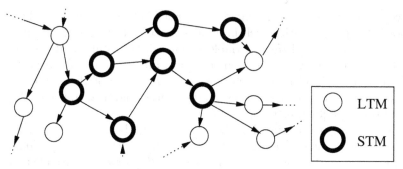

**Fig. 3.1.** Memory Model

*(STM)* of the individual. The elements of the STM are thus not spatially separated from the elements of the LTM (as it was assumed in older theories about the human memory [Shiffrin, 1973]), but rather differ from these only in their activation level. The major difference between the LTM and the STM is that the former has an unlimited capacity whereas the latter has a maximal size of approximately seven items [Miller, 1956]. In Figure 3.1, I have depicted a network of cognitive units out of which some are activated in the STM while the others remain passive in the LTM.

Although the LTM has an unlimited capacity, the size of the cognitive units should be kept at a minimum in order to speed up the retrieval process. The major technique for data compression is called *chunking* where a chunk is a collection of low level units that belong to the same mental construct. Thus, several simple units are encoded into a single, new item that is expressed in terms of these simple units and in terms of other chunks [Blum, 1992]. An example for chunking is that people remember words instead of syllables or letters or even phonetic impressions. However, the latter are linked to the higher level cognitive unit and can be accessed whenever necessary. Several studies have shown that chunking is a cognitive capability that has a large impact on cognitive performance. In one of these studies [Chase and Simon, 1973], novices and experts were asked to recall chess positions. While experts performed distinctly better on realistic game positions, the differences declined on random positions. The explanation for these results is that experts can compress more information into a single chunk then novices whenever they can use existing chunks such as sub-configurations on the chess board [Spada, 1990]. In [McKeithen et al., 1987], a similar experiment is reported where programmers are asked to recall Algol programs. Again, experts performed much better then novices on real programs but not on scrambled programs.

I have said before that the human memory is organized as in hierarchical levels of abstraction. While the representation of knowledge on low levels of abstraction is accomplished with little abstraction from the pure sensory impressions, knowledge on higher levels of abstraction is represented differently.

Single cognitive units are represented in so-called *schemata* where a schema is a knowledge packet with a rich internal structure [Détienne, 1990]. Each schema consists of several *slots* (variables) that can be instantiated with *slot fillers* (values). Partially instantiated schemata are *prototypes* for a particular concept, fully instantiated schemata are *exemplars* of this prototype. These exemplars can be ordered according to their semantic distance to their common prototype [Spada, 1990].

In the software engineering domain, schemata can be classified according to three different classes [Détienne, 1990]. The first class are *programming schemata* that are either *variable plans* or *control-flow plans*. A variable plan, for example, contains the semantic knowledge about the concept of a counter variable that is used in loops and a typical control-flow plan is the programmers knowledge about the general process of iterating over list of arbitrary elements. In a real program, the software engineer will need both schemata (amongst others) to implement a concrete function e.g. to sum up a list of integer values.

The second class of schemata are *application domain schemata* that represent the engineers background knowledge about the application domain. It is a crucial task in the software engineering process to match the application domain knowledge and the programming domain knowledge in order to develop or to understand a software system for the application domain.

The third class of schemata, finally, are *discourse schemata* that enable the software engineer to reason and communicate about programs besides functional aspects. These schemata include knowledge about general principles and conventions such as the convention that a variable should reflect its function or that particular variable names are used for certain tasks (e.g. i and j are typical variable names for loop variables).

For larger units of knowledge with many different interrelationships, schemata are not suited because of their rather descriptive nature. A more dynamic approach to the representation of large-scale cognitive units are *mental models* [Johnson-Laird, 1983]. These mental models contain declarative and procedural knowledge about a well-defined field and are often individualized scientific theories, e.g. about electricity [Spada, 1990]. Humans usually maintain a wide variety of these mental models and construct new models on demand, e.g. in the process of understanding the behavior of a complex system. The newly created models must be consistent with the existing models because these are resistant against changes and can only be revised with a certain learning effort [Spada, 1990].

### 3.1.2 Software Engineering as a General Design Task

A general design task is the process of arranging a collection of primitive elements according to a given design language in order to achieve a particular goal [Grenno and Simon, 1988]. Examples for general design tasks can be found in technical disciplines such as architectural design or electrical circuit design, but also in cultural areas, e.g. in music composition or in writing an essay. Thus, design tasks are complex tasks that entail multiple subtasks that draw on different knowledge domains and a variety of cognitive processes [Pennington and Grabowski, 1990].

Although these subjects appear to be rather different in their nature, they nonetheless share two fundamental activities that are exercised during the overall design process [Pennington and Grabowski, 1990]. The first general aspect is *composition*, i.e. the process of developing a design by describing associations between the structural elements of the design. In terms of a software engineering process, this step maps *what* a program should achieve onto a detailed set of instructions that specify *how* these requirements are implemented in a particular programming language.

The second, and equally important aspect, is *comprehension*. Comprehension means to take a particular design and to understand the associations between its structural elements. The input for this process may be a design that was produced by a third party, but often it is a design that was developed by the same person. Now, why should it be necessary for a designer to understand something that he or she has developed? Simply because it is almost impossible to anticipate all implicit relations that are introduced as side-effects of one explicit design decision. For example, creating a new function for a particular purpose may have the side-effect that other, already existing functions can be simplified by using the newly created function. For the software engineer, the process of understanding a design is to map *how* a program implements a specification to *what* this specification entails.

Please note that the software engineering process for a particular software system can start with any of these two fundamental activities. When developing a new system, the engineer will start with the composition of an initial design that is then elaborated in the course of the engineering activities. In the case of a maintenence task, on the other hand, the software engineer must first understand the existing software before changing it according to the new requirements.

The most important property of general design tasks is the evolutionary nature of the entire process. The design process is not sequential in that it proceeds from one intermediate product to the next until the design is completed, Rather, the process involves frequent revisions of previous decisions, re-structuring of the design elements or exploration of tentative solutions for particular sub-problems.

Therefore, the design process often starts with constructing a kernel solution and then incrementally extending this solution until it meets the initial requirements [Kant and Newell, 1984] [Ratcliffe and Siddiqi, 1985]. In software development, the kernel solution is often retrieved by re-using existing code fragments and the applying a series of repeated modifications to these fragments until the target system is constructed [Green, 1990].

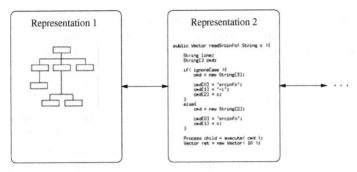

**Fig. 3.2.** Representations

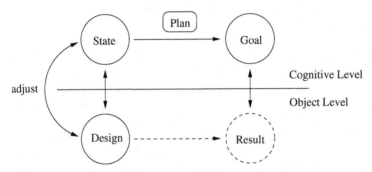

**Fig. 3.3.** Design and Model

### 3.1.3 Designs and Models

Before I describe a cognitive model of software engineering activities, I will outline a fundamental difficulty that is associated with the general task: the dichtonomy of the object that is worked on.

On one hand, we have a concrete *design* that is given in some external representation and that is manipulated by the process, e.g. the code of a software system, the draft of an essay or a piece of rock used by a sculptor. In the case of a software system, the design is often given in several external representations as shown in Figure 3.2. Ideally, these different representations are semantically isomorphic and differ only in their external form although in practical situations it is a major problem to keep the different representations synchronized. For the moment, however, we will not consider this problem and assume that the external representations are always consistent. We will return to the synchronization problem is Section 4.4 when we discuss a process model that deals with this question.

Besides the concrete design, we have the *model* (or the idea) inside the designers head that captures the intention of the final result of the design process as well as the current state of the design. As shown in Figure 3.3, the designer uses the state model and the goal model to derive a plan to reach the goal from the current state [Pennington and Grabowski, 1990]. But even if

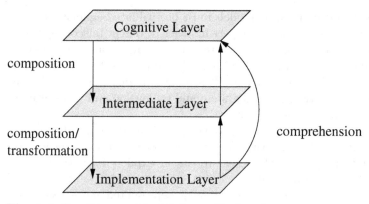

**Fig. 3.4.** Cognitive model of Software Engineering

we assumed that there is an error-free plan that transforms the current state into the goal state, the result will not be as expected. Why? Simply because the designers model of the current state does not correctly reflect the current state of the design. Ideally, these two objects should be isomorphic, but in the real world, there are so many details to consider that a true isomorphism will hardly be achieved. Because of this problem, the aforementioned comprehension process is crucial for the entire design task. It guarantees the necessary adjustment of the cognitive model in the designers head and the concrete design that is worked on. The goal of this comprehension process is to approximate existing mapping between the design and the model as close to an isomorphism as possible. The better the concrete design is understood, the better will be the result.

### 3.1.4 A General Model of Engineering

The cognitive model of software engineering that is presented in this section consists of three distinct layers as shown in Figure 3.4: the *cognitive layer* is the highest level of abstraction and operates on the various knowledge sources of the individual. The first of these knowledge sources is the background knowledge that contains general knowledge about computers and computations and technical aspects such as programming languages or hardware. Second, the cognitive layer also contains the engineers knowledge about the application domain for which a new software system is developed or where an existing system comes from. This knowledge is a crucial factor for the success or the failure of a software engineering task because it determines the bounds into which the software engineer can apply his or her technological abilities. If the problem domain is not sufficiently understood, the results will seldom match the intentions of the customer. Obviously, it is impossible for a software engineer to be an expert in any possible application domain and so the domain knowledge of the software expert develops during the design activities. The resulting implicit models must be evaluated against reality by external supervision of a domain expert in order to detect misconceptions.

Besides these major information sources, the cognitive layer also contains a mental model [Johnson-Laird, 1983] that has the same functional nature and structure as the system it models. This mental model is used for the simulation of processes within the real system and to develop and (pre-)evaluate hypothesis about the systems behavior.

The information structures within the cognitive layer are usually not represented explicitely. They are the sum of experiences of the engineer, often over years, and are thus hard to capture in an explicit form that can be communicated across individuals.

On the *intermediate layer*, the system is represented more technically in terms of the background concepts and the domain knowledge. This layer can be supported by an external representation although this is often omitted. If an external representation is used, software engineers tend to use highly individualized pseudo-languages [Petre and Winder, 1988]. These pseudo-languages are usually a collage of convenient formal or informal notations from several fields where each notation is selected on the basis of suitability for a particular task. The different notations are often partially inconsistent which makes it difficult to develop a general transformation scheme from the intermediate representation to a particular target language. This transformation process is therefore usually done manually [Kernighan and Plauger, 1974].

The intermediate layer is particularly important as it dictates the quality of the resulting design because it has been shown in [Petre and Winder, 1988] that the programming language has only a weak influence on the solution.

The lowest layer, finally, is the *implementation layer* that contains the code that is understandable by a computer. Obviously, the information on this layer must be encoded in an external form with a fixed syntactic format. In the usual software engineering practice, the communication across individuals takes place on this layer because of the standardized access to the information structures. The problem of this practice is, however, that information is lost during the transition from the intermediate to the code layer. Only particular associations between structural elements are transformed while others are lost and must be re-built by the receiver. We will return to this aspect in section 3.2 when we discuss the requirements for software engineering support systems.

Each of the above layers is subject to resource limitations that restrict the possible input and output of the process on a particular layer. Examples for these constraints are *cognitive resources* [Ormerod, 1990] such as the cognitive capacity which was already introduced in Section 3.1.1 or *knowledge resources* e.g. about the application domain or in terms of problem solving knowledge such as syntactical knowledge about the programming language or appropriate design patterns. The third form of resource limitations are *technical resources* which includes the expressive power of the programming language or tool support on the code level.

The information that is handled in each of these layers is provided as flexible *information structure* [Green, 1990] that represent the structural elements as well as their relationships. The most interesting property of the information structure is the flexibility in which the elements can be arranged. It is therefore possible to re-arrange the structure of the problem and solution descriptions according to the structure of the underlying task.

A good means to represent the structural design elements is provided by schemata as they were introduced in Section 3.1.1. Schemata are the basic elements for data generation, acquisition and manipulation that can be used in different ways. In the *forward use*, existing schemata are instantiated with problem related information in order to construct a concrete solution from abstract solution plans. The other form of schema usage is the analytical *backward use* where schemata are used to recognize particular aspects of the system and to either construct new schemata that describe these aspect or to instantiate existing schemata in the course of program understanding.

To illustrate the different layers that work together in the course of software engineering activities, consider the following example. A program for graphical manipulation of simple objects must be developed in a assembly language for an embedded system. On the cognitive layer, the engineer deals with concepts such as lines, squares or circles and their interrelationships. Assume further, that a particular function of the system requires to compute the diameter of a circle from the area it covers on the screen. On the cognitive layer, the engineer will combine this (domain) requirement with the background knowledge about geometric objects and retrieve the matching formula $A = \pi r^2$ from memory and rewrite it to $r = \sqrt{\frac{A}{\pi}}$ so that it yields the desired result. On the intermediate layer, this formula is used directly, probably by incorporating it into an external representation of the problem solving attempts of the engineer. In the subsequent transformation process, the elements of the formula are then broken up into parts that need no further refinement (e.g. division) and those aspects that are not provided by the underlying programming language and therfore need an explicit implementation (e.g. the square-root function).

We can already tell from this tiny example, that a lot of information is lost down along the line from the cognitive layer to the code layer. This gap widens as system gets bigger and it is the task of a software engineering support system to minimize the information loss as far as possible.

### 3.1.5 The Basic Engineering Cycle

A general design task as it was described in Section 3.1.2 is an *iterative, explorative* process that usually starts with a *fuzzy* specification of a *complex* goal. A cognitive model for working on these kinds of tasks was presented

---

**Process Model 1** The Basic Engineering Cycle (BEC)

---

1. **Select**
2. **Construct**
3. **Execute**
4. **Comprehend**
5. **Evaluate**
6. **Iterate**

---

in Section 3.1.4 and some issues regarding knowledge sources and knowledge representation were discussed. In this section, I will combine the introductory remarks of the previous sections into a generic process model that describes the general steps in building or in understanding a design.

As shown in Process model 1 and Figure 3.5, the resulting model consist of six steps: In the first step, the objective of the following iteration is selected. This can be a concrete entity such as design element that needs further elaboration but it can also be an abstract property or a functionality of the system that is to be analyzed for the purpose of understanding the property or functionality itself as well as its relation to the entire system. Then, either a solution for the sub-problem or a hypothesis to test the assumptions about the system is constructed. Note that different solutions for a particular problem may be tested and compared in subsequent iterations. After that, the solution is implemented or the test case for the hypothesis is run on the system. Then, the consequences of the implementation or the results of the test case must be understood before they can be evaluated according to given quality measures or test case specifications. After the evaluation is completed, a new iteration starts. In Figure 3.5, the steps of the process are shown together with the inherent flow of control and information.

To illustrate the generic process model, consider the task of understanding an existing program that implements a graphical editor. In the first step, a typical sub-problem of this task is identified e.g. to understand how a newly created element is integrated into the internal data model of the editor. Thus, the question to answer is "Which data stores are used and how is the new element linked to existing elements?".

In the second step, an hypothesis is created on the basis of the present code. The engineer may, for example, select several variables whose names suggest that these variables are involved in the process, e.g. a variable `elementList` would be a good candidate. Then, a test case is developed that generates a new element that is passed to the system. The major difficulty in developing test cases in general is to focus on the aspects in question and to leave the rest of the system untouched. During the test case specification, the expected results – based on the assumption that the hypothesis holds – are defined as well.

In the next step, the test case is run and the results are recorded. Running the test case may become a nontrivial task if the system requires some

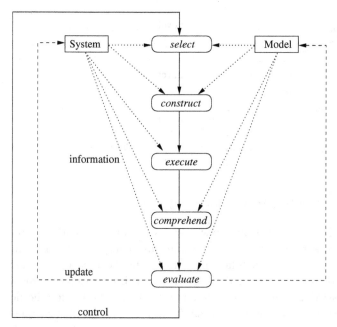

**Fig. 3.5.** The Basic Engineering Cycle

complicated start-up procedure before it is in the state to accept a particular test input. Especially distributed systems are sometimes difficult to bring to the desired start state.

The fourth step of the cycle is to understand the changes that occurred within the program. These changes are retrieved by a *before* and *after* analysis of the *relevant* aspects of the system. The relevance of particular aspects is usually given by the hypothesis that was defined earlier.

In the evaluation step, the results are checked for compatability with the expected results on the hypothesis is accepted of rejected on the basis of this evaluation process. A third possibility for the result of this evaluation is that the data is not sufficient to allow for a decision on the validity of the hypothesis and that additional test case are necessary before a decision can be made. After these steps have been performed, the process iterates back to the beginning to start a new cycle.

The basic engineering cycle that has been presented in this section is only a very general framework for engineering tasks. A concrete instantiation of the generic model usually depends on a specific application area such as civil engineering or, in our case, software development. Each of these application areas has some special skills that are necessary for a successful application of the basic engineering cycle. In the following section, I will therefore outline some of the basic skills that are relevant in the software development domain.

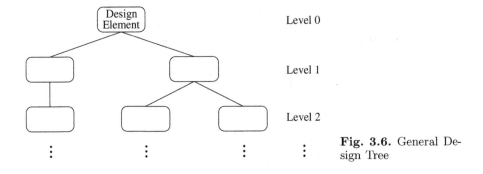

**Fig. 3.6.** General Design Tree

### 3.1.6 Basic Skills in Software Engineering

In this section, I will give a brief overview over technical skills and possible development strategies that have been identified as being relevant for the software development process. The following paragraphs are a loose collection that I have compiled from several sources and that I think capture the most relevant skills and strategies for software engineers. Thus, the reader should be able to recognize some of his or her own habits in this section. In the course of the section, we will start out with an overview over (generic) development strategies and then proceed with a list of individual skills that are more or less necessary for a successful software engineer.

*Development strategies* capture how individuals proceed with the engineering tasks on a particular subject, i.e. they describe, in terms of the basic engineering cycle that was presented in the previous section, how the next sub-problem is selected. In [Wisser and Hoc, 1990], these strategies are explained at hand of an n-ary tree as shown in Figure 3.6 that describes the current state of the design at different levels of abstraction.

However, the implicit assumption of this view is, that there exists a unique starting point of the design process, indicated by the root of the tree. In previous sections, I have argued that the information about the system that is used by the engineer is more likely to be represented in a flexible, network-like structure. This idea is consistent with the wide-spread view that "real systems have no top" [Sommerville, 1995], i.e. there always exist a large number of perspectives on the same system. Therefore, I suggest that there are multiple design trees that are projections of the net with respect to a particular relationship of the structural elements. Thus, as shown in Figure 3.7, we may have the *refinement-tree* that represents e.g. the refinement of system elements or we may have the *uses-tree* that describes the functional dependencies between design elements.

The strategies that are discussed in the following paragraphs are used in two ways: first to *select the relation* (and therewith the respective design tree) that needs further expansion and second to *select a particular design element* within the design tree that is to be worked on next.

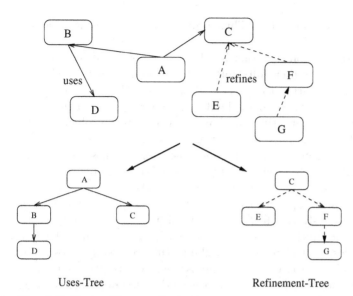

Uses-Tree                    Refinement-Tree

**Fig. 3.7.** Design Trees as Projections

In using a *top-down* strategy, the designer proceeds from the structural elements on the most abstract level to more concrete elements until finally the code level is reached. This strategy is very common with imperative models of computations (and sometimes in later phases of object-oriented approaches) and it is more or less formally capture in so-called Structured Programming approaches e.g. [Dahl et al., 1972]. This strategy is usually most appropriate whenever the designer is familiar with the problem domain and thus knows in advance what potential difficulties lure on lower levels of abstraction.

A *bottom-up* strategy, on the other hand, starts with a collection of low level design elements that are subsequently assembled into bigger units. This strategy is quite common in functional or declarative models of computations such as Lisp [Graham, 1995] as well as in early phases of object-oriented programming. An advantage of this strategy is that it can be used to detect implementation problems that can force a re-design on higher levels of abstraction to match the requirements of a particular platform.

The top-down and the bottom-up strategy describe *how* to proceed from one level of abstraction to the next. These strategies can be combined with another two strategies that prescribe *when* to proceed from one level to the next.

In a *breath-first* strategy, all design elements on one level of abstraction are developed before the next level is approached. This strategy is therefore particularly helpful to deal with interactions among design elements on the same level of abstraction. However, the problem is that these interactions can become too complex to be simultaneously considered by the designer

[Guindon et al., 1987], [Hoc, 1988]. Thus, a pure breath-first strategy is usually not feasible.

A *depth-first* strategy, on the other hand, aims at developing components of one or few branch(es) to their full depth and then going back to the highest level of abstraction to start with the next branch(es). This strategy is very good to explore particular aspects of the design in early stages of the design process and to develop alternative solutions for a particular problem.

The four strategies the have been discussed in the previous paragraphs are idealized and abstracted. In a real design task, none of these strategies is applied throughout the full development process. Rather, the developer usually chooses the best strategy for the next few steps [Wisser and Hoc, 1990]. This behavior is called opportunistic. In such an *opportunistic strategy* [Hayes-Roth and Hayes-Roth, 1979], the next sub-task is selected according to its utility and its cognitive costs [Visser, 1990]. If the information for handling the current design element is not available, the processing is postponed if the retrieval would be too costly (or impossible, because necessary other design elements are not even built). In this case, other design elements are expanded because it is "cheaper" then sticking to the plan which would dictate a context switch. Thus, an opportunistic strategy needs support for flexible switching between different task. We will return to this aspect in Section 3.2 when we discuss tool support requirements for the software development process

Besides these development strategies, which obviously influence the overall "flavor" of the engineering process, we have some other important skills that are used by the software engineer. In [Balzert, 1998a], one of the key capabilities of a successful software engineer is the ability to use *abstraction* . Abstraction (sometimes also called *modeling* ) is the process of deriving the general from the specific while leaving out unnecessary details. An important abstraction technique is *layering* , i.e. the process of decomposing the target problem into several, hierarchically related sub-problems where the sub-problems on a lower layer are refinements of those on higher layers. The problem of this technique, however, is to decide when to stop the decomposition in order not to run into a too detailed analysis.

Another important capability is *structuring* , i.e. the aptitude to define the relation between the whole and the parts as well as between the parts themselves. Structuring is closely related to abstraction in that it tries to find a reduced representation of a complex system such that the basic character is revealed. We distinguish between *static structuring* where the resulting structure remains fixed over the system lifetime and *dynamic structuring* where the structure can change during the system lifetime. A sub-category of structuring is the ability to *build hierarchies* by ranking, ordering or graduation of the parts of the system. Also related to this selection of capabilities is *grouping* or *modularization*. Ideally, the system is divided into self-contained functional groups that can be worked on in isolation whereas in reality, existing dependencies blur the ideal picture and require to model dependencies explicitly. Therefore, the designer must be able to identify and describe these dependencies in lucidly. Thus, the designer must have extremely good communicative skills and posses means of *verbalization* in order to express thoughts and ideas to bring them to his or her own as well as consciousness to transport them over boundaries of individuals. Thus, verbalization is very important for internal reasoning as well as communication between engineers.

Besides this list of quite general capabilities, there are a number of aspects that are specific for the software development process. *Simulation* [Adelson et al., 1984] , for example, is referred to as the process of mentally imitating the system behavior on the basis of the mental model that is constructed in the design or comprehension process. It can be used to predict potential interactions between design elements or is can be used in an opportunistic strategy to select the design elements that need expansion. Furthermore, simulation can support the comprehension process by using the mental model of the system to develop the expected results of a particular hypothesis before it is tested on the system. Simulation is also useful to roughly evaluate tentative solutions for a particular problem prior to implementing it. This is sometimes a cost-effective way to detect misconceptions before they are introduced into the system.

Another important aspect of software engineering is the *change of perspective* [Adelson et al., 1984], [Visser, 1987]. Thus, the engineer can either take the perspective of the user for a better understanding of the requirements or he or she can take the users perspective to develop hypothesis about the systems external behavior. Furthermore, the engineer can switch to the perspective of another software engineer in order to assess the structure and the comprehensibility of the current design. This can help to improve the maintainability of the final design.

The last important skill that I want to mention in this non-exhaustive list is to make use of *existing experience* and *software design re-use*. It is empirically validated that any software design is seldom generated from scratch [Visser, 1987], [Pennington and Grabowski, 1990]. Rather, the designer usually makes use of existing designs that are adapted to the current requirements. These design templates are either retrieved from the designers internal database, i.e. from memory, or they are take from external sources such as [Gamma et al., 1994]. Such re-use of working solutions is crucial for developing a design in always decreasing product life cycles.

In this section, I have briefly outlined some basic cognitive skills that are relevant for the software developer. The application and development of these skills can be greatly simplified by the use of adequate tools and methods that support the software engineer in his or her work. In the next section, I will therefore sketch some general requirements for such tools or methods.

## 3.2 Requirements for Softw re Engineering Su    ort

In this section, we will discuss some aspects that should be addressed by software engineering design tools or methods that are constructed according to the cognitive aspects that were presented in the previous sections.

The first major requirements deals with the *presentation* of the current state of the design. The presentation scheme of a tool or method should support a broad range of perhaps individualized notations. It should allow the designer to express his or her ideas in the most suitable form without imposing a particular syntactical structure. Experts want a notation scheme that allows them to express their ideas elegantly [Petre, 1990] and therefore often use individualizes schemes that were discussed in Section 3.1.4. Obviously, this requirements has the consequence that automatic tool support is difficult or even impossible. I will argue later, why the basic idea of individualized notations is still feasible although it requires some additional start-up effort from the designer. The second important aspect in conjunction with presentational issues is that a tool or method must support perceptual support for the contents of the design. For example, useful information should be highlighted and the information should be represented in redundant perceptual and symbolic forms [Curtis, 1989]. The information presentation should also support revelation, i.e. it should reflect the structure of the solution and perhaps the process that lead to the current state of the design. To document the evolution of the design to its current form can especially help an engineer to understand the design from a third party. Finally, the presentation scheme of a tool must support grouping mechanisms, i.e. strongly related components should be kept together. The difficulty with this requirement is that the term "strongly related" depends on the current focus of the engineer. Therefore, it is necessary to support dynamic re-ordering of the information structures according to the change of focus.

The literate programming approach proposed by Donald Knuth [Knuth, 1992] is a good example for the idea of grouping related aspects together in order to make them accessible to the programmer. The problem of literate programming, however, is that the relation between the parts remain static and thus prevent the programmer from choosing the most adequate relation for a particular situation.

Presenting information statically, however, is only one side of the medal. An equally important aspect that requires tool support is the *navigation* within the information structure that describes the current state of the design. Navigation through this information structure should be possible along various threads such as control flow, logical grouping, refinements etc. The navigation must be possible across levels of abstractions because expert software engineers want the ability to work with high-level constructs on abstract models as well as the ability to work on a low level such as hardware devices [Petre, 1990]. The navigation should be supported by additional cognitive aids that ease, for example, simulation of the systems behavior by providing mnemonics for variable values or that allow for symbolic execution of the program as demonstrated e.g. in [Sneed, 2000]. Finally, the navigation between different tasks should be backed by mechanisms for the management of the working memory [Wisser and Hoc, 1990], e.g. in case of an opportunistic refinement strategy by keeping a list of postponed sub-tasks.

The third major aspect besides presentation and navigation is *changing* the information structure that captures the current design state. Therefore, the presented information should be editable wherever it is presented, i.e. there should be no read-only presentations. Furthermore, any changes that are made to the design should be easily revisable [Curtis, 1989] and a tool or a method in general should not force premature commitment as it is often the case with existing development suites or methods [Green, 1990].

The last major requirement for tool or method support, finally, is that the information structure that is developed in the course of the design process is *accessible* on a technical level. Expert software engineers expect to build their own tools because understanding the difficult mechanisms of a particular Software Engineering Environment is usually considered to entail more work then building utilities up from a low level [Petre, 1990]. This easy access to the information structures then solves the above problem in conjunction with individualized notation schemes. The software engineer can build his or her own set of tool that transform the individual notation scheme to a particular target language and so express the design in an individual notation that is subsequently transformed into the target language. Although the initial effort to build the transformation tools is quite high, it quickly pay off because of the better internal management of the design object.

A good starting point for the development of tools and methods for software engineering, is to have a general model of the underlying process. Therefore, we will now skip our reflections about engineering in general and the required cognitive capabilities and address ourselves to the peculiarities of software development by starting with a general model of the software development process.

## 3.3 A General Model of Software Engineering

In Figure 3.8, I have depicted a general architecture for software development methods: the basic entity that is worked on during software development is the *product* as the intended outcome of the process. Typically, such a software product is constructed according to an abstract description that holds the general form for a particular class of products. Such a generic description is called a *product model*. Since each product model is a generic description of the parts and their interconnections for an entire class of products, it is quite natural that we have several generic product models, one for each class of applications.

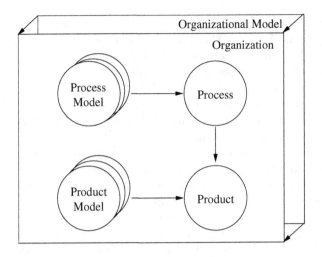

**Fig. 3.8.** A General Model of Software Engineering

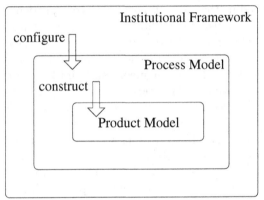

**Fig. 3.9.** The Structure of an Ideal Development Method

The instantiation of product model into a product is achieved by applying a particular *process*. Again, a concrete process is the instantiation of a particular *process model* that is an abstract plan of the software development activities. As with product models, we have several generic process models that are either general purpose models that can be used for any type of software, or specialized models for particular application classes. The software development process itself is usually part of a larger organizational structure that is used to manage the various product and process models as well as their concrete instantiations. This organizational structure can be built according to an *organizational model* which is again a generic description of the managemental entities or activities and their relations.

I will use this general model of software engineering activities to structure the following chapters as well as the ideas that comprise the software development method presented in this book. Following the above considerations, the basic structure of an –in my view– ideal development method is shown in Figure 3.9. It thus provides one or more product models that are used to describe the design and/or the implementation of a particular system, one or more process models that guide the developer in constructing the product models according to the user requirements and finally an organizational framework that guides the project management in selecting and supporting the development process to yield the best possible result.

In the next section, we will start our tour through the various aspects of the above model by inspecting the properties of generic product models.

## 3.4 Softw re Engineering Product Models

**Definition 3.4.1 (Product [Balzert, 1998b]).** *A* **product** *is the self-contained result of a manufacturing process that is intended for a particular customer.*

As I have said before, a product model is a generic description of the parts that make up a software product as well as their interrelationships. It serves as a means of communication between the participating parties within a software project. The resulting product of the software manufacturing process is thus an instantiation of a particular product model that is created by the process and the product model can therefore be interpreted as a description of the goal of the software production process.

Often – but not always – a product model is closely related to a particular process model. In the V-Model as described in [Rombach, 1994a], the product model resembles the steps of the process model that is used to construct the final product. The product model of the V-Model consists of six parts that can be directly mapped to the activities within the V-Model: the *Problem description* contains a high level description of the systems intended behavior that is subsequently refined into the *User requirements* which hold a more formal and more detailed specification that it is even more refined into the *Developer requirements*. This rather fine grained specification document serves as the basis for the high-level *System design* that is extended towards the *Unit design* which holds the blueprints for the individual components of the system. These *Executable components* are constructed during the coding phase of the V-Model and assembled to the *Executable system* that is brought into production after the validation against the initial specification, leading to the *Production system* as the final part of the product model of the V-Model. Note, however, that the structure of the product model does not determine the ordering of the steps that are taken to build the parts of the product model. Although this is the case in V-Model, the same product model can be used with a different process model that stipulates another sequence of activities.

### 3.4.1 A Generic Product Model

In this section, I will present a generic product model that is independent of a particular process model. As a starting point for such a generic model, I will use the following four questions that I think a product model should allow to be answered: (1) What should be done? (2) Where should it be done? (3) Who should do it? and (4) How should it be done?

The first question in the above enumeration aims at the system itself and the requirements that it must fulfill in order to be accepted as a solution for the problem under consideration. I will not impose any constraints upon the notation that is used to capture the system requirements to allow the system developer to chose the most appropriate notation for a particular case. The system itself, however, is only a part of the problem because no systems runs independently from its environment. Thus, there as usually a large number of external interfaces, constraints or prerequisites that must be taken into account when developing a software system.

Although stated above that the intended product model should be independent from a particular process model, it is an unrealistic goal to try to be completely independent. Therefore, I assume a minimal process model that consists of an *Analysis phase* and a subsequent *Design phase*. This minimal process model (if one could even call it a process model) is in my view the absolute minimum beyond simple hacking. An even in the case of hacking a program directly into the keyboard, I would still argue that the minimal process model is at least implicitly used by the hacker.

The above list of questions is often split out in a way that the system requirements and the system environment are usually broken down in the analysis phase of the software development process whereas the focus of questions (3) and (4) are the major concern of the design phase. In developing the system design, the software engineer must lay out the entities (who) that are involved as well as their interrelationships (what). The entities themselves can be anything from rather simple data structures, functions or objects up to complex entities such as agents. The range of relationships between these entities is equally broad and includes simple method or function invocation as well as message exchange between remote entities.

The separation of concern that is implied by the above list is shown graphically in Figure 3.10. In the figure, we can clearly see that there is a rather string relation between the system and its environment that are captured by the design on the one hand and the "who" and "how" of the implementation on the other hand. I will return to this separation into design and implementation in Section 4.2 where I will present the foundation of the MASSIVE product model in greater detail.

In this section, we have investigated the basic structure of a product model on a very high level of abstraction. However, the instantiation of a product model into a specific product can be achieved in many different ways with each of these ways using their own content language to describe

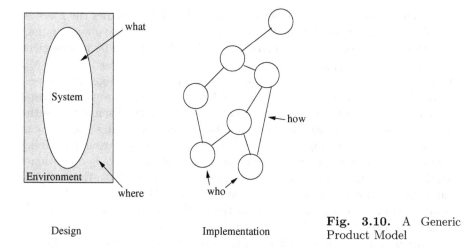

Design                    Implementation

**Fig. 3.10.** A Generic Product Model

the final product. Obviously, this approach has the serious drawback that developers tend to use the favorite notation schemes, making it difficult – if not impossible – to communicate with other developers. Especially in the object-oriented community, the drawback of multiple design languages stimulated the development of a common content language that integrates the main object-oriented notation schemes.

### 3.4.2 Software Blueprints: The Unified Modeling Language

A design tool that has recently gained major attraction in the software engineering community is a graphical language to describe the design of software systems. The *Unified Modeling Language (UML)* [Booch et al., 1999], [Rumbaugh et al., 1999] aims at a global standard for the description of software systems comparable to standardized blueprint languages that exist for electrical, mechanical or civil engineering for several years. The advantage of such a blueprint language for software systems that is built upon a set of symbols and mechanisms together with a well defined semantics for both of them, is that it enables software designers to express, exchange and work on their ideas without complicated translation processes that are necessary nowadays. Furthermore, a unified language increases the interoperability among software design tools and allows software developers to become more independent of particular development environments and thus allow them to assemble customized environments out of different tool suites. The UML combines original ideas with established features of other graphical design languages into a coherent framework that allows for the specification of a broad range of design aspects of a software system. In this book, I will use the UML in the case studies to describe parts of the system design.

The major goals of the UML as they are discussed in [Rational Software, 1999a] are to provide a ready-to-use expressive visual modeling language that is widely accepted and thus allows the users to exchange design models without loss of information or excessive work to map their models onto each other. Furthermore, the UML should be independent of a particular programming language or development process i.e. the UML should be able to support all reasonable programming languages as well as most existing process models. The UML should also provide a formal basis for understanding the modeling language. The formal semantics of the language constructs must, however, not be too complicated so that it can be applied by the average user. UML expresses the operational meaning of most constructs in precise natural language and thus avoids operational definitions that are equivalent to implementation specifications. Extensibility and specialization mechanisms are used in the UML to extend the core concepts by allowing the users to tailor the UML towards their specific needs without the need to alter the core definition or re-implement tools. The UML also supports higher-level development concepts such as design patterns, components or frameworks to support reuse of models and software and aims at encouraging the growth of the tool market by stimulating interoperability between the products of different vendors on the basis of a commonly agreed format and meaning of modeling constructs. All in all, it is the main goal of the UML to integrate best practices in industry.

The UML is currently undergoing a standardization process that will not be finished for several years. However, the basic functionalities seem to have settled during the past few years and are unlikely to be changed as they are already used in software development environments of all kinds. The building blocks that are currently defined in the UML are described below.

**Things** Things are first-class abstractions in models that are used to describe *structural, behavioral, grouping* or *annotational* entities. Structural entities are the static parts (either conceptual or physical) of a software design, e.g. classes, interfaces, collaborations, etc.; behavioral things, on the other hand, deal with the dynamic parts (i.e. behavior over space and time) and are described in interaction diagrams or state machines; groupings are the organizational parts of the software system (e.g. packages) and comments are used to describe, explain or illuminate facts that cannot be expressed in the UML itself.

**Relationships** The task of relationships is to tie things together by modeling their *dependencies*, i.e. the semantic relation between things where the change of one thing may affect the semantics of the other thing; their *association*, i.e. structural relationships that describe a connection between things (e.g. aggregation); *generalizations* that express the substitutability of a thing (the parent) for another thing (the child) and *realization*, i.e. a semantic relationship wherein one classifier specifies a contract with another classifier that guarantees to carry it out.

**Diagrams** Diagrams are used to group interesting collections of things. The diagram types that are defined within the UML are

**Fig. 3.11.** The Ideal Software Development Process

- *Class diagrams* for classes, interfaces and collaborations and their relationships,
- *Object diagrams* for objects and their relationships,
- *Use case diagrams* for actors and their relationships,
- *Sequence diagrams* for messages between objects with a focus on the time-ordering,
- *Collaboration diagrams* for messages between objects with a focus on the structural aspects,
- *Statechart diagrams* for a dynamic, event-oriented view of the system,
- *Activity diagrams* for emphasizing the control flow among objects,
- *Component diagrams* for the static implementation view and
- *Deployment diagrams* for the configuration of the run-time processing nodes and the components that live on them.

These concepts will not be explained in this work and I refer the reader to [Booch et al., 1999] for a full introduction to the UML. I will use the UML in this book to present some of the ideas and the resulting implementation of the case study at a high level of abstraction. These rather simple diagrams should be understandable without an intensive knowledge of the UML.

## 3.5 Softw re Engineering Process Models

The need for prescriptive plans for the development of software systems arose as it became clear that the software development process contains numerous difficulties that cannot be solved in an ad-hoc manner [Naur and Randell, 1969]. In the late sixties software community had slipped into what was called the "software crisis" and the need for engineering models that guide the software development process was raised. Since then, a large number of software engineering models have been proposed.

Ideally, software development as shown in figure 3.11 is achieved in three steps:

1. The designer develops an *abstract model* of the aspects of the real world that should be implemented by the software system.
2. The system is *constructed* (implemented) according to the model.
3. The operational software system is *installed* at the customers site.

The products that are generated in the course of this development process are the *design* that describes the designers view on the system and its environment as well as the designers intention of what the system is supposed to do and the *implementation* that realizes the design on a computer platform.

Unfortunately, things are not always that straight because of various difficulties that can occur during the development process. Therefore, the designer needs some pre-defined plan of how to execute the activities that are involved in the software development process and also plans of how to handle difficulties that arise in the course of these activities. Such a pre-defined plan is called a process model as defined below.

**Definition 3.5.1 (Process Model [Jalote, 1997]).**
*A Software Engineering* **process model** *is a formalization of the software design and implementation activities and of the products that are connected with these activities.*

A large number of different process models have been proposed since the need for these prescriptive plans became apparent. I have chosen some of these models to present them in subsequent sections either because they are fundamental and widely accepted and used in industrial contexts or because they are closely related to our development philosophy. Section 3.5.1 captures the classical process models that have been proposed at the beginning of the development of software engineering as a distinguished research field and although some of the models discussed there may appear outdated, the nonetheless have laid out the ground for the development of more elaborate methods. In Section 3.5.2, I will then discuss some of the most recent approaches towards software development. Literally all of the methods presented there have contributed to the software development method for multiagent systems that is described in this book. In Section 3.5.3, finally, I have assembled a overview over other software development methods that explicitly deal with multiagent systems in order to relate the method presented in this book to its "competitors".

### 3.5.1 Classical Process Models

In this section, I will present some of the most fundamental process models that have been developed in the early days of Software Engineering. I have decided to include these classical models because some the basic ideas that are incorporated in these models are still used – although mostly modified or hidden – in more recent models.

**Waterfall Model.** The Waterfall model [Royce, 1970] was initially created to describe the various stages that occur during the software development process and it is one of the earliest attempts to formally describe software development. The Waterfall model is a document-oriented top-down approach that models the entire software development process as a sequence of consecutive steps where the output of one step serves as the input of the next step. As depicted in Figure 3.12, the individual steps that are executed during the software development process are the *analysis* of the problem domain, *designing* the software system that solves the problem, *coding* the design into

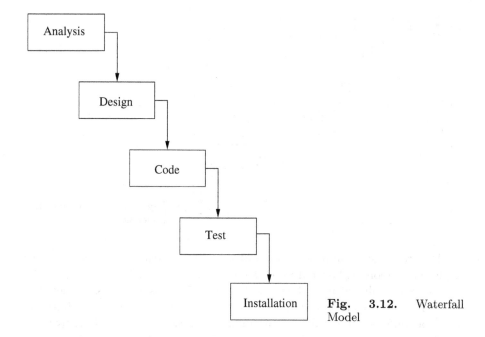

**Fig. 3.12.** Waterfall Model

a particular programming language, *testing* the code with respect to the requirements and finally *installing* the system at the user site.

The Waterfall model optimistically assumes that these steps can be executed in the given order, i.e. that all documents are complete and no problems occur that would require to trace back to a previous stage.

Due to its simple, sequential nature, the Waterfall model is easy to understand and to use, even by unexperienced programmers. Because of the non-existing interdependencies of the different stages, no complicated coordination among team members is necessary. This might explain why the Waterfall model is still widely in use in industrial projects of almost any size.

However, the Waterfall model has a number of serious drawbacks that limit its applicability. First, it is somewhat unrealistic to assume that all documents are complete and error-free upon the first creation. This assumption is often interpreted as a prescriptive requirement and thus the documents are not allowed to change once they are completed. This makes it impossible to correct design decisions that show to be sub-optimal. Second, the model does not feature any risk analysis that is helpful in order to identify potential problem areas of the software development process. In a way, this topic is closely related to the optimistic assumption that everything will go all right. The third major problem of the Waterfall model is finally, that the user often tends to see the documentation as more important then the system itself. Thus the focus of the development team shifts away from their initial goal to produce a software system to the goal of producing documents that describe the system.

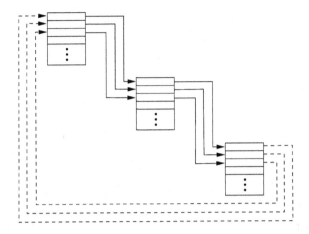

**Fig. 3.13.** Iterative Enhancement

Due to these limitations and problems of the Waterfall model, it was replaced by more elaborated process models.

Iterative Enhancement [Basili and Turner, 1975] is a process model that is similar to the Waterfall Model except for the fact that the Waterfall Model needs a complete and stable requirements definition while the Iterative Enhancement model operates in several cycles on a partitioned and incomplete system model. The incomplete model is iteratively enhanced (hence the name of the method) in each cycle as shown in Figure 3.13 for a three step process. The major advantage of this approach is that it takes into account that any specification is initially incomplete and usually undergoes frequent changes because of upcoming new information, external factors or simply because of human errors [Parnas and Clements, 1986]. Although the idea of Iterative Enhancement is pretty old in terms of computer science research, it is still developed further and used in software development methods such as described in Section 3.5.2.

**V-Model.** The V-Model [Rombach, 1994b], [Dröschel and Wiemers, 1999] is a direct successor of the Waterfall model and it was designed to fix some of the most obvious shortcomings of its ancestor. As a major enhancement, the V-Model adds explicit quality assurance mechanisms to the Waterfall model: *verification* is concerned with the correctness of individual products with respect to their specifications, and *validation* refers to the correctness of individual products with respect to the intended use of these products. Thus, verification and validation introduce explicit feedback loops if some process stages fail to achieve their goals.

Besides these enhancements, the V-Model provides a more fine-grained view on the process of software development. The basic idea is to model the members of a software development team by explicit *roles* with associated *activities*. These activities can generate or change the *products* that are produced during the process execution and that have already been mentioned in Section 3.4.

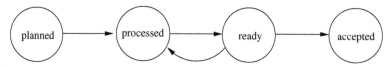

**Fig. 3.14.** Product-States

Each of these *products* has one out of four well-defined states; a product can either be `planned` if it does not exist at a particular step, `processed` during its construction or refinement, `ready` if the construction or refinement is completed or `accepted` when it has passed the quality assurance test mentioned above.

The possible transitions between product states are shown in Figure 3.14: when the process enters a state that generates a new product, the state of this product changes from `planned` to `processed` until a first version of the product is assembled and the product state changes to `ready`. If the product succeeds in the following quality assurance test, the state changes to `accepted`. If the quality assurance process fails, the product status is reset to `processed` and a new iteration is executed.

The possible *activities* within the V-Model as shown in Figure 3.15 are *development, verification* or *validation* where either of the activities can either generate a product, change the content of a product or change the state of a product. The generation and content change of a product are usually achieved by the development activities whereas the state-change of a product is associated with either a validation or a verification activity. Each of these activities is exactly documented according to a predefined scheme.

In the V-Model, *roles* are used to describe the required experience, knowledge and abilities for particular activities that are associated with a role inhibitor. The V-Model differentiates between *technical roles* and *management roles*.

The technical roles are the *requirements engineer* who is responsible for the definition of the requirements towards the software system, the *system architect* who designs the software architecture of the target system, the *designer* who is responsible for the design of individual components or entire sub-systems, the *code engineer* who transfers the designers specifications into executable code, the *verification engineer* who is responsible for the correctness of the code wrt. to the functional specifications, the *integration supervisor* who controls the assembly process of components and sub-systems and finally the *validation engineer* who assesses the correctness of the system or parts of the system wrt. to its intended use.

The management roles are the *product manager* who is responsible for a single product, the *project planer* who is responsible for planning the time lines and resource allocations of the project, the *project manager* who controls the project execution and keeps it synchronized with the scheduled activities

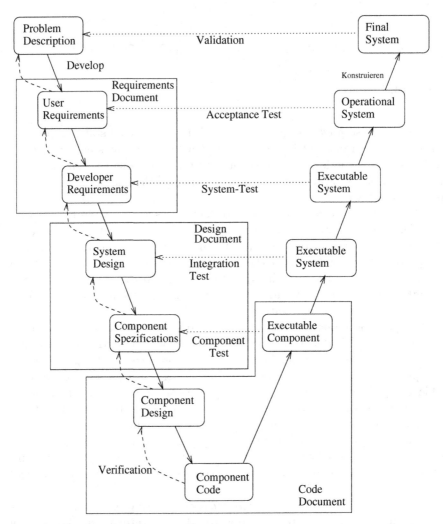

**Fig. 3.15.** The V-Model

and resource limitations and the *quality control manager* how is responsible for the maintenance of the quality standards.

The V-model is a very detailed model that is generic and customizable. It works well for large projects and is now a required standard for large industrial projects. It is a mandatory standard for military projects in Germany (and several other countries) and also for many public or government software projects. However, due to its degree of details, it is not suited for small or middle size projects because of the high institutional overhead that proportionally decreases with the project size. Furthermore, the model needs explicit tool support to handle the co-ordination processes between the various roles. Furthermore, the V-Model is not generally method-independent as

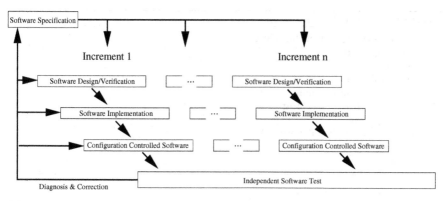

**Fig. 3.16.** The Cleanroom Model

it depends on a functional and a data-oriented decomposition of the problem to be solved [Balzert, 1998a].

**Cleanroom.** The Cleanroom software development process model [Mills et al., 1987], [Dyer, 1992], [Poore and Trammell, 1996], [Linger and Trammell, 1996] was originally designed to support the development of almost error-free software by introducing error prevention instead of error correction in the development process. In most other process models, one or more test-phase(s) are an integral part of the development process itself. The Cleanroom method, on the other hand, takes a different view on the matter of testing. The basic idea is to separate the software development process from the quality management activities. Thus, not the designer or the implementor of a piece of software is responsible for the quality of his or her product, but a completely different authority – the *tester*. This forces the designer to put more effort into the planning process of the products because errors cannot be "tested out" during the development process. The Cleanroom approach supports this idea by suggesting the use of formal methods of software design as far as possible. The tester, on the other hand, has no connection whatsoever to the design process as he or she is only responsible for maintaining the well defined quality standards through applying statistical testing methods to the software delivered by the designer. This separation of the two major activities in the software development process ensures a higher reliability of the final product and leads to a higher productivity because of the reduced work.

As shown in Figure 3.16 the Cleanroom process model divides the target system into several independent increments that can be separately worked on using an iterative refinement approach. The process model shown in the figure is summarized in Process Model 2.

In the requirements specification phase, the basic increments of the final software system are identified and the requirements towards each of these increments are defined. The specification should use formal method as far as

---

**Process Model 2** Cleanroom

---

1. **Requirements specification**
2. **Development**
   a) Design
   b) Implementation
   c) Configuration management
3. **(Independent) Testing**
4. **Quality test**
   If quality is sufficient goto (5)
   else goto (2)
5. **Done**

---

possible in order to allow for test specifications to cover all relevant aspects of the system.

In the development phase, the designers and implementors are not allowed to test their code. Some implementations of the Cleanroom approach even require that the development team is not allowed to *compile* the code produced. In order to prevent the "testing in" of quality, the only allowed techniques for the designers and implementors to check their design or code are code reading, walk-troughs and formal verification approaches.

The goal of the test phase is to verify that the previously defined quality standards are fulfilled by using functional testing with random input within the specification range. The randomization of the test data should be directed in a way that puts more emphasis on the parts of the system that are more important or more in use then others. It is thus based on the formal specification documents as well as use cases that describe the intended uses of the systems. Bugs that occur within the testing phase are not removed by the testing team. Instead, only feedback for the development team on where the bug occurred is provided.

The advantages of the Cleanroom process model are that it allows for the production of software with very high quality standards and is thus well suited for all kinds of safety-critical applications. The incremental approach that is applied within the development process allows for an efficient resource allocation throughout the entire project life cycle and supports the development of large scale systems.

However, the Cleanroom approach is a very complicated and costly method that requires an appropriate organizational infrastructure as well as experienced staff to work properly. Especially the use of formal methods is currently not wide-spread in industrial software engineering environments. Furthermore, the approach requires a high discipline within the project team to avoid "cheating" between the development and the quality assurance team.

**Prototyping.** Prototyping [Floyd, 1983], [Lichter et al., 1994], sometimes also referred to as rapid prototyping or rapid application development (RAD), is a Software Engineering method for the systematic support of the early

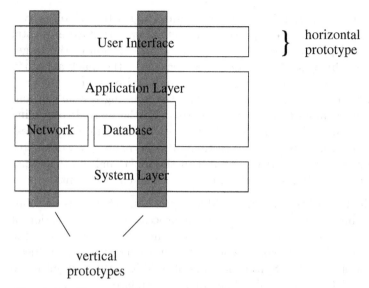

**Fig. 3.17.** Classes of Prototypes

development of executable software artifacts. Prototyping supports the user-designer communication and is often used in research and development, but also in an industrial environment, to demonstrate and evaluate requirements and design decisions. The executable system components enable the designer and the user to experiment with requirements and design decisions and to find more appropriate alternatives if some of these decisions do not reflect the intended use or fail to work properly.

Rapid Prototyping can have one out of two intents. First, it can be used to incrementally build a full sized product through the iterative enhancement [Basili and Turner, 1975] of the core system. Second, it can also be used to build a scaled down version of the target system in order to demonstrate and investigate crucial points.

As shown in Figure 3.17, two types of Prototyping can be distinguished. Whereas *horizontal prototypes* implement the functionality of a single layer of the final product to its full extent, *vertical prototypes* implement selected functionalities over all layers of the final product.

Prototyping is a valuable tool in order to reduce risks in the software development process because it allows the designer and user to identify critical requirements or design decisions. Therefore, prototyping is often used to support the planning process of a software development project. The early and intensive user interaction and the wide variety of existing tools make Prototyping an important technology besides other software engineering life cycle models.

However, using Prototyping alone is not sufficient for real applications but only in conjunction with some of the other methods described in this section.

First of all, Prototyping often invites the software designer to shift objectives during the software development process. Projects that started experimental version of the final product are silently used as a first version of the target system. However, this is seldom a good idea because of the quick-and-dirty techniques that are usually used on such prototypes and because of the poor documentation that is normally available. Thus, the resulting system will contain all these shortcomings throughout its lifetime. Furthermore, Prototyping often suffers from missing user interaction because of either missing interest or because of the wrong institutional settings. Prototyping only works with motivated users that have a strong interest in the functionality of the final product as for example in a research and development environment.

**Boehm's Spiral Model.** The Spiral Model [Boehm, 1988] aims at minimizing risks within the software development process by early detection of potential problem areas and by allowing a maximum degree of freedom in the choice of the process for each separate product that occurs within the project. Besides this major goal, the Spiral Model is also designed to minimize the resource usage and to ensure well defined quality standards.

The Spiral Model is an iterative model where the input of one cycle is the direct output of the previous cycle. The process model is oriented at four major activities that are sequentially executed in every cycle. As shown in Figure 3.18, these activities are

**Identify** This activity aims at the identification of goals, constraints and alternatives for the respective cycle. The goals define what should be done within the cycle and they also set the quality standards that must be maintained for any resulting product. The goals are usually subject to certain constraints that limit the possibilities on how to achieve the goals. However, there may still be several different ways to a goal and thus these alternatives must be outlined be the design team.

**Evaluate** During this activity, the alternatives that were outlined in the identification step are evaluated with respect to their risks and the implied costs. Risk detection is usually executed by applying prototyping or simulation techniques.

**Develop** After the most appropriate alternative is selected on the basis of the evaluation of the previous step, the goal products must be constructed. Thus, the first step during the development activity is to choose the most appropriate process model for the goal product. This selection should reflect the constraints and obey the quality standards that were defined at the beginning of the cycle. After the process model is selected, it is executed in order to construct the goal products.

**Plan** In the last activity of each cycle, the previously executed activities are reviewed and weaknesses that can be identified are reported. Then, the products and resources for the next cycle are planned. An important issue in this step is to commit the entire project team to the plan and to

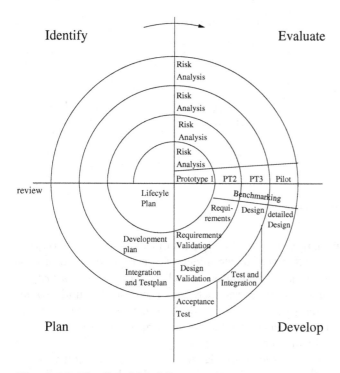

Identify                                     Evaluate

Plan                                         Develop

**Fig. 3.18.** The Spiral Model

clarify any uncertainties in order to minimize misunderstandings within the project team.

The major advantage of the Spiral Model is that it is capable of an early detection of errors and of ruling out sub-optimal alternatives. Due to the freedom of choice of process models for any product, the approach is very flexible and thus applicable in a wide range of software development projects. Furthermore, the incremental planning process that only considers the next cycle makes it easier to adjust the project plan to changing requirements then in other development process models.

However, this flexibility has its price which is in this case the high management effort that is needed to conduct software development processes according to the Spiral Model. Thus, the approach is not suited for small or middle-size projects.

### 3.5.2 Novel Trends in Software Engineering

In the previous section, we have seen a number of process models that have been developed at the beginning of Software Engineering. Now, we shall briefly look at more recent approaches in software development methods.

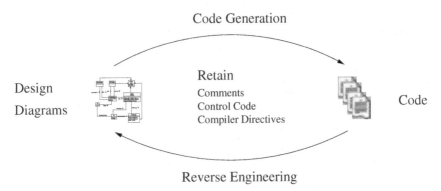

**Fig. 3.19.** Round-trip Engineering

**Round-Trip Engineering.** I have already said in the previous section that it became obvious soon after the development of the first software process models that purely sequential models are not well suited for the majority of projects. The main reason for this is the fact, that the designers understanding of the problem domain grows with the development of the system and that the increasing knowledge leads to discovering improper design decisions that must be rectified during the ongoing project.

Round-trip engineering as shown in Figure 3.19 is a general software engineering method that formalizes this process of trial and discovery. During a *Forward Engineering* phase, the software system or parts thereof are constructed from a specification that reflects the current state of knowledge. Then, when a testable version of the system exists, errors are discovered and corrected by changing the code such that the test pass. These changes are then analyzed in the *Reverse Engineering* phase order to adjust the specification. Thus, reverse engineering is the process of evaluating an existing body of code to capture important information describing a system, and representing that information in a format useful to software engineers and designers [Advanced Software Technologies Inc., 1999].

The main advantage of the round-trip approach is that it supports an incremental development of the system according the current knowledge of the designer. The changes that are applied to the code in order to correct errors is often a useful source of information and reflects the growing experience with the problem domain that is too valuable to be thrown away.

Round-trip engineering is a general method that is usually not used in isolation but rather in conjunction with other best practices. As we will see later, round-trip engineering is one of the building blocks of the method proposed in this book.

**DSDM.** The *Dynamic System Dynamic Modeling (DSDM)* method [The DSDM Consortium, 1998] is an attempt to define an industrial standard for the development of IT Systems with tight time scales on the basis of rapid application development (RAD). The method features an iterative, product-centered process model that is used to incrementally build the target system, it can be seen as an attempt to formalize the prototyping approach presented in the previous section. The DSDM method is a user-centered approach that relies on the integration of user input throughout the entire software development process.

DSDM is not designed as a general purpose method but instead as a specialized method for business applications where most of the functionality of the target system is visible or accessible through the user interface. Furthermore, the task of the target system should be decomposable into several sub-tasks and the method can only be applied when the classes of designated users are known in advance and when these users are accessible to the development team. If the population of designated users is represented by a small subgroup of users, this smaller group is referred to as the "ambassador user".

The DSDM method is build upon a number of basic principles that must be obeyed to in order to get the method working. First of all, the method depends on *active user involvement* which means that the ambassador users are not regarded as the customers but rather as equal partners in the software development process. Second, the software development team (=developers + users) should have *autonomy* in their decisions. It is essential that the development team knows that it is allowed to make any decisions that it regards as essential for the final product. Third, the method is built on the *frequent delivery of (interim) products*. The process by which the product is finally generated can be chosen according to the particular requirements of the product and is not pre-determined by the method. Fourth, all decision within the development process must be *reversible*, i.e. the development team must use some sort of configuration management that allows for backtracking or reconstruction of previous product versions. This is necessary to ensure that potentially risky decisions can be reversed at any time. Fifthly, the method requires *integrated testing and validation* throughout the development process which guarantees that the quality assurance process is built into the development process.

These are the major principles of the DSDM method, there are a number of additional assumptions that the method makes e.g. that the requirements of the target system are frozen at a very high level at the beginning of the project or that any deliverable must not be over-engineered in its functionality. These additional issues, however, are only of minor interest and are thus not explained in greater detail.

The life cycle model of a system that is constructed according to the DSDM method consists of five phases as shown in Figure 3.20. The first phase consists of a *feasibility study* that determines the suitability of a RAD approach and describes the technical and managerial conditions of the development process. The second phase is a *business study* that aims at the definition of high level functional and nonfunctional requirements, a system architecture outline and the definition of maintainability objectives. In the

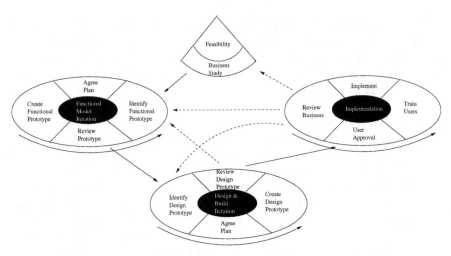

**Fig. 3.20.** The DSDM Method

*functional model iteration* phase, an incremental prototype is set up that is re-engineered during the *design and build iteration phase*. The goal of this phase is to evaluate the prototype with respect to the needs in the operational context of the customer. The last phase, finally, is the *implementation* of the system in the organizational structure of the customer and the user training. During this phase, additional project reviews that aim at learning from the experiences made during the project take place.

The advantages of the DSDM method are that it is far more formal then normal prototyping approaches and that it is independent of particular tools or techniques. Furthermore,the DSDM supports institutional learning which is a matter that is mostly neglected by other approaches. However, the DSDM is only suited for a specific class of applications and due to the heavy dependency on user interactions, it requires a particular institutional framework for the software development process.

**Booch's Model.** Although the software development model that is proposed in [Booch, 1996] is specifically aimed at object-oriented systems, some of the ideas are valid in non object-oriented environments as well. Basically, Boochs model distinguishes between two major aspects of the software development process:

The *Macro level process model* as depicted in Figure 3.21 spans over the entire life cycle of a project and focuses mainly on management activities within the project. Booch's model is somewhat related to the Spiral model that was discussed in Section 3.5.1: the basic idea of the macro process is that it should comprise the successive refinement of the system's architecture and that it should be steered in a risk-driven manner, i.e. that the highest risks are identified and the resources are assigned accordingly. Furthermore,

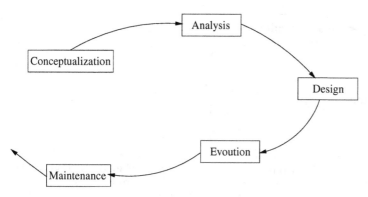

**Fig. 3.21.** Booch's Macro Process

the approach proposes a process of continuous integration (with tangible milestones) that leads to regular releases with extended functionality.

The macro process is divided into five main activities that cover the entire life cycle of a software system: The goal of *Conceptualization* phase at the start of a project is to establish the core requirements of the target system, to identify the main risks that may come up during the project and the proof of concept of the chosen solution strategy. In the *Analysis* phase, a model of the system's desired behavior is produced that is mainly based on scenarios describing the systems intended actions in particular situations. The main tool for the scenario-based analysis are *Use cases* as described in [Jacobson, 1992] or [Kenworthy, 1997] leading to *function points* that capture the systems indented behavior in terms of observable and testable behavior. Another goal of the analysis phase for which use case analysis has proven to be a valuable tool is to establish a common vocabulary between developers, domain experts and users. The analysis phase is then followed by the *Design* phase during which an architecture outline for the evolving implementation of the system is created. During the design activities, premature design decisions as well as delayed design decisions should be avoided as far as possible. However, in case of doubt, design decisions should be delayed until they are absolutely necessary. The architecture outline should be *executable* in the sense that it runs in a limited way and in that it is written in production quality code, i.e. Booch's model does not propose some sort of rapid prototyping. Furthermore, the executable architecture outline should consider pragmatic aspects early enough to identify potential problems. The main phase in the life time of a system is the *Evolution* phase during which the implementation grows through successive refinement of the system's architecture. The major activity during system evolution is clearly coding; pragmatic aspects of the development process become pre-dominant. As said earlier, constant integration is a must and thus releases are generated frequently and tested for the compliance with the systems requirements. When the system has reached a state where it implements its initial specification, it enters the *Maintenance* phase of its

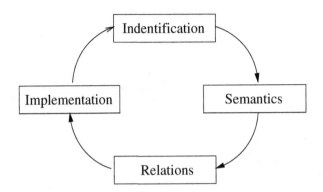

Fig. 3.22. Booch's Micro Process

life cycle. The goal of this phase is to manage post-delivery evolution and it is focused on localized changes that eliminate bugs and implement new requirements. Therefore, the maintenance phase can be seen as continuing system evolution without major architectural changes.

Whereas the macro process model as it was outlined in the previous paragraph concentrates on the management aspects of the project, the other part of the model is concerned with technical aspects of the software development process. The *Micro level process model* as shown in Figure 3.22 is more or less specific for object-oriented software development and is divided into four activities that are repeatedly performed in each phase of the macro process. Each of these activities contains three basic elements at varying intensity: its degree of *discovery, invention* and *implementation*. Booch uses this characterization to capture the nature of each activity within the four phases of the micro process model.

The first activity in each cycle is to *identify classes and objects*. Clearly, the task is mostly a matter of discovery when applied during the analysis phase of the macro process. It then requires to select the right abstractions to model the problem and to decide about what is part of the problem and what is not. If the micro process is applied during the design phase, the main objective is to create an object-oriented decomposition of the system's architecture that can be used as an initial architecture outline. In my opinion one of the best tips that Booch gives in his description of this activity is to remind the reader that there is no such thing as a perfect abstraction (see also [Pernici, 1990]), i.e. that every design is a compromise between various factors such as clarity, performance etc. The next activity in the micro process model is to *identify the semantics* of the classes and objects that have been described in the first step. This activity is about 45% discovery, 45% invention, 10% implementation and its main objective is to determine the distribution of responsibilities among the entities and to identify roles and responsibilities according to the semantic distance between entities. The key idea that should be kept in mind during this step is information hiding, i.e. to focus on semantic abstractions that have maximum cohesion. After the

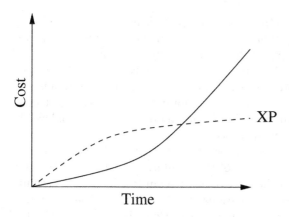

**Fig. 3.23.** Cost-of-Change Curves

semantics of the classes and objects have been clarified, the next task is to *identify relationships* between them. The goal of this activity that consists of about 90% invention and 10% implementation is to find dependencies among classes and objects or groups thereof and to exploit structural patterns that can simplify the overall architecture. Therefore, this activity is particularly concerned with the coupling between the design entities. In the *Implementation* phase of each iteration of the micro process, finally, the abstractions and mechanisms that have been developed earlier must be expressed in efficient and elegant code. Booch adds the important reminder to select existing algorithms and data structures whenever possible.

The major advantage of Booch's model is that it is developed by a practitioner and derived from experiences in real world projects. In my personal view, one of the strongest points in Booch's model is the emphasis on early feedback for the developers by starting with a code outline of the architecture in order to determine how it feels. This is a valuable tool for early risk detection in any software project. What I do not like too much about the process model is its focus on object-oriented software development especially in the micro process. I would prefer a more general method that can be applied to object-oriented system development but that is not limited to it. In the next section, I will therefore discuss a software development method that shares some similarities with Booch's model but that is more extreme in its general ideas.

**eXtreme Programming.** eXtreme Programming (XP) [Beck, 1999] is a relatively new software engineering method that aims at the integration of several best practices under a common umbrella. The basic assumption of XP is somewhat contradictory to traditional approaches in that XP assumes that the cost of change does *not* rise dramatically over time. In Figure 3.23, I have depicted the cost-of-change curves as they are assumed by most traditional approaches on the one hand and by XP on the other hand. As you can see from the figure, the traditional point of view is that the cost of changes are higher, the later the are made in the software development process. In

[Beck, 1999] the author argues that this assumption is not necessary valid any longer as the average development cycles become shorter e.g. due to improved tool support in form of integrated development environments or better and faster compilers. Therefore, the author concludes that it would be natural to interpret change as the only constant factor in the software development process and to shift away from software development models that put more emphasize on early stages and instead to favor a model that puts equal weight onto *all* phases of the development process.

The XP method is based upon four basic *values* that can be found in every phase of the entire method. The first of these values is *communication.* Bad communication habits within the development team lead to wrong assumptions, double work, wrong cost estimations etc. Therefore, the people within an XP team are encouraged to communicate their knowledge to the benefit of the entire group. As we will see later, the aspect of making knowledge public is a major goal of the activities that make up the XP process.

The second value of XP is *simplicity,* the fundamental question is thus "What is the simplest solution that could possibly work?". Again, this is a contradiction to traditional ideas where one of the major goals of a good design was to "implement for today, design for tomorrow". Thus, XP takes a different route in that it postulates to make things simple today and pay a little more tomorrow if a need to change arises. Instead of starting with the most generic solution that may be not necessary, XP starts of simple and changes the simple solution as needed.

The third value is *feedback* about the current state of the system instead of un-validated assumptions about that state. Feedback in XP is heavily based upon automated testing on the unit level and on functional testing on the system level. Automated testing refers to tests that check the validity of the test results automatically, requiring no intervention or manual checking by the user. Thus, the automatic tests can be run after every little change in order to validate that the system is still working properly. In my personal experience, the habit of writing automated tests for all major aspects of the system has proven to be an invaluable tool that reduces development time as well as debugging time. A prerequisite for generating feedback as early as possible is to start the productive use of the system as soon as possible in order to incorporate the end users in the development process.

The fourth and final value of XP is *courage.* While this value seems to be a bit odd in the context of software development, it is nonetheless necessary in order to produce a high quality system. Courage in this context means, that it is sometimes necessary to enforce decisions even if they are risky, i.e. to start with the development of a particular feature probably without knowing about every potential problem in advance. Also, courage is needed to try out several alternative solutions for a problem and to throw away bad or unnecessary code. Finally, courage means that the members of the development team must trust their abilities that they will be able to solve the problem at hand with the given resources.

After these preliminary remarks, it is now time to turn to the flesh and bones of XP. One of the major advantage of XP is that it is mainly a collection of best practices that can be individually chosen according to personal preferences or organizational or project specific constraints.

**The planning game** Planning in XP is an incremental process that is based on the ranking of system functionalities according to their current value for the user. Thus, the main objective of the planning process is to identify the most valuable pending requirement and to develop a plan how to implement them. The planning process of XP is related to hierarchical planning where aspects that refer to requirements that are not of immediate interest are only briefly sketched and then put on hold until their time has come.

A major aspect of the planning game is that it is jointly done by business and development people, i.e. the people controlling the budget are provided with input from the technical staff and vice versa. This approach avoids mutual misunderstandings about what is possible and what is not.

**Small releases** The release times of XP project typically range between one and two months. Obviously, these short time spans do not allow for major changes or enhancements between two subsequent releases. As it was already mentioned in the planning game, each release aims at the implementation of the most valuable business requirement(s), i.e. the requirement(s) that provide the highest effort/value ratio. As a general rule of XP releases, it is absolutely necessary that a feature must be completely implemented before it is released in order to prevent users from getting frustrated by half-working solutions that may endanger the acceptance of the entire system.

**Metaphor** Each XP project should have a system metaphor that relates the tasks and parts of the system to more accessible entities in the real world. This metaphor should be chosen from the application area and serves as a conceptual tool that allows for a consistent description of the system from a high level of abstraction. A good system metaphor usually not only improves the communication with the customer, but it is also a valuable tool for discussions with the development team.

**Simple design** As mentioned above, the design philosophy of XP is somewhat contradictory to most other approaches as it does not follow the guideline to "implement for today, design for tomorrow". Instead, XP promotes the idea of using the simplest design that can do the job at hand. However, as there is no general measure that expresses the complexity (or simplicity) of a particular design, XP is relatively fuzzy about what a simple design in fact is. The only hints that are given occasionally are that the design should run all test, that it should contain no duplicate logic or that it should have the fewest possible classes and methods.

**Testing** Testing plays a major role in the XP approach and serves two main purposes. Firstly, testing should increase the developers confidence in the system that is developed. By running the test cases frequently, the software developer can be sure that none of his or her changes have affected the system functionality. This assurance is important as it promotes the idea of frequent system integration that will be discussed below.

Secondly, the test cases serve as a coded version of the system requirements that can be used to decide about the state of the system in comparison of the planned state at a particular point in time. Therefore, the test cases for a particular requirement should be written *before* the component that is responsible for satisfying the requirements is actually implemented.

An important aspect of XP test cases is that they should be self-checking. Self-checking means, that the computer can run each test case and compare the result of the test with the result expected by the system developer. Automated testing is a powerful tool that can significantly reduce development time as it is possible to run the test cases at almost no additional cost.

**Refactoring** The goal of Refactoring [Opdyke, 1992], [Fowler, 1999] is to improve the structure of existing code. Central questions are thus how the programmer can change the code such that it makes the implementation of a new feature simple or how can the program be changed such that it is easier to understand and to maintain. A crucial aspect of refactoring is that it does not affect system functionality in any may. The observable behavior of the program must be the same after refactoring as it was before. The functional equivalence of the two versions of the system is usually ensured by running all test cases in order to check whether the program behaves as expected or not. As a general rule, refactoring should only be applied when it is necessary – e.g. when a new feature could be integrated easier if the code was refactored first – and not on speculation.

**Pair programming** On of the most controversial aspects of XP is the pair programming approach. In XP, all production code is written by two programmers on one machine with one keyboard and one mouse. It is the usual practice in XP projects that two people team up to implement a particular feature and that these two people are jointly responsible for all steps until the successful integration of the new code into the existing system. Pair programming teams encompass two roles: the *implementor*, who controls the keyboard and the mouse, is typically concerned with the question how to implement the particular feature, whereas the *strategist* is somewhat further away from the actual code and instead checks whether the overall approach is ok, which test cases are affected and whether it might be a better idea to refactor the code before implementing the feature.

Personally, I think that pair programming has some interesting aspects that make it worth considering applying it in a particular situation but not as a general practice over the entire lifetime of a project. The problem is that a full implementation of a pair programming approach usually requires a complete re-organization of the working style in a development team that may not be feasible.

**Collective ownership** Collective ownership is the manifestation of the idea that all developers within a development team are equally responsible for the overall product, not only for those parts that the have worked on. Collective ownership resides somewhat in between "no ownership", meaning that changes are made if they fit individual needs and nobody is responsible for other peoples code, and "individual ownership" where each piece of code has an owner who is the only person that is allowed to change it, others have to submit change request that are decided upon by the owner. The main goal of the collective ownership model is to make people responsible for what they do, but also to stimulate peoples interest in the parts of the system that are not directly concerned with. Obviously, not everybody in the team can know everything about the entire system, but a fair overview can increase the efficiency of the intra-team communication as there exists some common understanding about the system as a whole.

**Coding standards** As consequence of the collective ownership model explained in the previous paragraph, some means must be applied to enable the members of the development team to understand all parts of the system. A prerequisite for this understanding is that the code is kept readable by sticking to well defined coding standards. In [McConnell, 1993], the author explains that it is not the major point in coding standards how the finally look like (although he gives some impressive examples on good and bad ideas for coding standards), but that the major point is that they exist and that they are obeyed to e.g. by performing regular code reviews [Sommerville, 1995]. An important rule for introducing coding standards is that they should be developed by the development team itself and not imposed on them from the outside, e.g. by the team leader.

**Continuous integration** In an ideal XP project, the code of the system is tested and integrated at least every day, even better are integration cycles that lie within a few hours. The integration process of XP is strongly supported by the testing approach that was described above and that allows the integration team (integration is done as pair programming job as well) to decide whether the system is still working as expected or not. In the latter case, the integration team is responsible to bring the system back into sync with the test cases. Integration is incomplete until all test cases are running as before.

**40 hour week** As working overtime is a quite common phenomenon in most
software development projects, this requirement of the XP approach seem
to be a bit behind the times. However, as argued in [Beck, 1999], constant
overtime is a clear sign for a serious problem within the project that
should be identified and resolved instead of throwing additional resources
at it. In analogy to [Brooks, 1995] where the author claimed that "adding
more people to a late project makes it even later", XP argues for a change
in strategy rather than more man-power.

**On-site customer** On of the most overseen aspects of software development projects is that the software is usually not built for the people that
order it, but rather for people that have to cope with the resulting piece
of software as part of their daily job [Sommerville, 1995]. Therefore, XP
argues that is absolutely necessary to have at least one of the end users
in the project team during the development of the system. Especially because XP features a dynamic approach towards the system requirements
and planning of next steps, the customer within the team is responsible
for answering questions, resolve conflicts and set small-scale priorities.
Although most customer companies will argue that it is too expensive to
have a full-time employee in the software development team for a longer
time, this can be nonetheless cost effective as the on-site customer can
usually continue with his or her normal work and only support the software development team if needed – but with much better response times
as it would be the case if the team and the customer were geographically
separated.

The thing that I like best about XP is the fact, that it is merely a collection
of approved best practices that can be combined according to personal needs
and preferences. Although Beck suggests a particular life-cycle, it is quite
straightforward to adapt this cycle to the requirements of a given project. The
problem with the suggested practices is, however, that they heavily depend
on the business culture of the software development company. Applying XP
requires some boldness within the management because the proposed ideas
are sometimes very contrary to traditional ideas in Software Engineering and
there is obviously a risk that the development team will reject the ideas
instead of adopting them. Thus, XP can only work for a team of highly
motivated individuals that are willing to go new ways instead of relying on
established, but not necessarily optimal, methods.

### 3.5.3 Development Methods for Multiagent Systems

In this section, we will discuss approaches that were specifically build for the
development of multiagent systems. Some of the approaches presented in this
section are general-purpose methods for all kinds of multiagent systems while
others are the result of the analysis of the development process of a particular

system. I will present each of them according to the following scheme that makes it easier to compare individual aspects of the models.

**Scope** This aspect describes the overall goal of the method and the parts of the life cycle that are covered by the method. Furthermore, we will also indicate the origin of the method an whether a case-study was supplied in the original material that presented the idea.

**Models and Representation** After the first more introductory part, we will then become more technical and present the main models of the method as well as their purposes. We will also briefly discuss the different levels of abstraction that are supported and whether and how the static and dynamic aspects of a system are modeled.

**Process Model** Here, I will outline the process model that is applied in order to construct the models discussed in the previous aspect and explain the main steps in the proposed life cycle model.

**Assessment** This part of the description will summarize the major advantages and the shortcomings of each method. I will also apply a ranking scheme for general properties as they appear to the author. The properties that are evaluated are

   **Generality** i.e. the range of multiagent systems that is supported or the commitment to a particular technology or agent architecture,

   **Flexibility** which covers aspects such as the extensibility of the method or support for different process models or tools,

   **Granularity** captures the level of detail by which system aspects can be modeled and the supported levels of abstraction,

   **Formality** e.g. the use of formal methods or well defined semantics of modeling elements and finally

   **Tool support** which summarizes available tools for a particular method.

There is a wide variety of methods (see [Iglesias et al., 1998] for a rather in-depth survey of the field) and the selection of ideas presented in the subsequent sections can only show a small amount of the full picture. However, I have tried to include those methods that either have a unique view onto the topic or that are reasonably general to be applied in the general context of multiagent systems.

**Burmeister.**

**Scope** The approach presented in [Burmeister, 1996] is a development method for multiagent systems based on object-oriented techniques. The method is limited to systems of cooperative, directly communicating software agents. A short case study is provide to illustrate the basic ideas but no reference for an application of the method in an industrial application is given.

   The approach covers the analysis and design phase of the software development process and it does not assume a particular life cycle model, although the process model presented later suggest that a linear life cycle model is used by the authors. The distinction between the analysis and design phase are somewhat fuzzy and seem to make it difficult to organize them in a sequential process.

**Models and Representation** The Burmeister approach uses three models to describe the entities and their interconnections within a multiagent system. The *Agent model* describes the internal states, i.e. the goals or plans, of the agents and thus models the *dynamics in the small*. The *Organizational model*, on the other hand, defines the relationships among agents and agent types.

These relationships include the inheritance hierarchy, the roles that occur within the system and the relationships among agents based on the roles they play. The objectives of this model can be two-fold in that it is either used to structure the system into several sub- systems or to represent a real organization. The *Cooperation model*, finally, describes the *dynamics in the large* of the target system, i.e. the interactions among agents. The interactions (limited to communication) are modeled by protocols based on KQML messages. Furthermore, the method implicitly assumes a cooperative setting (i.e. benevolent agents).

The method does not suggest any special from of representation, however, CRC (classes-responsibilities-collaborations) cards are recommended for establishing the agent model and interaction or collaboration diagrams known from OOD are suggested for the cooperation model

**Process Model** The method defines a three step process model as shown in process Model 3 that corresponds to the three models mentioned above. Each of these steps should be executable in parallel as the models are claimed to be independent. It seems however, that the author assumes these steps to be completed in the given order.

**Assessment** The method is conceptually clear and intuitive and provides an easy access to the basic concepts because of the relation to OO techniques. However, it is not very detailed and some of the claims are not substantial. Most striking is the claim that the different models are independent and can thus be developed separately but for example, the cooperation model can only be developed after the entities (agents) that interact are defined and thus the cooperation model depends on defining the agents first. Additionally, the activities within a single phase of the process model are somehow incoherent. For example, in the organizational model, the role assignment to particular agent types is made before the agent types are defined. Furthermore, the method pays only little attention to the inter-operation of the system with its environment. This is however, an important issue if the target system is to be used in a organizational context and should be explicitly dealt with. The overall value of the method is hard to decide as it is not clear if the method has been tested in an industrial project.

## Process Model 3 Burmeister

1. **Agent model**
   a) Identify and characterize agents and environment
      This step mainly aims at the definition of the entities that should become the agents of the multiagent system and suggests to identify the active entities in the problem description.
   b) Define motivations of the agents
      The motivations of an agent are its interests, preferences, responsibilities, long-term goals etc.
   c) Define behaviors (predefined plans)
      The method defines the behaviors of an agent in terms of plan schemes that describe how a particular goal can be reached.
   d) Define knowledge and beliefs
      In this step, the knowledge and beliefs that are used by the agent to fulfill its tasks are defined.
2. **Organizational model**
   a) Identify roles within the scenario
      In this step, not only the roles that occur within the system are identified, these roles are also mapped to the agents or agent types that are supposed to play the roles.
   b) Build inheritance hierarchy
      Agents are classified according to their knowledge, beliefs, motivations and behaviors in order to set up an inheritance scheme similar to OO design that describes the static interconnections between agents.
   c) Structure roles within the organization
      In this step, the inter-role dependencies are modeled on the basis of the intended structure of the multiagent system or on the basis of a real organization that is to be modeled by an artificial system.
3. **Cooperation model**
   a) Identify cooperation partners
      For each joint task, the agents that are necessary to complete it are identified and the type of cooperation (e.g. Resource sharing, synchronization etc.) is defined.
   b) Identify message types
      The method suggest to use KQML messages to describe the messages that are exchanged between the agents.
   c) Define cooperation protocols
      The patterns of interaction between the agents are described by specifying the cooperation protocols that are needed to complete joint tasks of different agents.

|   | low | high |
|---|---|---|
| Generality | | ■ |
| Flexibility | ■ | |
| Granularity | ■ | |
| Formality | ■ | |
| Tools Support | ■ | |

---

**Process Model 4** Kinny and Georgeff

---

1. **Develop external models**
   a) Identify roles
   b) Define role responsibilities (= services)
   c) For each service: identify necessary interactions, speech acts etc.
   d) Define the agent hierarchy according to the previous steps
2. **Develop internal models**
   a) Analyze means of achieving goals
   b) Build the beliefs of the agents

---

### Kinny and Georgeff.

**Scope** [Kinny and Georgeff, 1996] present an object-oriented development method for BDI [Rao and Georgeff, 1995] agents and multiagent systems of BDI agents. The approach covers the analysis and design phases of the software development process and assumes no particular life cycle model.

**Models and Representation** The proposed method is centered around basic models that are in turn subdivided into several sub-models. The first basic model is the *External viewpoint* that describes the more coarse-grained aspects of the system and its dynamics in-the-large and consists of two sub-models. The *Agent model* defines the inheritance hierarchy among agent types and the instance model, e.g. role multiplicity, of the agent society. The *Interaction model* describes the responsibilities of each agent class, the services it provides and the message model in terms of syntax and semantics of the exchanged messages.

The *Internal viewpoint*, on the other hand, is concerned with the design of individual agents according to the BDI paradigm. The internal viewpoint consists of three sub- models: the *Belief* and the *Goal model* describe the domain-specific belief and goal set, respectively and the *Plan model* defines the actions that must be taken by the agents in order to achieve a particular goal.

The models that are developed in the method are represented as enhanced UML class diagrams for belief class models and finite state automata for plan models. Furthermore, formal definitions for beliefs and goals are provided but the system dynamics are not explicitly modeled in the method.

**Process Model** The proposed process model is a sequential model that consists of two major steps as shown in Process Model 4.

**Assessment** The proposed method provides a set of models that can be used to describe most aspects of a multiagent system. The object-oriented approach supports developers that are familiar with the basic concepts and also leads to a modular design.

However, the method is limited to BDI agents and provides only a very sketchy process model that leaves a lot of questions unanswered, e.g. how to identify the roles, etc. This is the crucial factor in the entire design process as all of the models that are developed in subsequent steps depend on these decisions. If, however, no guidance is given on how to actually find the fundamental roles, the entire design may fail because of wrong decisions at a very early stage of the development process. Furthermore, the proposed process model is very high level and does not provide guidance on how to perform the different steps.

|  | low | high |
|---|---|---|
| Generality | | |
| Flexibility | | |
| Granularity | | |
| Formality | | |
| Tools Support | | |

### DESIRE.

**Scope** DESIRE [Brazier et al., 1996], [Brazier et al., 1997], [Brazier et al., 1998] is a conceptual framework for the analysis and design of multiagent systems, the extensive case study that is provided describes a project that is concerned with the management of an electricity transportation network. Management means in this respect the monitoring, fault diagnosis and maintenance planning of the network. The full system consists of seven agents out of which four are presented in detail in the case study.

The method covers the analysis and the design phase of the software development life cycle and assumes no particular process model although a linear, sequential model is used in the case study.

**Models and Representation** The method takes a compositional view on agents and systems: the entire functionality of the system is designed as series of interacting, task-based, hierarchically structured components. Each task can either be primitive or it can be composite; a task hierarchy is constructed by applying a recursive top-down decomposition process on the initial system task. The compositional view on agents sees an individual agent as a collection of task-solving units (components). The terms "task" and "component" seem to be used interchangeably in the DESIRE documentation.

The DESIRE framework proposes two models that should be specified by the system designer. The *intra-agent* model contains the expertise descriptions for domain tasks, the knowledge requirements and the reasoning capabilities for solving these tasks. The *inter-agent model*, on the other hand, describes the expertise to perform and guide coordination, cooperation and social interaction among agents.

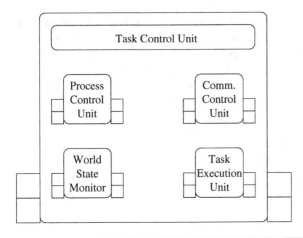

**Fig. 3.24.** The Generic DESIRE Agent Architecture

---

**Process Model 5** DESIRE

---

1. **Task decomposition**
   a) Define overall task hierarchy.
   b) Define individual task descriptions (inputs, outputs, meta-object relations, e.g. which task reasons about which other task, etc.).
2. **Information exchange model**
   a) Specify the information links between components.
   b) Define input/output relations, i.e. the input of which component is the output of which other, a translation mechanism enables to designer to use different languages for the task internal knowledge representation.
3. **Sequencing of sub-tasks**
   a) Describe task control knowledge (temporal order of tasks, effort to solve the task, etc.).
   b) Specify intra- and inter-agent sequencing of tasks
4. **Sub-task-delegation**
   a) Assign tasks to agents.
   b) Perform functional grouping of tasks.
5. **Knowledge structures** Define structures for the domain knowledge by providing concepts that describe the distinguishable objects in the domain and relations that describe how the concepts relate to each other.

---

DESIRE is centered around the generic agent architecture depicted in Figure 3.24 that consist of five elements. The *Task Control Unit* encapsulates the control knowledge of the agent, i.e. the relations between the components and the activation schemes that are enacted during the agents operation. The *Process Control Unit* is responsible for coordinating the agents reasoning processes, the *Communication Control Unit* manages for the social aspects of agent by handling incoming and outgoing messages, the *World State Monitor* constantly updates the world model of the agent by incorporating perceptions into the current model and a task-specific *Task Execution Unit*, finally, implements the particular skills of different agents.

The system dynamics are modeled by information links between the problem solving units, they can thus be used to model intra-agent information flow as well as inter-agent information flow. The concepts used in DESIRE can be formalized using temporal logic.

**Process Model** DESIRE proposes a five step process model as shown in Process Model 5 that is executed in sequential order.

**Assessment** The major advantage of the DESIRE method is that it provides a unified view on all entities within the system. The holonic approach makes it easier for the designer to think in functional terms rather then in agent-oriented concepts. However, the commitment of the method to a specific agent architecture and the strict process model limit its general applicability to a broader range of problems.

|  | low | high |
|---|---|---|
| Generality | | ▮ |
| Flexibility | ▮ | |
| Granularity | | ▮ |
| Formality | | ▮ |
| Tools Support | ▮ | |

## MAS-CommonKADS.

**Scope** MAS-CommonKADS [Iglesias et al., 1997] is a general purpose multiagent analysis and design method based on the CommonKADS design method for knowledge-based systems (KBS). CommonKADS supports most aspects of a KBS development project, including project management, organizational analysis, knowledge acquisition, conceptual modeling, user interaction, system integration, and design. The method is result oriented rather than process oriented and it describes KBS development from two perspectives. The *result perspective* captures a set of models that describe different aspects of the KBS and its environment. These models are continuously improved during a project life cycle. The *project management perspective*, on the other hand, features a risk-driven generic spiral life cycle model that can be configured and adapted to the particular project.

CommonKADS extends this framework by adding techniques from object-orientation (OMT, OOSE, RDD) and protocol engineering (SDL, MSC) and tailoring them towards the specific requirements of multiagent systems. The design method is primarily suited for systems of directly communicating software agent. An example application called the "Travel Agency" is provided in [Iglesias et al., 1997]. In the problem domain, a user requests a flight from the system and system finds the cheapest available flights with the lowest possibility of delays by querying the available

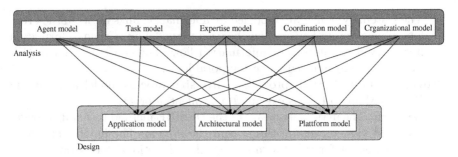

**Fig. 3.25.** Hierarchical Set of Models

flight carriers. The method covers the analysis and design phase of the
software development process and proposes a risk-driven, component-
based approach but no details of how this process can be implemented
are provided.

**Models and Representation** The MAS-CommonKADS method is centered around a set of different models as shown in Figure 3.25 that are
used to describe the target system. During the *Analysis phase* of the
development process, the first sub-set of models to be constructed contains the *Agent model* that describes the agent characteristics such as
the reasoning capabilities, the skills of the individual agent or the agent
architecture to be used. Second, the *Task model* defines the task decomposition within the problem domain and contains the task descriptions.
Thus, the task model is closely related to the *Expertise model* where the
basic knowledge requirements for carrying out the tasks are described.
The *Coordination model* captures the conversations between agents, their
interactions and the protocols used. The context of this coordination process is described by the *Organizational model* in terms of the structure
of the agent society or the agent hierarchy. The *Communication model*,
finally, covers the user interface of the target system.

During the *Design phase* of the development process, these initial models
are used as the basis for the design model, which is composed out of the
*Application*, the *Architectural* and the *Platform model*. The Application
model captures the overall structure of the target system, the Architectural model defines the networking and telematic requirements and the
Platform model describes the development platform for the system.

The method recommends a number of techniques to describe these models, for example

- *Use Cases* during the conceptualization phase to describe prototypical
  uses of the target system,
- *Class-Responsibility-Collaboration (CRC) cards* for the agent modeling
  process,
- *Event Flow Diagrams* and *Specification and Description Language
  (SDL) diagrams* for the coordination model or

- the *Conceptual Modeling Language (CML)* and *Inference Structure Diagrams* for knowledge modeling.

**Process Model** The process model of the MAS-CommonKADS method is shown in Process Model 6.

**Assessment** The MAS-CommonKADS method is very detailed and provides a conceptual framework for the analysis and design of multiagent systems that is based on an existing, working approach that is currently in use for the development of knowledge- based system. The method is not focused on the functional aspects of the target system, it also models the target environment and important aspects such as agent management aspects.

On the other hand, the method lacks a bit of an overall structure and sometimes appears as a collection of models with no explicit links between them. This makes it hard for the less experienced user to fully understand the structure of the model and to identify the most suitable model for a particular aspect of the target system.

|  | low | high |
|---|---|---|
| Generality | | |
| Flexibility | | |
| Granularity | | |
| Formality | | |
| Tools Support | | |

### Gaia.

**Scope** [Wooldridge et al., 2000] propose a method for the development of multiagent applications with the following characteristics:

- The application is coarse-grained, i.e. the computational resources that are available to a single agent should be comparable to those of a UNIX process.
- The problem domain is an optimization problem where all agents share the common goal to minimize or maximize some given measure. The problem domain does not contain true conflict situations that must be solved.
- The agent society is heterogeneous, i.e. agents may be implemented in different programming languages or on different platforms.
- The multiagent system is relatively small, i.e. less then 100 agents.
- The agents do not exhibit mobility.

The proposed method covers the analysis and design phase of the software development process on a very high level. The resulting design is intended to be used as the input for traditional software engineering methods that refine the high-level design into a particular implementation.

---

**Process Model 6** MAS-CommonKADS

---

1. **Conceptualization**
   This phase yields a preliminary description of the problem area and an informal requirements definition.

2. **Analysis**
   This step performs a requirements specification by developing several of the above mentioned models.
   a) *Agent model* In this step, initial instances of the agent model are created by performing a semantic analysis of the problem description and applying conceptual distance heuristics based on the determination of shared knowledge structures, organizational or geographical distribution etc. to the initial problem description.
   b) *Task model* The goal of this step is the task decomposition and goal determination of the agents using a top-down decomposition. The resulting task descriptions include the name, input/output data, control structures, frequency, preconditions, required skills of the performer etc.
   c) *Coordination model* This model describes the interactions and coordination protocols by specifying prototypical situations identifying messages and exchanged data in the form of SDL diagrams.
   d) *Knowledge model* This model contains the domain knowledge (declarative knowledge of the problem domain), the inference knowledge (what sorts of inferences are needed e.g. diagnosis, assessment, search, etc.), the task knowledge (order of inference structures) and the problem solving method(s) (define the implementation of each inference type needed) that occur within the target system.
   e) *Organization model* The result of this step is a static description of the relationships between agents as well as the organizational structure of the enterprise before and after the introduction of the MAS, i.e. the given structure of the enterprise and the target structure.

3. **Design**
   The design model refines the models of the analysis step and constructs the three design models mentioned earlier.
   a) *Agent network design model* This model describe the infrastructure (network, coordination facilities etc.) of the MAS, the network facilities (naming service, security, encryption, etc.), knowledge facilities (ontology servers, knowledge representation translators, etc.) and the coordination facilities (protocol servers, group management facilities, resource allocation, etc.) within the target system.
   b) *Agent design model* In this step, the most suitable architecture for each agent is determined. The method suggest a generic agent architecture that consists of a user-communication unit for the interaction between the agent and the user, an agent communication unit for the interactions among agents, a deliberation and reaction unit for the reasoning of the agent and an external skills and services unit that provides the agents services to the other agents.
   c) *Platform design model* In this model the software and the hardware platform for each agent are selected and described.

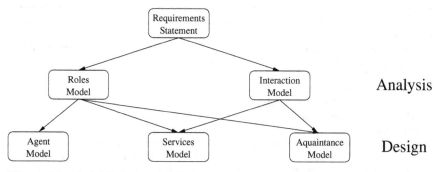

**Fig. 3.26.** Model Relations in Gaia

**Models and Representation** The method features an integrated view onto the system as a computational organization of interacting roles. Roles are dynamically assigned to agents and an agent can play several roles at the same time. The main models that are developed in this method are discussed below, the relationships between the individual models are shown in Figure 3.26, the process model itself is outlined in Process Model 7.

The *Roles model* contains several abstract descriptions of an entities expected function. Each of these descriptions defines the *permissions* of the role, i.e. the resources that *can* be used in the course of problem solving as well as the resources that *cannot* be used during this process. Resources in this respect are usually information or knowledge structures that are either available or not. Second, the role is defined by its *responsibilities*, i.e. what it has to do within a well-defined context. The responsibilities are defined in terms of *liveliness conditions* that express what has to be done while the role is active and in terms of *safety conditions* that describe invariants that must be maintained at all time during the lifetime of a role.

The *Interaction model* describes the links between individual roles and the protocols that are used to interact. Each of these protocol descriptions is given by its *purpose*, e.g. "information request" or "assign task", its *initiator*, i.e. the role that starts the protocol, the *responders* that follow the protocol initiation, the *input* information that is used by the initiator, the *output* information that is supplied to the responders and the *processing* that is performed by the initiator.

The *Agent model* defines the *agent types* by aggregating roles, e.g. to increase the efficiency of the application. The agent model does not support inheritance relationships between roles as they are regarded not necessary by the authors because the granularity of the application will seldom require other mappings then one-to-one mappings from role to agent type.

---

**Process Model 7** Gaia
_____

1. **Analysis**
   The goal of this phase is to understand the structure of the target system without referring to a particular architecture.
   a) Identify role prototypes
   b) Identify the protocols of each role
   c) Elaborate the roles model
   d) Go to 1a until finished
2. **Design**
   The goal of this phase is to transform the models from the first phase into sufficiently low level to serve as an input for traditional design processes.
   a) Create the agent model by aggregating roles
   b) Develop the service model
   c) Develop the acquaintance model

---

The _Service model_ describes the functionality of an agent. Functionality in this respect refers to a single, coherent block of activities and is defined by the _inputs_, the _outputs_ and the _pre-_ and _post-conditions_. Note that this description is still on a very high level and does not prescribe any particular implementation of the functionality.

The _Acquaintance model_, finally, defines the _communication links_ between agents, the goal of this model is to identify potential communication bottlenecks.

The method proposes some formal language to represent the liveliness and safety conditions of a role and some templates for role schemata and protocol definitions.

**Process Model** The process model that is used within the method consists of an iterative analysis phase that is followed by a sequential design phase. The relation of the models to these two phases of the development process are shown in Figure 3.26

As already stated above, the resulting design is thought as a high level description that must be refined in subsequent steps in order to yield to the final design. The proposed process model is shown in Process Model 7.

**Assessment** The advantage of the Gaia method is that it provides a detailed set of models that capture almost all relevant aspects of the target system. It is also straightforward to apply even by unexperienced users. Furthermore, the method is not committed to any particular technology such as BDI agents etc.

However, the major problem is the attempt to define the method on top of other software engineering techniques. The potential problem of this idea becomes apparent if is not possible to find an adequate implementation for the high level design. The entire design (perhaps even the analysis) has to be revised in order to develop a model that can actually be implemented. This problem could be weakened if the proposed set of models contained a model of the environment of the target system but still this would bear potential problems if the refinement from a high level to a low level design and finally to an implementation is not straightforward.

|  | low | high |
|---|---|---|
| Generality | | ▮ |
| Flexibility | | ▮ |
| Granularity | | ▮ |
| Formality | | ▮ |
| Tools Support | ▮ | |

### 3.5.4 Discussion

Most of the models outlined in the previous sections are *normative* models. They define – from the (subjective) point of view of the respective author – which activities make up the software engineering task, the temporal ordering of these activities, the involved products and often also the notation that must be used. However, the problem with this approach is clearly pointed out in the following quote from [Zemanek, 1985]: "One cannot standardize thinking and one should not even attempt to do so."

Furthermore, this fact usually limits the applicability of a particular method whenever there is a deviation of the prerequisites of an actual project and the prerequisites of the method to be used. In short, these methods focus on software engineering processes as they *should be*, not as they *are really like* [Carroll and Rosson, 1985]. Therefore, it seems to be a more promising idea to follow the suggestion from [Green, 1990] to " ... concentrate on what it seems that people really do, not on what they might do if they were perfect.". This approach can lead to more *pragmatic* software engineering models that are based on an explicit cognitive model that supports individualized strategies and notations.

However, before we turn towards the software development method that is presented in this book and that tries to follow the above remarks, I will briefly discuss another important aspect of a software development method: quality management, learning and re-use.

## 3.6 Qu lit  M n gement  nd S stem tic Le rning

Quality assurance and quality management are topics that were neglected in the software development process for a long time. Recently, however, the idea of integrating quality measurement in the software development process has shown to pay in terms of faster development cycles and lower maintenance cost. Another important issue that has come up in the software development process is organizational learning. Based on the insight on how dependent an organization is on the knowledge that is informally stored mostly in their human resources, methods were introduced to collect and to enlarge the organizational knowledge in a permanent learning process throughout the entire organization.

In this section, we will discuss two ideas that were developed in the context of software development to ensure high quality software and knowledge preservation over project boundaries.

### 3.6.1 The Quality Improvement Paradigm

The *Quality Improvement Paradigm (QIP)* [Basili et al., 1994] is a methodological framework for systematic improvement of products and processes within software development projects. The QIP is oriented at *Total Quality Management (TQM)* [Ishikawa, 1985], a conceptual framework that was developed in Japan and that aims at introducing quality assurance mechanisms into industrial production processes. However, the QIP goes a bit further then TQM as it also defines how to integrate learning feedback into the quality assurance process.

The QIP should only be applied in software development environments that can be unambiguously characterized, i.e. that allow for a clear description of all sub-processes and their interdependencies as well as for the clear identification of the products that are involved in the process. Furthermore, the QIP relies on a realistic definition of quality goals. This implies that the desired quality standards must be quantifiable in order to decide whether the process has met the quality goals or not.

The QIP can be viewed as a development process "wrapper" that is put around a particular development process model in order to support systematic learning. Basically, the QIP consists of six steps as shown in Figure 3.27 and Process Model 8.

The QIP features two feedback cycles, one is *project feedback* that is provided during the execution phase (step 4) and the other is corporate feedback that is provided by the models that are constructed on the basis of past experiences. However, no institutional framework is provided by the QIP itself and this makes it sometimes difficult to apply it in industrial projects. To overcome this limitation, the next section will introduce a flexible institutional framework for constant quality improvement and organizational learning.

### 3.6.2 Experience Factory

The *Experience Factory* [Basili, 1989], [Basili et al., 1994] is a framework that supports systematic learning within an organization and that is already in use in large scale industrial environments [Houdek et al., 1998].

The basic idea underlying the Experience Factory is closely related to case-based reasoning [Kolodner, 1993] and operates on similarities of software

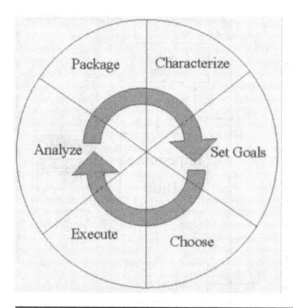

**Fig. 3.27.** The Quality Improvement Paradigm

---

**Process Model 8** Quality Improvement Paradigm

1. **Characterize**
   In this step, the goal products, the development environment, available data, used tools, etc. for a particular project are collected and documented.

2. **Set (quantifiable) goals**
   After the characterization is completed, the quality standards must be defined in terms of quantifiable properties of the involved products. The resulting goals should be ordered according to their relevance.

3. **Choose processes**
   The processes that are to be applied within a particular project are chosen in a goal-oriented manner [Basili, 1993] on the basis of their quality properties and on previous experiences.

4. **Execute**
   The selected processes are executed in order to build the target system. This step is the actual software development process as usually defined in the software engineering literature.

5. **Analyze**
   The resulting project data and determined problems are analyzed in order to make recommendations for future projects with similar characterizations.

6. **Package**
   In this step, either new models are defined or existing models are refined on the basis of the experiences made during the project execution phase.

---

development processes. In case-based reasoning, the specification of a problem to be solved is compared to specifications of problems that were previously solved and if a sufficiently similar problem specification is found, the previous solution is adapted in order to fit the usually slightly different new problem. If the adapted solution is sufficiently different, it is added to the repository for further use.

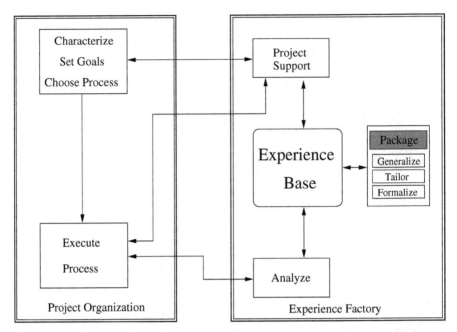

**Fig. 3.28.** The Experience Factory

The process idea of the Experience Factory is almost the same, but instead of just proposing the idea of experience reuse, the Experience Factory also offers an organizational framework for this process. As shown in Figure 3.28, the Experience Factory method differentiates between two organizational substructures: the *Project Organization* is responsible for the project work on the basis of software development process according to the QIP and on the basis of the process models presented in the previous sections. The *Experience Factory*, on the other hand is completely independent of the project organization and is responsible for analyzing and synthesizing all kinds of experiences and to provide the organization-wide repository of experiences.

Experience packages that are stored in the repository include *Product packages* such as programs, architectures, designs etc., *Process packages* describing process models, methods, etc. or *Relationship packages* that contain cost and defect models, resource models, etc. Furthermore, there also exist *Tool packages* that are divided ito constructive packages that cover tools such as code generators, configuration management tools, and analytic packages with tools such as profilers or static dependency analyzers. *Management packages* contain Management handbooks, decision support models, etc. and *Data Packages*, finally, hold project databases, quality records and the like. These experience packages are then used to *characterize and understand* new projects , to *evaluate and analyze* existing structures and processes, to *predict and control* the software development processes or to *motivate and improve* processes.

The major advantage of the Experience Factory is that it provides a single interface to the knowledge that exists within an organization and a central authority that collects and updates this knowledge. Furthermore, an Experience Factory can be introduced in parallel to the ongoing business of an organization and does not require complicated synchronization processes nor does it disturb the normal operational business. Finally, the idea of an Experience Factory is highly scalable. It can be used by an individual programmer who will then play several roles in order to store his or her personal experiences for later reuse, or it can be introduced into a large company as strategic department that increases the resource efficiency of the company.

The knowledge structures that will be presented in the course of this book can serve as basic structure for an experience base in order to store the experiences that are made during the development of multiagent systems.

## 3.7 Summ r

In this chapter, I have outlined some major Software Engineering concepts starting with a cognitive perspective on engineering in general and software engineering in particular. Then, we saw a general model of software engineering and discussed product and process models as the building blocks of this model. Finally, we have discussed some aspects of quality management and organizational learning.

In the next chapter I will demonstrate how some of these concepts are adapted to the specific case of multiagent systems and how they are assembled into a uniform framework.

# 4. T e Conce tu l Fr mework of MASSIVE

The ideas and concepts of the previous chapter constitute the basis of general Software Engineering methods which will now be refined for the particular case of multiagent system development. To this end, I will now explain the basic concepts and ideas of the MASSIVE method how its building blocks are assembled into a coherent method that can be used to develop multiagent applications.

## 4.1 T e Found tions of MASSIVE

In this book, I propose a pragmatic method for the development of multiagent systems that accounts for the specific requirements mentioned of MAS as they were mentioned in the introduction in Chapter 1. The building blocks of the MASSIVE method are based on the following ideas:

**View-oriented vs. model-oriented** All of the MAS specific process models that have been discussed in Section 3.5.3 develop several distinct models of the target system that must be subsequently integrated in order to construct the final system. This integration process is not always trivial, as the links between the models are usually neither explicitly defined nor obvious. Thus, I suggest adopting a view-oriented approach instead. A view-oriented method deals with the system as a whole and uses different perspectives on the entire system as fundamental abstraction. The system is not decomposed but rather viewed from different angles with different foci on particular aspects. The advantage of this approach is that it avoids the integration process because the model is always consistent from any view as changes in one view are always directly propagated to other views.

**Iterative vs. sequential** A sequential process model has the optimistic assumption that everything will work out as desired and that all documents are complete, correct and consistent once they are created. This assumption may hold in well-understood problem domains for which a lot of systems have been constructed, but it is unlikely that it holds in the case of multiagent systems because this class of systems is not well-understood at all until now. Any process model that is to be used in this context

J. Lind: The MASSIVE Method, LNAI 1994, pp. 97-120, 2001.

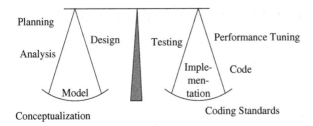

Fig. 4.1. Balanced Approach

should therefore reflect the fact that the system requirements and design documents are normally incomplete, incorrect and inconsistent due to the limited experience with this class of systems. To overcome these difficulties, it is a good idea to iterate the processes that are applied to construct the documents and to evaluate the results of each iteration according the explicit quality measures that are defined early in the development process. Although this approach does not guarantee that the documents capture all relevant aspects in the correct way, it nonetheless reduces the risk of errors because of the repeated quality evaluations.

**Balanced vs. biased** Traditional Software Engineering methods are often biased towards the modeling aspects of the problem in question and neglect the coding part of the resulting system. Figure 4.1 shows a simplified view on the situation: modeling the system is usually concerned with high-level tasks such as conceptualization or planning whereas for the implementation part of the system aspects such as performance or successful testing are more relevant. The traditional software engineering process models that have been discussed in Section 3.5.1 put most of their emphasis onto left hand side of the figure and treat the implementation of the system as a "simple" transformation of the model into code. Novel trends in the Software Engineering community, as they have been discussed in Section 3.5.2, especially the Object-Oriented approaches, feature a more code oriented point of view and tend to favor the right hand side of the figure.

In this book, I will adopt a point-of-view that treats the model and the code that implements the model as equally important parts of the whole. The MASSIVE development method clearly relates the parts of the model and the matching parts of the code and thus supports the construction of code that is well-structured and easy to maintain because of the explicit links between requirements and implementation.

**Requirements-driven vs. technology-driven** In a requirements-driven development approach, the requirements of the target system determine the technology that is to be used for the system design and implementation and not vice-versa. Thus before committing to a particular technology such as multiagent systems, it is necessary to analyze whether the intended technology is appropriate for the particular problem or not. This is clearly pointed out in [Wooldridge and Jennings, 1998] where an excellent overview on various problems that may come up with the development of multiagent is provided. Thus, the designer must not limit himself to a particular technology if it is not appropriate to the problem under consideration.

Consequently, a requirements-driven approach starts earlier in the life cycle of the target system when the fundamental characteristics of the problem under consideration are analyzed and then it is decided, which technology is the most appropriate to tackle the problem. In a rigorous requirements-driven approach, a functional analysis leads to a system decomposition that is developed without a particular technology in mind. After the system is decomposed, objective decision functions are applied in order to find the most appropriate technology for the task. However, the basic difficulty of this idea is that until now, no decision functions that decide whether a multiagent solution is appropriate exist and are thus subject to further research in the multiagent community [Jennings et al., 1998], [EURESCOM, 1999].

The resulting development method continuous previous work reported in [Lind, 1999a]. However, I still do not attempt to invent a uniform method for all types of applications (the "silver bullet") but I move modestly towards making my experience in the design of multiagent systems available to other system designers. In particular, the MASSIVE method provides a specific multiagent system product model, a nested process model that consists of a macro process model that covers the entire life cycle of the system development as well as several micro process models that are used to describe particular aspects of the target system and a framework for institutional learning in the development of multiagent systems.

After this introduction to the conceptual foundations of MASSIVE, I will now proceed to the more technical details on how these ideas are implemented in a software development method.

## 4.2 Knowbbles

The fundamental building blocks in the MASSIVE method are so-called *knowbbles* – with the term being comprised of "knowledge" and "bubble". Knowbbles represent all kinds of information that are available to the software engineer, ranging from conceptual entities such as design decisions or design constraints over implementation details up to test cases or information about physical entities such as system components or hardware devices.

Although we have claimed earlier that we only have a single design that captures all aspects of the system under consideration, it is often convenient to attribute knowbbles according to their major purpose. Therefore, we will first differentiate between *design* and *implementation* knowbbles in order to capture the dichtonomy that was explained in Sections 3.4.1 and 4.1. Design

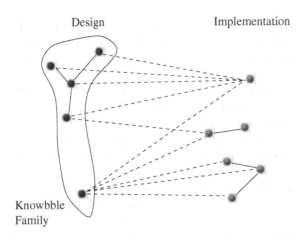

Design    Implementation

Knowbble
Family

**Fig. 4.2.** Connections between Design and Implementation

knowbbles are more conceptual entities that allow for a general description of the aspects of the system under consideration. For example, the class hierarchy of an application is a central aspect of the system design that is often represented as collection of knowbbles that are expressed in terms of some graphical notation such as the UML. Implementation knowbbles, on the other hand, are more specific e.g. to a particular programming language and therefore they are often the result of applying some sort of transformation process to the design knowbbles. Essentially, however, these two representations are isomorphic, i.e. design knowbbles and implementation knowbbles describe the same system.

Furthermore, we can classify the knowbbles as either *task specific* in that they capture properties or entities that are specific to the task at hand or as *task independent* knowbbles that describe general properties which do not pertain just to a particular application but to an entire class of applications. Background knowledge about the application domain are thus task specific knowbbles whereas background knowledge about developing computer programs in general is represented by task independent knowbbles.

Because of the isomorphism between design and implementation described earlier, the MASSIVE method sees the design and the implementation that realizes the design as a single collection of knowbbles. These knowbbles are linked in a flexible way that allows knowbbles of one group to be mapped onto knowbbles of the other group. This mapping is not unique as shown in the *Knowbble map* in Figure 4.2 where a single knowbble of the design is linked to several knowbbles of the implementation and vice versa. A collection of either only design or only implementation knowbbles is called a *knowbble family*, i.e. such a family is limited to knowbbles of a particular class. Depending on the type of the involved knowbbles, the links that are shown in Figure 4.2 can have different meanings. For example, a link from a design knowbble that represents a particular algorithm to an implementation knowbble means, that the implementation knowbble represents the code that

Design                    Implementation

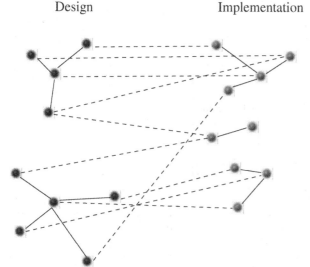

**Fig. 4.3.** Knowbble
refinement

implements the algorithm. If, on the other hand, the implementation knowbble represents information about a particular hardware device, the link to the
design knowbble usually means that the design knowbble depends on particular properties of the hardware device and that a change in the hardware
causes a change in the design.

Knowbbles are recursive structures that can be refined or aggregated. The
transition from Figure 4.2 to Figure 4.3 illustrates the idea of *knowbble refinement*. The single knowbble in the lower left corner of Figure 4.2 is refined into
five design knowbbles in Figure 4.3 and the single implementation knowbble
in the upper right corner of Figure 4.2 is refined into four implementation
knowbbles in Figure 4.3. The inverse process where several knowbbles are
combined into a single knowbble is called *knowbble aggregation*.

The MASSIVE method allows to define, alter, refine or aggregate knowbbles up to the desired level of abstraction and it is the task of the system
designer to identify the relevant knowbbles of the target system and to find
a structure for the software systems that implements these knowbbles.

## 4.3 Views

In this section, I will present one of the fundamental abstractions used in
the MASSIVE method to analyze and design the target system from different
points-of-view. I will first introduce the basic idea in a very general sense and
then refine the generic ideas for the case of multiagent applications.

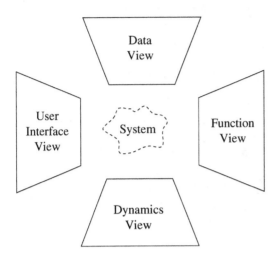

**Fig. 4.4.** A Generic View System

### 4.3.1 What and Why?

Knowbbles are a valuable tool to describe and to model the basic properties of a software system, but they are too general a concept for particular application areas. Therefore, we need a terminology that is more closely related to the particular need of multiagent systems design.

Knowbbles groups, as they were introduced in the Section 4.2 are not suited for this task for mainly two reasons. First, knowbble groups are limited to a particular class of knowbbles (either design knowbbles or implementation knowbbles) and second, knowbble groups only capture the refinement process that is performed during system development.

The terminological framework that I propose in the MASSIVE method is therefore based on so-called *views*. Views (sometimes also referred to as "viewpoints" or "viewports") have been discussed in the literature e.g. in [Sommerville, 1995] or [Balzert, 1998b] where each view is a representation of a different perspective on the system. However, although all of these approaches share the same terminology, they still have different ideas of what is meant by a "view". [Balzert, 1998b], for example, differentiates between four different views that a developer can have on the target system. As shown in Figure 4.4, these four views are the *Data view*, the *Function view*, the *Dynamics view* and the *User Interface view*. Although it is claimed that the above views can be applied to any application, I will later argue why I think that a more specific system of views that is oriented at the basic requirements of the problem class is more adequate.

In [Sommerville, 1995] some possible interpretations are listed: a viewpoint is either a *data source or sink* within a system, a *receiver of services*, i.e. viewpoints are external to the system and receive system services or provide data for performing these services or it is a *representation framework* such

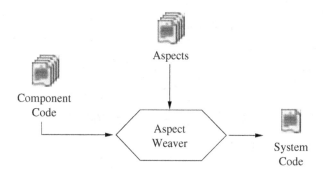

**Fig. 4.5.** Aspect Weaver

as an Entity-Relationship model or a Finite-State Machine that describes a (sub)set of the system properties.

Before I will explain the interpretation of the term that is used in this book, I would like to take a brief excursion to a relatively new idea in software development: Aspect-Oriented Programming [Kiczales et al., 1997].

Aspect-Oriented Programming tries to solve a problem for procedural programming languages as well as for object-oriented approaches. The problem that is dealt with are design decisions that effect several, functionally distinct parts of the system at the same time. A prominent example for this phenomenon is error-handling: the error handling strategy of a software system is usually the same throughout the entire system without being explicitly modeled anywhere. Thus it is hard to alter the strategy without major changes to most parts of the system – a process that requires a high effort and that is error-prone. If, on the other hand, the error handling strategy was explicitly modeled, the designer could change it easily and then use tools to re-build the system automatically. It is the goal of the aspect-oriented programming research to develop the mechanisms and tools for this process.

Aspect-oriented programming differentiates between two classes of entities that make up the system design. *Components* are the functional units that emerge through the functional decomposition of the target system whereas *aspects* represent the design decisions that cannot be encapsulated into a single functional unit. The idea of Aspect-Oriented Programming is to express aspects as meta-rules over the set of components and *weave* the system code from the code of the components and the aspects as shown in Figure 4.5.

While this idea seems to be quite natural, it bears a number of problems that have to be solved before aspect-oriented programming can become an accepted and established programming paradigm. The major problem is the mutual dependency of the programming language of the code, the rule language to express the aspects and the aspect weaver itself. In the current state of the development, a rule language and an aspect weaver must be developed for each target language. Furthermore, it is still not clear what expressive power the rule language must have and whether or not all relevant aspects of a particular system can be modeled with the basic approach.

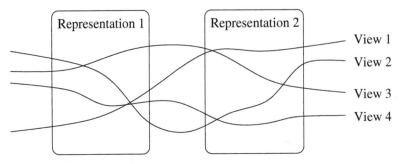

**Fig. 4.6.** Views

Because of these shortcomings, we will not use the full idea of aspect-oriented programming but rather borrow the basic observation that in every system there exist aspects that *cross-cut* all functional decompositions. My interpretation of the term view is therefore closely related to the properties (aspects) of the system under development and not so much on the observable behavior that is captured by interpreting viewpoints as services as mentioned above. The interpretation as representation framework is also not applicable as this seems to be a to narrow interpretation for my taste. It is well possible (and sometimes necessary and extremely helpful) to describe the same aspect of a system using different notations. For the same reason, the idea of interpreting views as data sources or sinks is too narrow as well because different data sources or sinks can belong to the same conceptual block of the system and a separation into different views can easily appear to be rather superficial or even distracting.

Therefore, I have decided to approach the problem of decomposing the system into several views from the direction of the design process. During the development of the system design, the designer will soon discover that some design aspects are more closely related to one another then to other aspects. These "natural" collections of aspects seem to be characteristic for a particular class of applications and it therefore suggests itself that these empirical decompositions capture the nature of an application class quite well. For these reasons, my personal idea of a view is therefore to see a view as an collection of knowbbles that cross-cut functional boundaries as well as different representations.

To illustrate this property, recall Figure 3.2 from Section 3.1.3 where I have said that a software system is usually described using several (ideally) isomorphic representations. In Figure 4.6, I have extended the original figure by adding four views that vertically cross the two representations of the target system. Views are thus a more general concept of grouping things together under a common semantic concept then knowbble groups alone and extend the original idea of linking related aspects of the system together.

Design                              Implementation

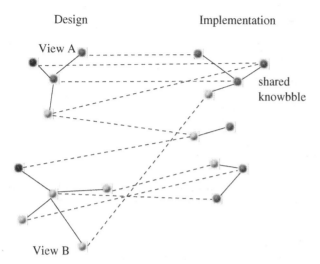

View A

shared
knowbble

View B

**Fig. 4.7.** Knowbbles
and Views

Ideally, the target system can be decomposed in several independent views
with well defined interfaces. In MASSIVE, each view represents a set of conceptually linked knowbbles, a view is thus a projection of the design onto a
particular subject. This interpretation is supported by results from programming experiments in cognitive psychology were it was found that different
abstractions (views) are used for different sub-tasks of the software development process [Pennington and Grabowski, 1990]. A collection of views that
achieves a logical decomposition of the target system is called a *view system,*
the interfaces between the views are modeled as explicit connections between
views by the use of so-called *shared knowbbles.* Shared Knowbbles belong to
two or more views at the same time and represent the interface between their
parent views.

The basic ideas are illustrated in Figure 4.7. View A (indicated by the
dark grey squares and circles) and view B (indicated by light gray) have a
shared knowbble in the upper right corner that indicates that these two views
jointly determine or depend on a particular entity of the implementation.

It is important to note that the property of a knowbble to be shared
between several views is not inherited by knowbbles that refine the shared
knowbble. As illustrated in Figure 4.8 for a knowbble that is shared between
two views and that is refined into two new knowbbles, the new knowbbles can
(a) belong to one of the views that share the parent knowbble, (b) belong to
different views (c) can be shared between the views or (d) can be shared with
a third view. The non-inheritance of the "shared" property of a knowbble
ensures the proper encapsulation of the abstractions within the knowbble
and is necessary to maintain the separation-of-concern among the views as
far as possible.

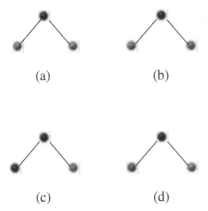

(a)                (b)

(c)                (d)

**Fig. 4.8.** Shared Knowbbles and Knowbble Refinement

### 4.3.2 View-Oriented Analysis

In [Sommerville, 1995], view-oriented analysis as it is shown in Process model 9 is described a two-step iterative process that is related to viewport analysis [Finkelstein and Fuks, 1989] and [Kotonya and Sommerville, 1992].

In the first step of a view-oriented analysis, the analyst will try to identify potential views. A technique that has shown to be quite effective for this task are simple brainstorming sessions were every aspect that comes to mind and that is related to the problem area should be written down. Customers and end users should participate in these sessions as far as possible because their input is very important for starting with the right thing. In the next phase of the view analysis, the aspects that have been identified during the brainstorming sessions are grouped together according to their conceptual distance. Obviously, this is a fuzzy process as there is no real measure that can be applied to decide how related two aspects are. Nevertheless, it is usually possible to allocate each aspect to a particular conceptual abstraction and these abstractions are then the views that separate the various aspects of the system. Aspects that cannot be allocated to a particular view or that could be allocated to several views at the same time are usually a sign for a missing view. Furthermore, aspects that have been overseen earlier may become obvious later. Therefore, the entire process is iterated until a stable state is reached. A general rule in the view-oriented analysis process is that the granularity of the resulting view system should neither be too coarse nor too fine.

In the previous paragraph, I have explained view-oriented analysis as it would be done for a particular problem under consideration. But this is only one aspect where view-oriented analysis can be applied successfully. As I have said above, it is often possible to find generic view systems for entire classes of applications and here, view-oriented analysis can be used as a tool to analyze such an application class in order to find a generic view system that covers most systems in that class. In the next section, I will present such a generic

**Process Model 9** View-oriented Analysis

1. **View identification**
2. **View structuring**
3. **Iteration**

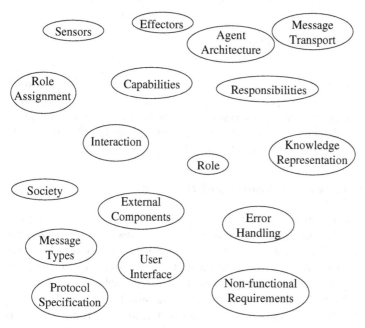

**Fig. 4.9.** Example for a Generic View Analysis

view system for multiagent systems that was found during the analysis of several multiagent applications.

As an example for the view-oriented analysis, consider Figure 4.9 where I have depicted an excerpt of the analysis map that lead to the generic view system for multiagent systems. According to the previously explained process model, this analysis map is the result of a brainstorming session for the view identification process. In the second step of the view-oriented analysis, the relevant aspects of the system under consideration are grouped together according to their semantic relation. In Figure 4.9, for example, the terms *role, role assignment, capabilities* and *responsibilities* are closely interrelated and are thus grouped together under the overall concept of a *role view* onto the system. Another example is the *interaction view* that covers things such as *protocol specifications, message types* and *message transport*. These initial groupings are then extended in subsequent iterations of the process when new aspects are discovered either by adding to existing concepts or by introducing a new general concept.

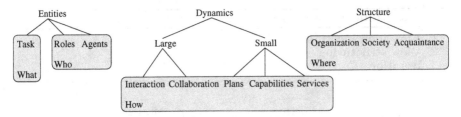

**Fig. 4.10.** Coverage of MAS Models

The major point in developing a general purpose view system for multiagent systems is to take specific applications and to abstract away from domain specific aspects while preserving the generic ones. The careful analysis of various application that are discussed in this book has finally lead to the generic view system that I shall present in the next section.

### 4.3.3 A View System for Multiagent Systems

Views are a general concept to arrange knowbbles with respect to a logical decomposition of the application class and I will now instantiate the general framework for the application class of multiagent systems. Before doing so, however, I will define some basic requirements that the resulting view system should comply to. First of all, the view system should help the designer to analyze the system with respect to the four fundamental questions from Section 3.4.1: what, where, who and how? However, the focus of these questions is very broad and thus we need a more fine-grained conceptual framework that separates the knowbbles of the target system as far as possible and that covers all relevant aspects of the target system. In order to develop an idea about the nature of an ideal view system, we shall return to the software development methods for multiagent systems that were discussed in Section 3.5.3 and review the product models that are proposed by those methods. Each of the presented approaches suggests several (sub-)models on either the analysis or the design level that deal with a particular aspects of the target system. Together, these (sub-)models constitute the full product model. All of the presented approaches take a model-oriented point-of-view that assumes a reasonable degree of independence between the models, sometimes even viewing the sub-models as being completely independent of each other and thus able to being worked on in parallel. However different the names and the coverage of the sub-models may be, they can all be classified according to the following scheme that is illustrated in Figure 4.10.

*Entity models* describe the fundamental entities that make up the target system and are thus concerned with more static aspects of the system. Common names for these models are either "Task" model for more fine-grained models, or "Role" or "Agent" model for the description on a higher level of abstraction. While some approaches make a clear distinction between these two models, others mix them up. Sometimes, architectural decisions such as an inheritance hierarchy are included in these models as well. Furthermore, while the concept of roles appears in many of the models, it usually refers to different ideas in each of them.

*Dynamics models*, on the other hand, are intended to capture the dynamic aspects of the target system on various levels of abstraction and can be divided into two distinct classes. Models in the first class describe the dynamics-in-the-large of the multiagent system and are usually referred to either as "Interaction", "Co-operation" or "Collaboration" model. Models of the second class are usually more fine-grained and describe the problem solving mechanisms of individual agents. Common names for these models are "Capabilities", "Services" or "Plans".

*Structural models*, finally, are used to either to describe the basic structure of the target system in terms of the connections between the agents or the knowledge an agent has about other agents, but also to describe the organisational context of the target system. The models of the first class are called "Society", "Organisation" or "Acquaintance" models whereas the others are referred to as "Organisation" or "Context" models.

Using the product models of the multiagent specific software develepment methods as guideline, we can derive the following requirements for a view system for multiagent systems.

**Separation** Separation in this context means, that the view system should support "separation of concern", i.e. changes in one part of the system should affect as few other parts of system as possible. In the knowbble oriented approach I have presented in the previous section, this property can be expressed by using as few shared knowbbles as possible. Generally speaking, the view system should provide a high cohesion among the knowbbles that are grouped together in the view and achieve a low coupling with other views.

**Coverage** The view system must be able to cover all aspects of the target system. For example, the view system should reflect the fact that the target system is not developed or used in isolation but rather in a well-defined development and operational context. Thus the view system must allow to specify and model not only the properties of the target system but also the properties of the environment of the target system.

Furthermore, the view system must allow the designer to specify functional as well as nonfunctional properties of the target system.

**Flexibility** The view system should allow the designer to model a broad range of multiagent systems ranging from multi-robot applications to systems of directly communicating software agents. Furthermore, the view system should not be limited to a particular technology, e.g. a specific agent architecture or a particular agent framework.

**Size** The size of the view system is a crucial factor with respect to acceptability in the development community. If the system is too fine-grained

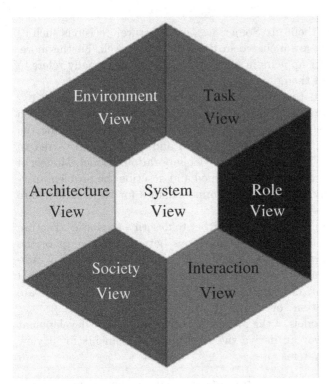

**Fig. 4.11.** MASSIVE Views

it is likely to be too complicated to be used. If, on the other hand, the model is too coarse-grained it will not be used because it provides no added value to the designer in comparison to an unstructured approach.

**Naming** The names that are used within the view system should be suggestive, i.e. they should cover the semantic attributes of the objects referred to as far as possible. They should also be distinguishable in a way that the designer is able to clearly associate a particular group of attributes with each view.

The view system that I will present now has matured over several years during our work on the design and implementation of multiagent systems. As shown in Figure 4.11, the system consist of seven views that are briefly described in the following paragraphs. A full description of each view together with the application of the views to a case study are presented in the next chapter.

**Environment view** In this view, the environment of the target system is analyzed from the developers perspective as well as from the systems perspective. These two perspectives usually differ as the developer has global knowledge whereas the system has only local knowledge. In the RoboCup domain [Noda, 1995], for example, the developer has access to the complete state of the system and its environment and this state is completely deterministic from this point-of-view. From the perspective

of the individual agent within the system, on the other hand, only parts
of the environment are accessible and the state transitions appear to be
nondeterministic because of ongoing activities that cannot be perceived
by the agent.

**Task view** In the Task view, the functional aspects of the target system
are analyzed and a task hierarchy is generated that is then used to determine the basic problem solving capabilities of the entities in the final
system. Furthermore, the nonfunctional requirements of the target system are defined and quantified as far as possible. Note that this view
does not assume that a multiagent approach is used for the final system
and therefore provides a rather high-level analysis of the problem.

In the case of a compiler application, for example, the basic functional requirement is that the system translates a program specified in a high-level
language to a particular assembly language. The quality of the resulting
code or the maximal tolerable time for the compilation are nonfunctional
requirements and the basic problem solving capabilities are for example
lexical analysis or code generation.

**Role view** This view determines the functional aggregation of the basic
problem solving capabilities according to the physical constraints of the
target system. A role is an abstraction that links the domain dependent
part of the application to the agent technology that solves the problem
under consideration. In my view, an agent consists of one or more role
descriptions and an architecture that is capable of executing these role
models which makes it important to aggregate the basic capabilities according to physical constraints.

In a robotics application for a storage area, for example, we may find
robots that are capable of carrying containers from one area to another
and others that are capable of stacking containers onto each other. Therefore, the roles of "carrier" and "stacker" cannot be assigned to a single
agent because of the physical constraints of the robots unless a third sort
of robot exists that can execute both basic problem solving capabilities.

**Interaction view** Interaction is a fundamental concept for a system that
consists of multiple independent entities that coordinate themselves in
order to achieve their individual as well as their joint goals. In this view,
interaction within the target system is seen as a generalized form of
conflict resolution that is not limited to a particular form such as communication. Instead, several generic forms of interaction exist that can
be instantiated in a wide variety of contexts. The developer is encouraged
to analyze the target problem with respect to the applicability of these
generic forms before designing new forms.

The most popular example for interaction is of course a communication
protocol, simply because communication protocols have been studied for
quite some time. However, multiagent systems that simulate physical
environments or real physical multiagent systems such as robots or ma-

chines have many other possibilities of interaction besides communication and these forms of interaction must be allowed for in a general purpose method as well.

**Society view** A society is a structured collection of entities that pursue a common goal. The goal of this view is to classify the society that either pre-exists within the organizational context of the system or that is desirable from the point-of-view of the system developer. According to this classification and to well defined quality measures for the performance of the target society that depend on application specific aspects, a society model is developed that is consistent with the roles within the society and that achieves the defined goals.

To illustrate how the quality measure affects the desirable society structure, consider, for example, Internet trading. In order to achieve the best trade, the number of participants in the trading process should be rather high in order to increase the chance of finding a profitable trade. On the other hand, a high number of participants also increases the computational and communicational overhead and thus a clustering of trading agents would increase the communicational and computational efficiency of the system. The final structure of the agent society (flat or clustered) thus depends on the quality measures (quality of the solution vs. efficiency).

**Architecture view** The Architecture view is a projection of the target system onto the fundamental structural attributes with respect to the system design. The major aspects that are dealt with in this view are the system architecture as a whole and – due to the size and complexity of this particular aspect – the agent architecture. The system architecture is described according to various aspects and includes things such as agent management or database integration. The required agent architecture is characterized according to the requirements of the problem to be solved and it is strongly recommended that the system developer should at first try to select one of the numerous existing architectures before trying to develop a new architecture from scratch.

An important aspect that has to be dealt with in this view is to find the appropriate segregation between agents and objects. Just because agents provide a means for structuring a problem does not mean that they are necessarily the best means to do so [Collins and Ndumu, 1998]. Sometimes, it is better to implement particular abstractions as ordinary objects and thereby increase the system performance by avoiding the inevitable overhead associated with turning an object into an agent.

**System view** This view, finally, deals with systems aspects that affect several of the other views or even the system as a whole. The System view, for example, handles the user interface that controls the interaction between the system and the user(s) whose the task specific aspects are usually the input specification and the output presentation whereas task

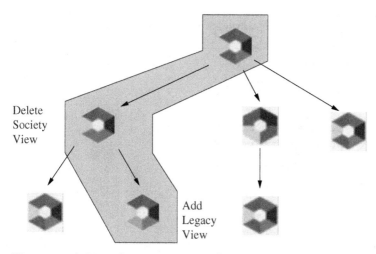

**Fig. 4.12.** A View System Tree

independent aspects deal with the visualization of the system activities in order to enable the user to follow the ongoing computations and interactions. Other aspects that are described in this view are the system-wide error-handling strategy, performance engineering and the system deployment once it has been developed.

According to the previously posed questions on the general nature of a product model and the classification illustrated in Figure 4.10, we can see that the Task view models *what* the system should do, the Environment view describes *where* the system should perform its tasks, the Role view defines *who* should do what and the Interaction, Society and Architecture views, finally, define *how* the tasks should be executed.

However, the view system shown in Figure 4.11 is not stable over time. Rather, it is intended as the root of a tree of view systems as shown in Figure 4.12. The tree emerges from the generic base model by adding view systems that have additional views or view systems that have one or more views deleted. Consider, for example, a multiagent system that has only a small number of agents. In such system, the Society view may be omitted because of the limited size of the agent society. A followup project may have similar characteristics as the original project (i.e. few agents) but it may furthermore need some sort of legacy software. In this case, the Society view is omitted as well, but also a new view, the Legacy view which deals with the integration of legacy systems in the multiagent environment, is added to the view system. The development of the original view system to the new view system is illustrated in Figure 4.12 by the shaded area.

The tree of view systems reflects the evolutionary idea of the Experience Factory presented in Section 3.6.2: the initial view system is altered in order to make it fit the particular needs of a specific project. Then the adapted

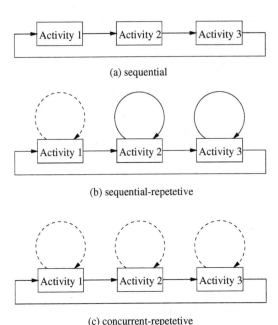

(a) sequential

(b) sequential-repetetive

(c) concurrent-repetetive

**Fig. 4.13.** Models of Iteration

view system is filed away in case that a later project will have the same characteristics as the project for which the view system was originally adapted. The goal of this constant learning process is to acquire a collection of view systems that cover a large variety of multiagent application domains.

After this outline of the product model that is used in MASSIVE, I will now present the process model that uses the view system discussed in this section.

## 4.4  ter tive View Engineering

Before we proceed to the process model of MASSIVE I will explain the origins of some ideas that have found their way into the iterative view engineering approach that is presented later. First of all, it is necessary to define what I mean by *iteration*. In Figure 4.13, I have depicted three possible approaches to the general concept. In its *sequential* interpretation, a process that consists of several activities is called iterative whenever the sequence of steps is executed one after the other and starting again from the beginning after the last step in the sequence has been completed. However, although this interpretation is straightforward and intuitive, it is also very rigid. If, for example, only a single activity within the process should be carried out several times, the other activities must be run through (although with no effect) as well. Therefore, we might introduce a more flexible iteration scheme that I would call *sequential-repetitive* . In this scheme, a single activity within a

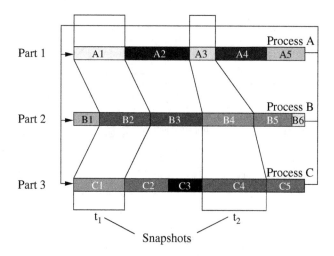

**Fig. 4.14.** Micro Processes

sequence of activities can be executed several times before proceeding to the next activity. Although this scheme adds some flexibility to the initial idea, it is still not optimal. For example in a case where some of the activities are independent from each other, a strict sequential interpretation of the ordering of activities unnecessarily delays the overall completion time. Therefore, I favor a third interpretation of iteration that I call *concurrent-repetitive*. In this form, the sequence of activities is worked through in the specified order. However, instead of completing an activity to its full extend before proceeding, the activity is simply spawned off the main chunk of processing and is worked on as parallel thread. Following activities can then be spawned off the main track as well an proceed unless there arises a resource conflict with an activity that has been started earlier. In this case, the second activity is put on hold until the first activity has is completed and the resources are freed. This, in my view, most general interpretation of an iterative process model is the conceptual basis of the view engineering process of MASSIVE.

Generally, iterative view engineering is a product centered software engineering process model that combines Round-trip Engineering and Iterative Enhancement discussed in Sections 3.5.2 and 3.5.1, respectively. However, the iterative enhancement approach that was presented in Section 3.5.1 assumes that all artifacts of the model are constructed with the same process model. This is not always optimal. Therefore, I propose an extension that sees the Iterative Enhancement as a *macro* process that encapsulates several *micro* processes that are used to construct individual parts of the model. This idea is illustrated in Figure 4.14 which shows a product model that consists of three parts where each part is iteratively constructed with potentially different process models. Part 1 of the model is constructed according to process model A which consists of 5 different activities, part 2 of the model is constructed according to process model B with 6 activities and finally part 3 that is constructed according to process model C with 5 activities. The vertical

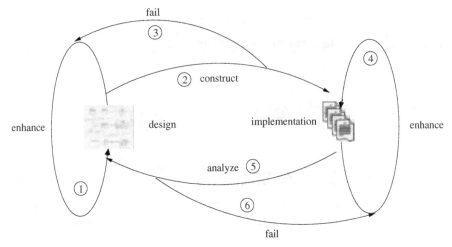

**Fig. 4.15.** Iterative View engineering

boxes represent snapshots of the entire model at times $t_1$ and $t_2$, where the parts of the model are in different stages of the processes that are used to construct the respective artifacts.

Combining these ideas into a concurrent-repetitive model as outlined above, results in the Iterative View Engineering model shown in Figure 4.15. The Round-trip steps are oriented along the horizontal axis of the figure and the Iterative Enhancement steps are depicted on either side of the figure.

The Iterative View Engineering process model is the following: Initially, the design and the implementation are empty. In a first cycle of Iterative Enhancement (①), the software engineer specifies the first version of the design probably by using different micro models for each view.

Note that it is not compulsory for the designer to work through the views in a predefined order. Independent parts of the design can be worked on in parallel, i.e. several micro processes can be active at the same time. However, experience suggests especially in early stages of a project that a cyclic ordering is quite useful. In the following step (②), parts of the initial design are implemented. If an error occurs during the construction phase, the design has to be refined (③) until it can be implemented. Next, the initial implementation is tested. During the test phase, it often turns out that the design specification was incomplete (even for the parts that were generated) or wrong. In this case the implementation is changed or enhanced (④) in order to meet the intentions of the initial design. After the test and enhancement phase of the implementation is complete, the results must be integrated into the design during an analysis step (⑤). If the implementation cannot be reverse-engineered (e.g. because the changes of the code are incompatible with some basic requirements of the design), e.g. because the expressive power of the modeling language is too limited for a particular feature of the imple-

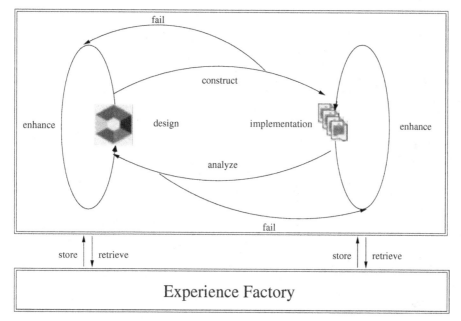

**Fig. 4.16.** The MASSIVE Method

mentation, the implementation must be changed (⑥) in order to comply to the modeling language. After this step, the next cycle is executed until the entire system is fully implemented.

The advantages of this life cycle model are that it can deal with an incomplete problem specification because of the iterative enhancement approach. The approach is also useful for early risk detection because parts of the design are incrementally implemented and can direct the project managers view to critical regions.

## 4.5 Putting  t All Toget er

Now that we have seen the individual concepts and entities that are part of the MASSIVE method, it is time to assemble these fragments into a coherent picture as shown in Figure 4.16 that captures the overall structure of the MASSIVE method: the product model that was described in Section 4.3 is integrated into the process model from Section 4.4 which is itself embedded into the framework of the Experience Factory outlined in Section 3.6.2. The resulting overall development model is given in UML notation in Figure 4.17 and a textual description is provided in Process model 10.

The core of the MASSIVE method is the view system that was outlined in Section 4.3 and that will be discussed in detail in Chapter 5. The view system is the conceptual basis for a wide range of product models that are

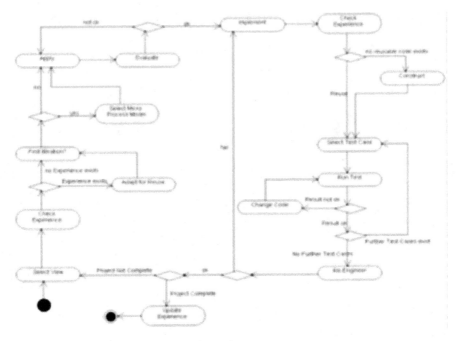

**Fig. 4.17.** The MASSIVE Method (UML)

developed and refined throughout the software projects that are carried out according to the suggested process model. The main idea of the process model is an Iterative View Engineering approach that is itself based on Iterative Enhancement and Round-trip Engineering. A macro process encapsulates several small micro processes that are used for individual activities within the design process for a particular view and that can be executed in parallel.

In Section 5.4, for example, we will discuss a micro process model for the role modeling activity within the design of the Role view. Such a nested process model was also suggested in [Booch, 1996] but there only a single micro process model is embedded into the macro process.

The macro model as well as the micro models of the MASSIVE method are in no way fixed for the entire lifetime of the project model, they are also subject to changes and refinements during the course of time. In order to preserve these and to make them accessible to others, the process model and the product model are both embedded into a larger organizational structure called the Experience Factory. The Experience Factory provides the formal framework for a permanent learning process that takes place over project boundaries and that eventually models the multiagent experience of an organization in terms of specific product and process models for various domains.

## Process Model 10 MASSIVE

1. **Select View** In the first step of the Iterative View Engineering process, the developer selects the view that will be refined to from the view system that describes the current state of the development process.

2. **[Select micro process model]** The micro process model assists the developer in the refinement of the previously selected view. Usually, the micro process for a particular view is selected upon the first iteration of the macro process and remains fixed until the end of the development process. It is, however, possible to change the micro process that is used for a view when it turns out, that the initial decision was not adequate.

3. **Check Experience Base** Before a view is initially developed or refined, the Experience base is checked for packages that contain knowledge about artifacts with similar specifications. If one or more of such packages are found, the results that are stored in these packages is adapted to the specific needs of the new problem and reused to construct a solution for the problem in question.

4. **Apply** In this step, the previously selected micro process model is applied to the selected view in order to generate the first version of the view or to refine an existing version either from a previous iteration or from the Experience Base.

5. **Evaluate** The current version of the view is evaluated according to well-defined quality measures. If the quality is not sufficient, the micro process is re-applied to the view until the quality standards are met.

6. **Implement** If the view has reached a sufficient degree of maturity, it is transformed into executable code. In this step, the Experience Base is used for the second time in order to find knowledge packages on the code level that can be reused for the implementation. If no matching code fragments are found, the implementation must be started from scratch.

7. **Test** The goal of the test phase is to ensure that the code that has been constructed in the previous step complies to the specifications that are captured in the design.

   a) **Select test case** The test cases are specified in features that are associated with each view. The Test Engineer selects one of these features for each round of testing.

   b) **Run test** Running a test means to set up the system environment and system state according to the test case specification and then executing the code. The results of the test execution are the analyzed to discover errors in the implementation.

   c) **Adapt** If the results obtained in the previous step differ from the expected results as specified in the test cases, the code must be changed until the results from re-running the test provide the desired result. If the results match the specifications, the test phase is complete.

8. **Re-engineer** The test phase of the system can result in changes of the code that are not captured in the design. Thus, this step aims at identifying these differences and adapting the design in such a way, that it adequately describes the current code of the system. This step is necessary to ensure consistency of the design and the code.

9. **Iterate** If not all specifications are implemented and have passed the quality checks, the entire process is repeated from the first step.

10. **Update Experience Base** After the completion of the entire process, the Experience Base is updated according to the new experiences that were made during the development of the new system.

## 4.6 Summ r

In this chapter, I have presented the basic ideas of the MASSIVE development method such as knowbbles that represent conceptual or physical entities, e.g. design decisions or system components. Knowbbles are conceptually linked into views that constitute a projection of the complete model onto particular aspects. Iterative View Engineering was then presented as the process model that is used to construct the product model built upon these views. The overall framework of the entire development process is the Experience Factory which supports systematic learning over project boundaries.

In the next chapter, we will focus on the view-oriented product model that was already outlined in this chapter. Each view will be discussed in detail and the basic ideas will be illustrated using the TCS/MAS system as a case study.

# 5. MASSIVE Views

The product model of MASSIVE is the core of the entire method. It allows the system designer to break the target system down into several views that concentrate on particular aspects of the system and abstract away from others. In each of the following sections, we will at first discuss the general nature and the intended scope of a view as well as a number of features and design patterns that belong to a view. However, the features and patterns that are presented are by no means an exhaustive collection, they rather represent the current state of my personal experience in designing multiagent applications. According to the basic idea of the Experience Factory, the potential user of the MASSIVE method is encouraged to add new aspects that are necessary or to remove aspects that are not important in a particular context. In each of the following sections, the general considerations are applied to a case study in order to demonstrate how the theoretical concepts are used in a practical situation.

Before I explain the views that constitute the view system of the MASSIVE method in detail, however, I shall clarify how these views relate to multiagent specific questions. Any of the subsequently discussed views covers some agent or multiagent specific aspects of the target application, but the degree varies greatly over the set of views. In Figure 5.1, I have sorted the views of the MASSIVE Product model according to their relation to multiagent technology.

The most general and thus most technology independent view is the Task view because it models the system from a purely functional point-of-view. The System view and the Environment view also deal with very general properties of the target system and contain only few multiagent specific features. The Architecture view in the middle can be interpreted as the link or the interface between the more technology independent views and the more specific views. The first view in the latter class is the Role view that explicitly models the agents and their properties, followed by the Interaction view that captures the ongoing inter-agent processes. The most multiagent specific view, finally, is the Society view that explicitly deals with collections of agents.

Although it seems to be a natural idea to construct a software product by proceeding from the general to the specific views, this approach is not the best for building the target system for the reasons explained in Chapter 4. This is simply due to the fact that some decisions in a more general view are

J. Lind: The MASSIVE Method, LNAI 1994, pp. 121-204, 2001.
© Springer-Verlag Berlin Heidelberg 2001

Task View

System View

Environment View

Architectural View

Role View

Interaction View

Society View

**Fig. 5.1.** Views and Multiagent Systems

**Table 5.1.** Views and the Minimal SE Process

|  | Task View | Environment View | Role View | Interaction View | Social View | Architecture View | System View |
|---|---|---|---|---|---|---|---|
| Analysis | X | X |  |  |  |  | X |
| Design |  |  | X | X | X | X | X |

refinements of aspects of a more multiagent specific view. For example, the roles and interactions in the target system constitute design decisions that have major influence on the architecture of the final system.

Furthermore, some of the views are more closely associated to the analysis phase of the software development process while others belong more to the design phase. In Table 5.1, I have marked the respective views of the MASSIVE product model according to the phase of the minimal software development process model introduced in Section 3.4 that they are more closely related to. The relations that are indicated in the table, however, are not exclusive as a particular view may contain analysis and design aspects at the same time. According to the principle of selecting the best strategy for a given problem, the views can thus be worked on in any order, switching back and forth between views as necessary.

Before we discuss the views that constitute the solution for the problem under consideration, however, I will provide a brief introduction to the problem that is used in the case study to illustrate the basic properties of each view.

## 5.1 A  rief  ntroduction to Tr in Cou ling-  nd S  ring (TCS)

Efficient transportation — be it of persons or goods — is a key issue in todays industrial world [Carroué, 1997]. Because of the immense amount of transportation tasks, it is necessary to use the available resources most effectively.

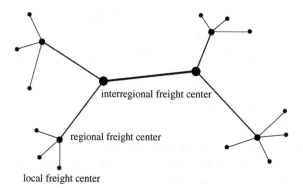

interregional freight center

regional freight center

local freight center

**Fig.  5.2.**  Hierarchical freight haulage

Thus, computer aided — or entirely controlled — scheduling systems are key technologies not only for telematics.

Conventional wagon load traffic as it is performed today is shown in Figure 5.2: a company that wants to ship something via rail to its customers delivers the freight to the local freight center (usually a railroad station) where it is stored until enough freight from other companies has arrived to justify a train to the regional freight center. At the regional freight center, wagons from other local freight centers that have the same direction are assembled and sent to the next interregional freight center where another re-assembling process takes place. The decomposition of the trains is achieved in reverse order.

This approach has some serious drawbacks. First of all, the wagons of individual customers must wait at the local freight centers until enough freight is delivered to make a train to the next local freight center profitable. Second, the re-assemblance of trains in regional and interregional freight centers is a very time consuming process that introduced additional delays in the producer-to-customer route.

An  alternative  approach  [Kracke et al., 1995],  [Fabel, 1996], [Voges and Mierau, 1997] to the classical freight transport process uses small railroad *transportation modules* (e.g. the CargoSprinter [Windhoff AG, 1996]) instead of conventional trains. Whereas a normal train is made up of one locomotive and several freight wagons, a transportation module consists of two power units on either side of the module and up to three permanently coupled intermediate vehicles with a fixed number of loading spaces. Thus, a transportation module is a single unit of limited size. When a company wants to deliver some freight to a customer, it orders a transportation module at a local freight center and loads its goods onto this module and the module itself is then responsible to find its way through the railroad network.

A transportation task is served by a transportation module and we assume that each task can be served by a single module, i.e. there is no need to hook two or more modules together to serve a single task. Vice versa, we

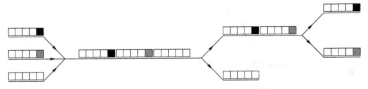

**Fig. 5.3.** Train Coupling and Sharing (TCS)

assume also that a module cannot serve more than one task at a time. All tasks occurring in the system are transportation requests in a railroad network; a network is graph consisting of several nodes connected via so-called *location routes*. In the current version of the system, an abstracted map of the German railroad network with approximately 250 nodes and 350 links is used to simulate the underlying railroad network.

Whenever the system receives a transportation task, it assigns the task to a free module which in turn computes the path from the origin to the destination node with a shortest path algorithm. The module then rents the intermediate location routes for a certain time window from the network manager. The time window for each location route is uniquely determined by the earliest departure time and the latest arrival time of the transportation task. The problem is now, that a location route in a railroad network cannot be used by two independent modules at the same time. Either a route is blocked while being used by a single module or two (or more) modules share a route by hooking together at the beginning of a location route and splitting up afterwards as shown in Figure 5.3. In order to use the underlying railroad infrastructure most efficiently, the railroad modules should share as many location routes as possible while taking care of their local constraints.

The main advantage of this approach is that it avoids a central planning authority that schedules all transportation modules. Instead, each module is autonomous and tries to achieve its goal, which is to deliver its freight to some destination node in the network. Thus, each module performs local optimization of the network throughput by sharing as many location routes with other modules as possible. The local optimization process of all modules eventually leads to a high, though usually only suboptimal, degree of resource efficiency. Besides this major advantage, a decentralized approach implies less coupling operations during the train composition process, a high degree of customer accessibility and lower costs because of the effective location route usage.

The basic idea of the TCS approach for freight transportation in a railroad network that have been outlined in this section are a good example for using multiagent systems technology in a real world problem. I will therefore use the TCS/MAS system throughout the next sections to illustrate the basic ideas of each view and develop the fundamental design of the system in the course of this chapter.

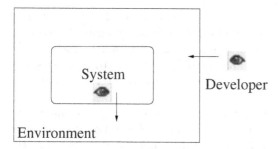

System

Developer

Environment

**Fig. 5.4.** Perspectives on the Environment

## 5.2 Environment View

The goal of this view is to model the environment of the target system from two distinct points-of-view as shown in Figure 5.4. First, the environment will be analyzed from the perspective of the developer and a general characterization of the environment as it appears to the developer will be generated. Second, the environment will be described from the systems point-of-view in terms of input/output or sensor/effector specifications.

### 5.2.1 Developers Perspective

This part of the Environment view describes the environment of the multi-agent system from the developers point of view. The main aspects are the organizational context in which the system will be used, the general characteristics of this context as far as it is relevant for the application and a technical assessment of the runtime environment of the operational system.

**Organizational Context.** The first step in modeling the environment of the target system is to clarify the organizational context that determines how and where the target system should be used within the customers organization. If, for example, the target system is meant as a prototypical evaluation of a new approach or some other technology that will not be used in an operational context, it surely directs the focus of the final design onto more functional aspects then onto nonfunctional aspects such as stability or user friendliness.

It is hard – if not impossible – to specify concrete rules of how to specify the organizational context because the relevant concepts are extremely fuzzy. Therefore, the major contribution of organizational context specification in this view is to provide the designer with a feeling of how the system should be used and what is important with respect to the field of application of the target system.

In order to characterize the development context of the TCS/MAS system, we will at first analyze the customers ideas of what the system should be used for. According to the Deutsche Bahn AG, the TCS/MAS is intended as a strategic tool to evaluate the basic characteristics of Train Coupling- and

Sharing. "Strategic" means, that the system is not intended to be used in an operational context in order to plan and organize freight transport according to the TCS approach. Instead, the system should be used to identify the relevant parameters and their optimal settings according to a given set of quality measures (e.g. cost of a particular schedule or average number of coupling activities).

Furthermore, the TCS/MAS system was also developed to evaluate the technology behind it, namely multiagent techniques for distributed problem solving. This evaluation is done from the functional point-of-view, i.e. the customer wants to find out whether multiagent technology can solve the TCS specific scheduling problem or not. From the nonfunctional point-of-view, the customer is also interested in the question of how good the multiagent solution is. The quality of the solution depends not only on functional measures such as overall cost, but also on nonfunctional quantities such as response time to a new task.

The necessity to evaluate the TCS approach in general results in many constraints towards the organizational context of the TCS/MAS system because the system is required to obey the most important railroad operation regulations. These regulations affect the network specification of the underlying railroad network as well as specifications for coupling activities, maximum train lengths or maximum train speeds. A special case is resource allocation within the TCS/MAS system. The resources that must be scheduled among the competing modules are the location routes between any two nodes in the network. For these location routes, a predefined schedule exists that must not be violated by the resource assignment algorithm. Furthermore, the assignment algorithm must respect the minimal distance that two trains must keep when they are using the same location route.

**Characterization.** [Russell and Norvig, 1995] propose a very general scheme to describe the environment of agent-based applications that uses five dimensions to capture the characteristic features of the environment.

**accessible vs. inaccessible** In an accessible environment, the agents can perceive the full state of the environment at any time. In a an inaccessible environment, on the other hand, only partial information is available to the agents.

**deterministic vs. nondeterministic** This feature describes how the agents perceives the development of its environment, i.e. whether the next state of the environment is completely determined by the current state (as perceived by the agent) or not.

**episodic vs. nonepisodic** An episode is a single perception-action cycle performed by the agent. In an episodic environment, these cycles are unrelated, i.e. the action of one cycle does not have any impact on the next cycle. Thus, episodic environments are much simpler then nonepisodic environments because they do not need the ability of the agent to plan ahead.

**static vs. dynamic** In a static environment, the environment cannot change while the agent is not acting (i.e. while the agent is deliberating) whereas this assumption does not hold in a dynamic environment.

**discrete vs. continuous** In a discrete environment, the agent has distinct, clearly defined percepts that (partially) describe the environment. This is not the case in a continuous environment.

These features can be used to characterize a broad range of environments. The physical world, for example, is inaccessible, nondeterministic, nonepisodic, dynamic and continuous, whereas a virtual world that is inhabited by software agents is also nondeterministic, nonepisodic and dynamic but it is usually accessible and discrete.

Characterizing the environment according to the above features can help the designer to anticipate basic problems that are likely to occur in a particular class of environments. Dynamic environments, for example, require a much more sophisticated reasoning mechanism that is capable of integrating newly perceived state information in the ongoing reasoning process.

Using the characterization scheme given above, we can classify the environment of the TCS/MAS system as nonaccessible because no single entity has a complete model of the entire system, nondeterministic because of the incomplete view of any entity, the entity is not able to predict the next system state, nonepisodic because the actions performed in one cycle (forming of unions out of modules) affects the possible actions of the next cycle, static because the tasks are integrated one after the other and discrete because of the granularity of the planning process.

The organizational context and the general characterization of the environment of the target system usually depend on the particular problem domain. Another important aspect of the system environment from the perspective of the developer that will be discussed in the following section, however, is domain independent.

**Runtime Environment.** This aspect of the system environment deals with technical aspects of the runtime environment of the target system. These characteristics are often neglected because they are considered unimportant and could therefore be left out without loosing generality. But this is not true! The runtime environment can have an enormous impact on he final design and performance of the system and should thus be explicitly modeled as early as possible. A good example for the impact of the runtime environment on the final system is the TEAMWORK LIBRARY discussed in Section 6.1. The original approach used simulated broadcast messages because physical broadcast was not offered by the communication platform (Ethernet). It was assumed that simulated broadcast would do as well. This turned out to be a mistake because the performance and value of the teamwork approach relied on the fast transfer of large amounts of data. Thus, the entire system had to undergo a re-design phase that added mechanisms and protocols for physical broadcast. To avoid such expensive error-corrective work, the runtime environment must be carefully characterized and evaluated.

First of all, the designer must specify the programming model that is used in the target system. Programming models can be classified according to their degree of concurrency: a *sequential* programming model admits for no concurrency at all; functions are called strictly one after the other. This kind of programming model does not require synchronization mechanisms and it is sufficient in case the multiagent paradigm is solely used for design purposes, i.e. to structure the target system. A *pseudo-parallel* model, on the other hand, typically uses light weight processes (threads) within a single operating system process to achieve concurrent execution of program fragments. This kind of programming model is well suited for multiagent applications because it allows for a reasonable degree of parallelism while still being easy to handle with respect to debugging and traceability. A fully *distributed* programming model, finally, distributes the computation space over several computers connected via a communication network. This model is quite hard to handle because it often requires complex synchronization and fault tolerance mechanisms. However, for real world applications, this might be the only possible choice.

In the next step, the designer has to describe the communication platform that will be used within the target system. The choices for the communication platform are usually limited by the choice of the programming model; a sequential system, for example, will usually be limited to internal communication using ordinary method invocation mechanisms. In the case of a pseudo-sequential programming model, the choices are broader because such a programming model usually requires asynchronous message exchange to exploit the (pseudo-)parallelism provided by using several threads of execution. Asynchronous message invocation methods are usually not offered by the programming language and thus the designer must define a method that is best suited for communication between the entities of the target system. The widest range of choices, however, is given in the case of fully distributed systems. The entities can communicate using network protocols such as TCP/IP or radio transmission protocols such as GSM to exchange messages.

Finally, the choice of the appropriate programming language is an important issue. The programming language need not necessarily support a particular programming paradigm, e.g. object-oriented programming in order to built a multiagent application. However, a cleaner, more structured code will be generated if the programming language supports particular features that are characteristic for multiagent systems.

In the TCS/MAS system, the technical development environment features a pseudo-parallel programming model because it offers a reasonable degree of flexibility and concurrency while still being relatively easy to monitor and debug. The chosen programming language is a functional, constraint based, multi-threaded language called Mozart [Programming Systems Lab, 1999],

[Smolka, 1995] and the communication platform uses Mozart threads to achieve asynchronous message exchange between the agents. The system platform is Linux .

However, as it was said in the introduction to this section, the developers perspective is just one aspect that is dealt with in the Environment view. Therefore, we will now discuss the other main aspect of this view – the system that is situated in an environment and that somehow perceives and acts upon this environment.

### 5.2.2 Systems Perspective

Specific parts of the system may have a very different perception of the environment given their physical or conceptual constraints. Usually, the system (and later the agents) perceive their environment through a number of sensors and operate on the environment by using effectors. First of all, this very general concept of an input/output specification must be clarified with respect to the characteristic needs and requirements of the target system. Second, the designer must develop a model of the environment that is internally used by the agents to represent their environment and to reason about it.

The definition of the mechanisms that enable the entities in the system to perceive and act upon their environment should be general enough not limit the choice of assigning particular sensors and effectors to the roles within the multiagent system defined later (see Section 5.4). In this view, only a general model of the sensors and effectors that allows the designer to get an overview of how the systems inter-operability with its environment can be arranged should be produced.

The model of the sensors and the specification of the individual percepts then leads to the choice of the data structures that are needed to capture an internal world model depending on the functional requirements of the target system. Sometimes, an internal model is completely obsolete [Brooks, 1991] whereas in other cases the agents must be equipped with a rather fine-grained model of their environment and their fellow agents.

In the TCS/MAS example, the perception and action possibilities of the system (and later the agents) are rather limited as it is often the case with systems of communicating software agents. The agents can perceive all other agents that are currently active within the system and the only action that is allowed for an agent is to send a message to another agent. The knowledge structures that are needed to model the agents knowledge about the environment are therefore very simple and consist only of a list of peer agents that are currently active in the system.

## 5.3 T sk View

The goal of this step in the MASSIVE method is to identify what the target system should do. We should therefore try not think in terms of "agents" or "goals" because this could too easily restrict our view for other possible solutions. Ideally, the result of this step in the method should be the basis for the decision of the designer whether a multiagent approach is the best solution for the given problem or not.

As explained in Section 2.4, agents are kinds of abstractions that should be viewed in a broader context then just under a functional point-of-view. The functional abstractions that are modeled in this step can spread over several agents and multiple functional abstractions can be encapsulated in a single agent. These decisions, however, are not the subject of this view that only models the basic requirements of the target system.

Requirements analysis is a difficult task, mainly because of the communication gap between developers and users. In the next section, I will therefore introduce a technique that was developed to bridge this gap.

### 5.3.1 Use Case Analysis

Use Case Analysis or Use Case Modeling as, e.g. presented in [Jacobson, 1992] [Kenworthy, 1997] or [Kulak and Guiney, 2000], is a powerful tool to capture the system requirements from the point of view of the people that will use the system after or during it is developed. But even for systems with limited user interaction, use case analysis can be a valuable means to describe the intended behavior of the system. In the latter case, however, the name "use case" is somewhat misleading and can be replaced by a more neutral term such as in [Booch, 1994] where the term "scenario" is used to capture essentially the same aspects as in a use case.

Basically, each use case is a very high-level description of *what* the system is supposed to do. It is *never* a means of describing *how* the intended behavior can be achieved! Therefore, use cases are not a functional decomposition of the system but rather a decomposition of system behavior from the users perspective that can subsequently be refined into a functional specification of the system behavior.

In the first step of Process Model 11, the end-users of the system to be developed are identified and separated into user groups. Then, the interaction patterns with the system are described for each of these user groups, leading to an initial set of use cases. Each of these initial use case is then informally described first in its normal course of operation and second in alternative paths according to exceptional situations that may occur. The informal description should ideally follow and easy scheme such as "The user does X, the system does Y. Then the user does Z, the system does ... ". Again, the designer must be careful in order not to specify how a particular system reaction should be provided. After the use cases have been specified

---

**Process Model 11** Use Case Analysis

---

1. **Identify actors (users)**
2. **Identify self-contained interaction scenarios (use case)**
3. **For each use case**
   a) **Define the "normal" course of operation**
   b) **Create additional cases for exceptional situations**
4. **Identify commonalities between use case and aggregate**
5. **If not complete, go to 1.**

---

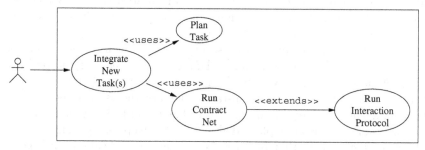

**Fig. 5.5.** Use case example from the TCS domain

in an initial description, the designer should try to identify commonalities between case and eliminate them by generating an extra case that is jointly used by the others. Similarly, the designer should try to identify <<extends>> relation between two cases where one of them is an extension of the other. The entire process is then iterated several times until the collection of use cases becomes sufficiently stable. In can also be repeated in the course of the development process as soon as new requirements are identified or when the details of previously unspecified use cases become obvious.

As an example for a use case analysis, Figure 5.5 shows an excerpt from the full document that holds the use cases of the TCS domain. In the example, the user wants to integrate a new task into the existing schedule. To this end, the system performs some local planning in order to find a valid schedule for the new task. Optionally, the system can also try to do some optimization by running the contract net protocol with the new task as the manager and the other modules as contractors. This dependency relation is expressed by adding the keyword <<uses>> to the arrow that links two use cases. Also shown in the figure is an <<extends>> relation between two use cases where the use case that runs the contract-net protocol is a specialization of the use case that runs an interaction protocol in general.

### 5.3.2 Functional Requirements

Functional requirements are a specification of what the system should do. To obtain a first sketch of the functional requirements, it is often useful to analyze the intended workflow in the broadest sense. To this end, he designer can use the specification of the organizational context that was discussed in Section 5.2.1. The result of this analysis should be an abstract definition of the input and output of the system and allow for a precise description of the system task(s). A potential problem that arises in this context is that many multiagent system as continuous systems, i.e. systems that doe not simply transform input data to output data but that continuously act upon their environment. A solution of this problem is to break down the continuous operation into episodes that are defined in terms of the state of the environment before and after a particular operation. Therefore, even continuous systems can be described by a functional approach.

A tool for the functional decomposition of the problem to be solved are *task trees* that capture the fundamental functional aspects of the problem domain. A task tree for a given problem is constructed by decomposing the overall system task into several sub-tasks that are themselves decomposed until a sufficiently low level of detail. Note that I avoid to talk of "goals" in this respect for the reasons explained above. The concept of a goal implies the existence of some entity that pursues the goal and thus leads to an "agent-oriented view" that I wish to avoid in this early phase through the back-door.

Figure 5.6 shows an example for a task tree as the result of the task analysis process. The tree describes some of the tasks that may occur in a mail order company that maintains a stock of goods and a database of customers that; the tree is embedded into a larger organizational structure indicated by the dashed line at the top of the figure. One can see in the figure how a particular task is decomposed into several subtasks, e.g. the task "Manage Customer" is decomposed into "Manage Address" and "Take Order". These sub-tasks can be decomposed further as shown in the Figure.

The construction of the task tree follows the general idea of a hierarchical decomposition according to functional aspects of the problem domain. The granularity of the decomposition process depends on the specific problem but it should not become a specification of a particular algorithm. The task tree only provides a general picture of the activities that will be present in the target system, individual algorithms are designed later. The functional decomposition of tasks can be supported by the use of Structured Analysis [DeMarco, 1978] or related methods.

From the task decomposition captured by the task tree, the next step is to derive a mathematical formalization of the problem domain. Mathematical formalizations are an extremely valuable tool in studying and describing the transformations performed by any software system and should be used whenever possible. To obtain an initial formalization of the problem domain, the entities of the domain are defined as precisely as possible while abstracting away from unnecessary details. Then, the functional transformations (tasks) are expressed in terms of these basic entities. However, this initial formalization of the desired functional behavior is usually not complete nor is it

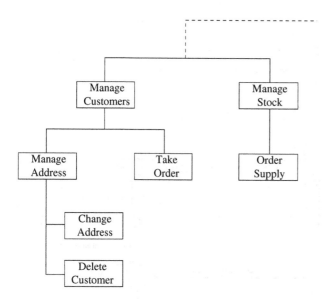

**Fig. 5.6.** Example for a Task Tree

detailed enough to allow for an immediate implementation of the system. Therefore, the model will go through a refinement process. To achieve a complete model of the desired behavior, several iterations of the entire modeling process are likely to be necessary because the complete model needs input from the other views as well as user feedback.

Besides the functional modeling of the behavior of the target system, it is also important to quantify functional properties of the output (in the most general sense) of the system. Quantification means that the designer – ideally together with the user – must identify qualitative features of the solution that can be quantified by defining appropriate measures to decide that a solution generated by the systems satisfies particular requirements. Identifying the features that determine the quality of a solution and defined measures for these features is sometimes very difficult and should be done in close collaboration with the user to avoid the risk of designing a system that does not capture the users intention. This holds especially true in the case of optimization problems.

One of the most important rules for the functional modeling of the target system is to avoid any kind of control flow specifications. In this view, it is not important – sometimes even harmful – to think about *how* something has to be done. The goal of this view is solely to specify *what* is to be done. Furthermore, it should always be kept in mind that a complete functional specification is not possible in the first iteration and consequently, the initial design should not be overloaded by modeling features that show to be of less importance during the course of modeling the other views onto the system.

I will now illustrate the approach that has been discussed in this section by applying it to the TCS example. I will start with a workflow analysis of

Customer                    Carrier                              Net Provider

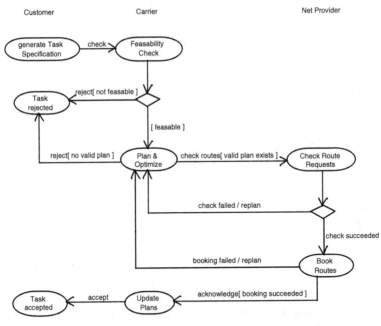

**Fig. 5.7.** TCS Simulator Workflow (UML)

TCS and then derive the task tree that represents the various tasks within the target system. Then, I will demonstrate how the formalization of the TCS domain is accomplished.

The workflow of a customer request for a transportation service according to the TCS approach is shown in Figure 5.7. First of all, the service provider checks whether the request can be satisfied due to technical constraints (e.g. if the customer requires a special wagon type, e.g. cooled). If the required resources are available, the user request becomes a transportation task (or simply task[1]) and is added to the task list of the service provider. A task is served by the service provider by finding a plan that satisfies additional user constraints such as freight availability or delivery deadlines and that also minimizes the cost for the service provider. If no plan can be found that satisfies these additional requirements, the task is rejected by the task dispatcher. If, on the over hand, a valid plan exists, the service provider must try to allocate the external resources that are needed to complete the task. The external resources in our case are the location routes that are used by the union that serves a particular task. If the resources can be allocated successfully, the task is finally accepted and scheduled for execution when the time is up.

The focus of the TCS/MAS system in this scenario is the service provider which is given a list of task specifications that must be satisfied. The set of

---

[1] Not to be confused with the task decomposition discussed earlier.

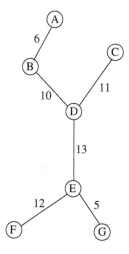

**Fig. 5.8.** Example railroad network

tasks is not fully known to the system at start-up time, new tasks arrive during the planning process and may require a revision of the already assembled plan in order to reduce cost. In order to have a more realistic simulation of the environment, the resource allocation process should be modeled as well. Furthermore, the system should be capable of simulating the resulting schedule as well as failures that occur during the execution of the schedule such as location route failures, i.e. the case that an allocated resource is not available upon plan execution time and a process of dynamic re-planning must take place.

In Section 5.1, I have introduced the basic ideas of TCS. Recall that fundamental idea of TCS is location route sharing, i.e. the idea that two or more modules hook together at the beginning of a location route (or of a sequence of consecutive routes) and split up afterwards.

For this case study, we shall use the seven node network shown in Figure 5.8 to illustrate the basic ideas of the TCS/MAS system. The numbers on the routes in Figure 5.8 indicate the distance between two nodes connected via a location route. To illustrate the idea of route sharing, consider the following example with two transportation tasks from $B$ to $F$ and from $C$ to $G$, respectively. If the two modules serving the respective tasks act independently, the transportation costs for the first module are 35.0 units and 29.0 units for the second. If, on the other hand, the two modules decide to cooperate and to share the common location route between node $D$ and node $E$ and assuming that the cost for shared routes are equally distributed among the participation modules, the transportation cost reduces to 28.5 and 22.5, respectively.

The computational problem in conjunction with location route sharing is to identify sets of tasks (i.e. their respective modules) that can share location routes. The limiting factors are the compatibility of transportation paths and

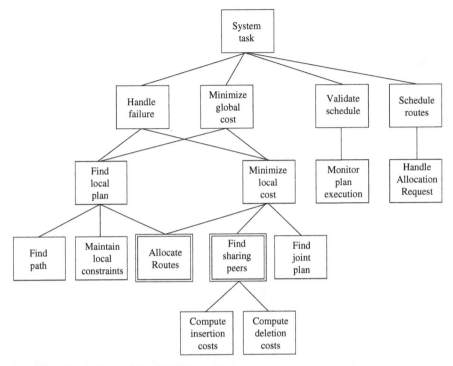

**Fig. 5.9.** Task Tree of the TCS Domain

time windows. We shall refer to sets of cooperating modules as *unions* where each union is determined by the participating modules.

The functional requirements are now informally given as follows:

1. The system should be capable to plan the union formation process. Union formation means, that the system is able to find task specifications that can be combined into larger units according to the TCS approach.
2. The system should be capable of dealing with an incomplete problem specification.
3. The system should be able to simulate the execution of the resulting schedule.
4. The system should be able to simulate failure situations such as the unavailability of a particular resource.

The task decomposition of the TCS/MAS system is shown in Figure 5.9. The activities in the leaf nodes of the task tree shown in the figure correspond to the basic problem solving capabilities that will be developed in the course of the role modeling process described in the next section. The double box indicates a leaf node that requires the collaboration of several problem solving entities and that are thus not subject to this view. Joint capabilities will be dealt with in Section 5.5.

We will now construct a formal model of the TCS domain that enables us to define the basic problem solving capabilities more precisely.

**Definition 5.3.1 (Time Window).** *A* **time window** *$TW$ is a tuple $\langle \underline{t}, \overline{t} \rangle$ that consists of a lower bound and an upper bound with $\underline{t} \leq \overline{t}$.*

**Definition 5.3.2 (Path).** *A* **path** *is a sequence $\overline{A_1, \ldots, A_n}$ of node identifiers such that there exists a link between any two nodes $A_i$ and $A_{i+1}$ for all $i \in \{1, \ldots, n\}$.*

**Definition 5.3.3 (Task).** *A* **task** *is a tuple $\langle O, D, TW, AT \rangle$ consisting of the origin node $O$ and the destination node $D$, a time window $TW$ that specifies the earliest possible departure time and the latest allowed arrival time and finally a time stamp indicating when the task is announced to the system.*

**Definition 5.3.4 (Module).** *A* **module** *$M_i$ is specified by its unique identification number $i \in \{1, \ldots, m\}$ and a tuple $\langle P, S, L \rangle$ denoting its current plan $P$, the maximum speed $S$ of the module and its length $L$.*

**Definition 5.3.5 (Plan).** *The* **plan** *of a module $M$ is a sequence $[PS_1, \ldots, PS_n]$ of plan steps where each plan step $PS_i$ is given by a tuple $\langle N, TW, A \rangle$ that consists of a node identifier $N$, a time window that specifies the earliest possible arrival time and the latest allowed departure time from the node and a list $A$ of coupling actions with other modules that must be executed in the node.*

**Definition 5.3.6 (Action).** *An* **action** *is a tuple $\langle T, P, D, TW \rangle$ that specifies the action type $T$, the peer modules $P$, the action duration $D$ and the time window during which the action must be executed.*

**Definition 5.3.7 (Union).** *A* **union** *$U_j$ is a collection of several modules $M_{i_0}, \ldots M_{i_n}$. Each union has a unique identifier $j \in \{1, \ldots, k\}$ and is written as $U_j^{i_0, \ldots, i_n}$.*

*Unions are-meta level concepts; a union emerges when at least two modules decide to cooperate by sharing location routes and it ceases to exists when all modules within the union have completed their respective tasks.*

**Definition 5.3.8 (Failure Specification).** *A* **failure specification** *is a tuple $\langle L, TW \rangle$ consisting of the location route identifier $L$ and a time window $TW$ that specifies when the location route is blocked and when it can be used again.*

**Definition 5.3.9 (Schedule).** *A* **schedule** *is a sequence of tuples $\langle L, TW^* \rangle$ consisting of the location route identifier $L$ and a sequence of time windows $TW_i$ where each time window specifies when the location route is used by a train.*

The elements of the data structures are accessed using the dot notation scheme where the list elements are referenced by their index number. For example let

```
[
(NodeId:A, t:10, t̄:16, actions:nil)
(NodeId:C, t:10, t̄:16, actions:[(type:join peers:[M₂ M₃] duration:4
t:11 t̄:15) ])
(NodeId:D, t:10, t̄:16, actions:nil)
]
```

be the plan of module $M$. Then we have $M.A.\bar{t} = 16$ or $M.C.actions.1.peers = [M_2\ M_3]$.

This initial formalization of the basic entities in the TCS domain will be used later when we define the basic capabilities that are needed by the agents within the TCS/MAS system. However, although the functional requirements of a software system are usually predominant in the system specification, some other aspects need attention as well.

### 5.3.3 Nonfunctional Requirements

The nonfunctional requirements define meta-level properties of the target system, i.e. properties that usually specify additional constraints that cannot be modeled in the solely functional context. Typical examples for nonfunctional requirements are the stability of the system, security aspects, portability, extensibility etc. Nonfunctional requirements often affect a system as a whole. Because of their global nature, they should be specified only if it is absolutely necessary as they usually impose severe limits on the system design [Rombach, 1994a].

Because of the fact that the TCS/MAS system is only a prototype, there are only few nonfunctional requirements of system. The only relevant nonfunctional requirement is that the integration of a new task into an existing schedule should be within a time span of few minutes to make sure that an operational system that is built upon the foundation of the prototype allows the task operator to answer to a customer request quickly.

## 5.4 Role View

Up to now, a characterization of the environment where the system will be running after it is developed as well as the tasks of the target system have been specified without committing to a particular technology to solve the given task. In this section, we will now look at this and start with modeling the system according to the role concept of the multiagent programming paradigm as presented in Section 2.4. We will not only discuss the problem of finding role abstractions given the functional and physical constraints of the problem specification, but we will also look at the problem of how to assign particular role(s) to agents of the target system.

## 5.4.1 Role Definition

I have already mentioned in Section 2.1.2 that a major problem in the field of sociology is the delimitation of roles that occur within a society. In the design of a multiagent system, the software engineer is faced with the problem of role delimitation as well. He or she is given a functional specification and is the asked to transform this functional specification into a society of interacting roles.

In this section, we are concerned with the definition of the *functional roles* within the multiagent system, i.e. roles that are defined in terms of the tasks that must be carried out. A second group of roles in a multiagent system called *interaction roles* are prototypical roles that are used in the definition of interaction protocols that are used within the multiagent system. In the contract-net protocol [Smith, 1980], for example, the generic interaction roles *manager* and *bidder* must be implemented according to the particular context. Interaction roles, – despite of their name – however, are not a genuine part of the role view and are therefore discussed in the Interaction view in Section 5.5.

In the course of defining the functional requirements of the target system, it is recommended to build a task hierarchy of the problem domain. Usually, this process leads to a task tree with the overall system task as the root of the tree that is decomposed into several sub-tasks. The leaves of the tree are either atomic activities that can be handled by a single problem solver or they are joint activities that require the collaboration of several problem solvers. The activities of the second group are handled in the Interaction view discussed in Section 5.5 whereas the activities of the first group are subject to this view.

Each of the atomic activities given in the task tree is specified on an algorithmic level that uses the abstractions of the formal model to describe a particular problem solving strategy. The basic capabilities that are defined here will later be combined and used as the basis for the role delimitation process.

There are three potential ways to achieve this goal. The first approach is the classical *top-down* processing of the functional specifications [Barbucean and Fox, 1995]. The specifications are decomposed into hierarchical sub-groups and these groups are then declared as the roles. This approach has the advantage that it is straightforward and that it usually leads to satisfactory results. Unfortunately, the approach assumes that the designer has the full flexibility in grouping the functionally decomposed units. However, this assumption does not hold for example in the case of a robotic application where the physical entities limit or even define the functional grouping.

functional
grouping

physical
grouping

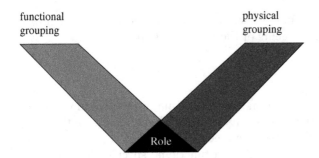

**Fig. 5.10.** Hybrid Role
Identification

Therefore, the designer may decide to go the other way round, namely to follow a *bottom-up* approach to identify the roles within the system. This approach [Parunak, 1997], [Parunak, 1999b] starts from the physical grouping that is usually determined by the environmental context of the target system or by the physical capabilities of the existing entities and tries to create the interactions that fulfill the functional requirements. The idea outlined in [Parunak, 1999b] is to apply linguistic case theory analysis on an informal task description as it is e.g. given by the Task view (Section 5.3). First of all, Linguistic Case Theory [Cook, 1979], [Parunak, 1995] assigns a set of slots to each entity in the problem domain. These slots are typically filled with nouns associated to each verb in the informal description and each slot reflects the semantic connection of the role inhibitor to others. The verb and the collected nouns then become potential candidates for role descriptions. Although this approach is in accordance with the organizational or physical constraints of the target system, in its pure form it is only applicable if such a physical grouping really exists.

In the Massive design method, I have tried to combine the advantages of these two approaches and to avoid their limitations as far as possible. First of all, we need a new definition that combines the role concepts according to both strategies.

**Definition 5.4.1 (Role).** *A role is a logical grouping of atomic activities according to the physical constraints of the operational environment of the target system.*

Definition 5.4.1 tries to combine the top-down and the bottom-up approach towards role delimitation by equally weighting the existing functional and physical groupings. Figure 5.10 illustrates the basic idea of our *hybrid strategy:* the functional decomposition and the physical structure are integrated into a common role that fulfills the functional as well as the physical requirements. The resulting micro process for role modeling in Massive is pretty much straightforward as shown in Process Model 12.

In order to demonstrate how this micro process is applied, recall the task tree for the TCS domain as it is shown in Figure 5.9 on page 136. From this task tree, we can derive the following set of roles.

---

**Process Model 12** MASSIVE Role Modeling

---

1. **Identify functional groupings** In this step, the basic capabilities are grouped together into functional roles such that each role represents a coherent cluster of functions that is sufficiently different from other clusters. [Collins and Ndumu, 1998] suggest two rules of thumb that can support this process:
   - The *Sphere of responsibility test* aims at identifying local resources that are used by a group of functions and to associate this group with a particular role.
   - The *Point of interaction test*, on the other hand, is used to separate the different functional groupings from each other in order to achieve a high degree of partitioning of the target system.

   Thus, the two rules of thumb clearly relate to the concepts of coupling and cohesion.

2. **Identify physical groupings** In the second step, the physical constraints that are present in the problem domain are identified and documented. The physical groupings are usually determined by the system environment e.g. hardware devices or geographical constraints.

3. **Identify basic problem solving capabilities**

4. **Integrate** In the final step of this micro process, the functional roles are unified with the physical entities. It is important for the designer to define a mapping from one group onto the other that achieves a high degree of resource efficiency i.e. that does not overload a particular resource while others are not used to their possible extend. If, for example, a workstation represents a physical role, the functional roles that are mapped onto this workstation should not be of a computational complexity that cannot be handled by a single computer nor should they be so lightweight that the machine is idle most of its time.

---

The task of a *TCS module* (or simply module) is to transport goods within a railroad network. To achieve this task, the module has to perform a local planning process that yields a plan through the railroad network and that satisfies the customer constraints with respect to freight availability and freight delivery deadlines.

As already mentioned in Section 5.3, a *TCS union* is a meta-level structure that emerges whenever two or more modules decide to share a particular location route. A union integrate additional modules if there are sharing possibilities with the union members and thus reduce its costs by performing a local optimization process. Furthermore, a union can also release one or more of its members from the union if this allows the union to integrate another module thats cost saving potential is higher then the saving that was gained with the original module. Global optimization within the society of unions emerges from the local optimization steps of the individual unions.

The *task manager* is responsible for handling incoming transportation requests. The task descriptions are externally specified; each task has a time stamp that indicates, when (i.e. in which clock cycle) the task should be announced to the system. This mechanism allows to simulate time varying task arrival-times.

The *net manager* controls the location route usage by serving the route allocation requests of the unions. It has direct access to the underlying railroad network. The major task of the net manager is to guarantee that no location route is allocated to more than one module or union during a particular time window. Furthermore, the net manager is responsible for managing an existing schedule on the location routes (i.e. passenger trains) and thus limit the available time windows for some location routes.

With this set of functional roles, we can now go on and identify the physical constraints that are present in the problem domain. In the TCS/MAS system, this is straightforward as the physical structure of the problem domain is not important for the structure of the target system because the system implements a virtual multiagent system that is running in a single process.

In future extensions of the TCS/MAS to a fully operational system, however, there is the possibility to distribute the agents to physical entities, for example the transportation modules that handle the transportation tasks or to remote machines that handle the resource management process. Thus, the design of the multiagent solution should reflect this possible extension and be flexible enough to serve as a basis for a transfer of the software architecture to the physical world.

The next step in the micro process for role modeling in MASSIVE is to define the basic problem solving capabilities that are needed by the agents. The capabilities that are described in this section are the basis for the subsequent role aggregation process for the roles of TCS agents.

The main capabilities that are needed by the agents are as follows.

**Planing algorithm for a single task** This capability is needed by a transportation module to find a path through the railroad network from the source node of the transportation task to the destination. Additionally, the local planning operator must determine the time windows (i.e. the earliest possible arrival time and the latest possible departure time) for each intermediate node in the path that must be maintained in order to deliver the goods on time.

**Plan integration operator** Whenever two or more modules want to share location routes, their individual plans must be synchronized by inserting join and split operations into the start and end nodes of the shared routes, respectively. This process requires a sophisticated and flexible planning mechanism that allows for the integration of as many modules as possible into a union.

**Decision functions** The decision functions of the modules and unions determines which of the potential sharing peers offers the biggest cost saving potential. The computational complexity of the decision function should be as small as possible as it is likely to be used many times during the planning process.

**Plan execution simulation** This capability, finally, is used for the visualization of the schedule such that it can be evaluated by the system operator. A dynamic animation of the plan execution process can provide a much better impression of the global schedule then a collection of static plans.

I will not discuss these capabilities in detail here, the interested reader may refer to Appendix B.1 for a thorough presentation.

The final step of the MASSIVE micro process for role modeling is to integrate the functional and physical groupings together with the basic problem solving capabilities into roles. The functional and the quasi nonexistent physical groupings presented in the previous paragraphs suggest that it is quite natural to use the functional decomposition as the final role models. This natural practice is justified in the case of the task manager and in the case of the net manager as these roles are independent of any other functional role and so they can be modeled in isolation. However, this is not the case with the modules and unions. These roles have a rather tight coupling and this coupling should be reflected in the system design.

We have assumed so far that a union emerges when two or more modules decide to share a location route. Even though this view reflects the basic idea of the TCS approach, it is not really appropriate in the design of the software system that implements the approach. For a more clearly structured design, it is a better idea to view each individual module as a special case of a union – simply a union with a single module, in the context of this work referred to as a *degenerated union*. Applying this scheme results in a much simpler system design because it allows us to treat modules and unions uniformly. Thus, we have less abstractions and less complexity in our design. Abstractions, on the other hand, are of course extremely valuable when a problem must be decomposed into several parts. But this example demonstrates that an extensive use of abstractions can lead to difficulties that can be circumvented if some abstractions are merged together into larger units.

However, the unions are not the only functional roles in the TCS/MAS system as we also have the task manager and the net manager that controls the resource handling process. As described above, the net manager is responsible for accepting incoming location route requests and computing a schedule that uses the underlying resources most efficiently. Because of the fact that there are no other related tasks in the system, the entire functional role is determined by a single activity. This holds also for the task manager which does not have related functional aspects and is thus also mapped in a one-to-one manner to the functional role. This completes the role modeling process for the TCS domain. The problem that remains to be handled in the role view is then to assign these roles to agents.

### 5.4.2 Role Assignment

Role assignment is the process of mapping roles as they were introduced in Section 2.1.2 and discussed in the previous section onto agents. By defining agents as the sum of the agent architecture and the potential roles the agent can play as it was suggested in Section 2.1.4, we are now faced with the task to group the roles in way such that each group of roles can be played by a single agent.

This role assignment within a multiagent system can either be *static*, i.e. the agent is assigned a particular role at system start-up or it can by *dynamic*, i.e. the role assignment to an agent can change during the agents lifetime. Furthermore, an agent can play its different roles sequentially or it can have several roles at the same time.

Static role assignment has the advantage that the system designer need not think about how the agents internal state changes during a role change can be modeled. The agent is bound to a fixed task and no intra-agent conflicts of any kind can occur. However, static role assignment is not feasible if different roles share particular resources, for example cognitive structures. The knowledge transfer from one agent to another can be prohibitive for a static role assignment and so a dynamic scheme must be applied. An example for this case is discussed in Section 6.1.

Dynamic role assignment becomes a very difficult problem if all agents have the same capabilities and the role assignment process should be arranged by the agents themselves. In [Fischer, 1993] this problem is discussed in depth and a generic interaction protocol for the dynamic assignment process is presented.

In the TCS/MAS system, a static the role assignment scheme is applied because of the natural mapping from the functional roles to agents. There is no need for an agent to switch between functional roles in the application and thus the role assignment can be hard-coded into the implementation.

## 5.5  nter ction View

The roles that have been developed in the previous section are the fundamental abstractions that decouple the functional aspects of the system from the agents. However, some functional aspects require the collaboration of several agents in order to be fulfilled and these collaborations must be specified by the system designer in one way or another.

In Section 2.2.1, I have defined conflict resolution as the general purpose of any interaction between agents. Now, I will describe how a system engineer can track down the abstract ideas behind the conflict resolution process into a concrete implementation. To this end, we shall decompose the interaction design process into three layers of abstraction as depicted in Figure 5.11. The design process thus proceeds from the most abstract level towards an

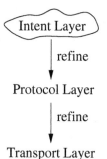

refine

Protocol Layer

refine

Transport Layer    **Fig. 5.11.** Layers of Abstraction in Interaction Design

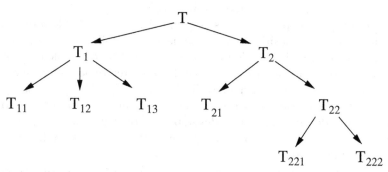

**Fig. 5.12.** Task Decomposition

implementation by refining and extending the concepts on the next higher level.

### 5.5.1 Intent Layer

The intent layer is the highest level of abstraction of the interaction design process where the system designer specifies the general nature of the interaction process, i.e. the purpose of the interaction. The interaction purpose describes *why* the agents interact with one another. For example, the purpose of interaction can be *co-operation* where the agents will usually work together to jointly solve a given problem. The agents are thus usually not self-interested as long as the overall system task is solved. A typical example for such a situation is *task decomposition*. This interaction scheme achieves a hierarchical decomposition of the overall system task into sub-tasks. Ideally, these sub-tasks are independent from each other and can thus be worked on separately. Figure 5.12 illustrates the basic idea: the overall system task $T$ is split up into two sub-tasks $T_1$ and $T_2$ that are divided in turn.

Whether a task decomposition is feasible usually depends on the structure of the problem domain which is mainly characterized by its coherence. A very dense problem space is usually non-separable i.e. it cannot be split into several parts and is thus resistant against task decomposition. A separable problem

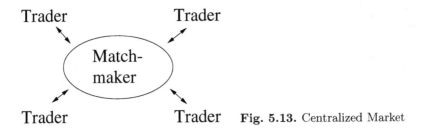

**Fig. 5.13.** Centralized Market

space, on the other hand, often offers a natural decomposition into several independent parts that can be worked on in parallel.

Therefore, task decomposition is usually in suited for separable problem domains where the decomposition requires some sort of explicit co-ordination. A certain degree of direct interaction between the agents is desirable but not necessary. The approach scales rather well and can therefore be used in small agent systems as well as in larger ones. The co-operative behavior that is necessary to achieve a smooth task decomposition can either be built into the agents by the designer or it can develop over time in that the agents learn that co-operative behavior usually pays [Rovatsos and Lind, 1999], [Rovatsos and Lind, 2000].

Another possible purpose of agent interaction is *competition*. In that case, the agents usually interact to optimize an external property and simulate a market-place where (abstract) prices for resources are negotiated. Ideas such as Market-Oriented Programming [Wellman, 1996] are attempts to capture problems of distributed resource allocation with little information. The major advantage of these approaches is that the agents need not provide internal information to external authorities as the only information that is exchanged is the price.

Market-based mechanisms can be implemented in a centralized form as shown in Figure 5.13 where the agents interact with a matchmaker agent that is responsible for bringing together sellers and buyers. This form of Market-Oriented Programming has the advantage that the degree of communication is low because all agents are linked to the matchmaker. Furthermore, the trade can be performed anonymously.

In its decentralized form as shown in Figure 5.14, each agent is linked to any other potential trading partner and the agents negotiate directly without using an intermediate matchmaker. Although this approach has a higher degree of communication overhead it has the advantage that no global pricing scheme takes places which can help the individual agents to increase their profits.

In any case, Market-Oriented approaches are well suited for competitive agent societies that interact directly. The structure of the problem domain is not as relevant but the idea of a market suggests that a separable domain is preferable. Whereas a decentralized market scheme is suitable for small agent

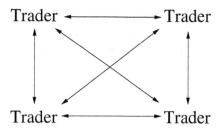

Fig. 5.14. Distributed Market

societies, a centralized scheme scales rather well as long as the matchmaking process is sufficiently simple and can thus be better used for larger societies.

Another high level decision that must be made before going into more specific details of the interaction design is the mode of interaction that will be pre-dominant in the application. The agents in the multiagent system either interact directly, for example by direct peer-to-peer communication or they interact indirectly via the environment. Direct interaction usually requires some facilitator that brings together the agents that want to interact with each other. Such a service is often provided by the agent management framework, e.g. FIPA [FIPA, 1997]. Indirect interaction, on the other hand, is typical for a real or a virtual environment where the agents meet for some purpose. It is not limited to verbal communication alone; the agents can communicate without explicit message exchange making it more flexible and suitable for agents that have only limited communication skills.

The last important requirement to be analyzed on this level of abstraction are *scalability* requirements. Scalability is of the interaction scheme is an important issue that has seldom been addressed in the existing literature [Lee et al., 1998], [Gerber, 2000]. In small systems, it is feasible that any agent can communicate with any other agent in the system. But as the systems grows, the exponential growths of message exchange that is introduced into the system can easily become prohibitive. Designing a system that works well for 10 agents is often a straightforward task; however, scaling the system up to, say, 10000 agents is often a completely different matter and may require a re-design of major parts if the operational size of the system was neglected during the design and test phase. The question of scalability is usually handled in the Society view of the system but it also play are role in the design of the interaction schemes. If the system is likely to be large, it is necessary to find scalable forms of interaction in order to ensure later the scalability of the entire system

The TCS domain is clearly an optimization problem that can be solved with a market based approach. An analysis of the input data (transportation tasks) has shown that the problem domain is almost non-separable because the routes of the tasks are highly overlapping. The application will feature a direct interaction scheme between the software agents that will be built upon a proprietary agent management framework. Furthermore, the system must scale up to 500 agents.

After these high level requirements on the interaction processes have been laid out, the system designer should have a fairly good – although still very rough – idea about how to proceed. Therefore, we can now turn the a more specific characterization of the interaction schemes.

### 5.5.2 Protocol Layer

Protocols are means to describe the general control flow within an interaction. Generally, an interaction protocol consists of two distinct phases. In the first phase, the agents (or at least one of the agents) must be able to signal a request that it wants to start an interaction scheme with one or more other agents. This part of the interaction is usually covered by the agent framework such as FIPA [FIPA, 1997], [FIPA, 1998] and it will therefore not be treated in this section.

Another aspect that I would like to mention only briefly in this section is the problem of the mutual understanding between agents from different sources. Several agent communication languages have been proposed [MacGregor and Bates, 1987], [Bussmann and Müller, 1993], [FIPA, 1996], but it seems that the KQML (Knowledge Query and Manipulation Language, [Finin and Fritzson, 1994], [Mayfield et al., 1995]) has become a defacto standard as agent communication language. However, I will only give a short introduction to the basic ideas of the KQML and direct the interested reader to the original sources as cited above.

The goal of the KQML project is to develop a method for distributing information among different systems that clearly separate the semantics of the domain-independent protocol from the semantics of the domain-dependent messages [Neches et al., 1991]. KQML messages have a fixed structure that allows each receiving agent to understand the message structure. To understand the content of the message, the agent must have additional knowledge.

The basic structure of any KQML message is the following:

```
(<KQML-Performative>
                    :sender     <word>
                    :receiver   <word>
                    :language   <word>
                    :ontology   <word>
                    :content    <expression>
                    ...)
```

Each message consists at least of a so-called *performative*. Performatives were introduced in speech act theory [Searle, 1969] to describe the illocutionary force (i.e. the intended meaning) of an utterance. Speech act theory was discovered by multiagent researchers as a valuable tool to describe the meaning of messages that are exchanged between agents [Werner, 1988].

The structure of a KQML message is divided into several fields that have fixed semantics. In the above example, the :language, :ontology and

:content field define the language in which the message is expressed, the vocabulary of the language and the message itself, respectively. The content language can be anything from user defined data structures up to LISP or PROLOG Programs or SQL queries. One of the most common content languages is the Knowledge Interchange Format (KIF) [Genesereth and Fikes, 1992].

KQML messages or any other types of messages define single messages that are exchanged between the agents, a more complicated matter is to organize the orderly exchange of sequences of messages. Therefore, we will no turn to the main part of this section and discuss how these interaction protocols can be specified in a natural and manageable way.

For an example of an interaction protocol, consider an English auction. There, an auctioneer offers a product at a particular price to a group of bidders. Each of the bidders individually decides to accept that price or to decline the offer. If one of the bidders accepts the current price, the auctioneer raises the price by a fixed rate and asks the group of bidders again if any of them accepts the new price. If this is the case, the price is raised again and the cycle repeats until none of the bidders is willing to pay the current price. Then, the last bidder who accepted the price is given the product.

In this example, we can identify the major elements of interaction protocols. First, we can separate the participating agents into different groups. In this case, we have two groups: the auctioneer and the bidders. Each group has a set of associated incoming and outgoing messages an internal functions that decide about their next action. We will refer to the set of messages and behaviors that are associated with a group of agents as a role that can be played by an agent. Please note that the roles that are discussed in this view are interaction roles as opposed to functional roles as they were discussed in Section 5.4.1. Note also that just with functional roles, agents are not limited to a single interaction role. For example, the auctioneer in the English auction can be a bidder in another auction at the same time.

The second important aspect of an interaction protocol besides the participating roles, is the temporal ordering of function evaluation and the messages that are exchanged. For example, it would not make sense or would be impossible for the bidder to decide on an offer and to decline it before it has even received the offer. Therefore, the interaction protocol determines the flow of control within each role as well as between different roles.

It is precisely the dualism mentioned in the previous paragraph that makes protocol design a difficult task. There are not only role-internal aspects to consider during the design process, but also external effect induced by the other roles. Even worse, there is currently only little Software Engineering support for the design of interaction protocols. A number of protocol description languages (PDLs) have been proposed ranging from specification languages for low level communication protocols [The International Organization for Standardization, 1997], [Holzmann, 1991] up to high level specification languages for multiagent applications [Burmeister et al., 1995], [Kolb, 1995]. Up to now, however, none – perhaps except for Estelle – of these languages has gained wide-spread acceptance.

One reason for this lack of acceptance is probably the fact that the above languages only provide text-based representations for the interaction protocols. This makes it hard, especially for complex protocols, to understand the flow of control within the protocol. An alternative for these text-based languages are therefore graphical languages that make the described protocols more accessible for the reader. As mentioned in section 3.4.2, the UML allows the Software engineer to specify almost all aspects of a software system. The key term in the last sentence, however, is "almost all" as the field of interaction protocols is one of those areas that are not treated adequately by the UML.

Due to the strong focus on object-oriented software design, the UML is not right away suitable for agent-based systems. In order to make it fit some special requirement of agent-oriented software, there are two possible ways to be taken. One way is to extend the UML by providing new structural elements and diagrams that enhance the expressive power of the base language. This way is favored by the OMG/FIPA in the development of GENTUML [OMG and FIPA, 1999] which proposes an extension of the UML with respect to agent-oriented concepts. As part of the GENTUML in the FIPA standard, [Bauer et al., 1999] suggests an extension of the UML by a completely new diagram type called *protocol diagrams*. These diagrams combine elements of UML interaction diagrams and state diagrams to model the roles that can be played by an agent in the course of interacting with other agents. The new diagram type allows for the specification of multiple threads within an interaction protocol and supports protocol nesting and protocol templates based on generic protocol descriptions.

This approach, however, has the major drawback that it violates the idea of the UML as a general design language. If each group within the computer science community added their own UML extension according to their particular needs, the base language is likely to be split up in several increasingly unrelated dialects. The result, as it can be observed with programming languages such as Basic, is a collection of inconsistent language fragments. Besides this not being the idea of a standard language, it introduces the additional difficulty of having to learn a new dialect when switching between two specialized application fields.

As a consequence from the above considerations, I decided to take another approach to protocol specification in MASSIVE, resulting in a two stage process that uses a graphical notation based on UML diagrams for the abstract protocol specification and a textual representation for the concrete implementation.

One of the goals of my work on using UML as protocol description language is to change the standard as little as possible and only within the

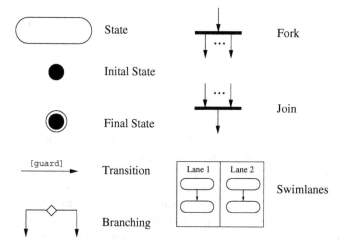

**Fig. 5.15.** Structural Elements of UML Activity Diagrams

boundaries of changes that were explicitly admitted by the language designers [Booch et al., 1999]. Thus, I do not introduce completely new diagram types or the like but instead rely on the provided structural elements and use them to model the system of agent-based applications.

**UML Activity Diagrams as PDL.** Activity diagrams in UML models provide a number of structural elements as shown in Figure 5.15 to describe algorithms in a flowchart like manner. To this end, each computation is expressed in terms of states and the progression through these states. In order to allow for a hierarchical modeling, the UML distinguishes between two classes of states. Action states are atomic entities that cannot be decomposed and that relate to atomic statements in a programming language, e.g. variable assignment. Activity states, on the other hand, represent a collection of atomic states and can thus be decomposed into these atomic states. Furthermore, the execution of an activity can be interrupted between any two subsequent states. In terms of programming languages, actions relate to statements and activities relate to subroutines.

The states of an activity diagram are linked with each other through transitions that indicate the control flow within the activity diagram. Each transition can have a guard condition that controls the flow of control in that it only allows a transition to fire if the guard condition is true. Because of the basic requirement that each transition must have at least one start and one end point, special states are introduced that represent the beginning and the end of an activity diagram, respectively.

The control flow within an activity diagram is not necessarily linear, otherwise it would be impossible to express anything other then trivial algorithms. Therefore, *branching* elements that represent the decision points within a di-

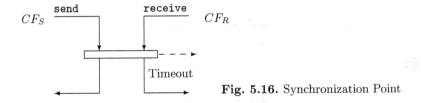

**Fig. 5.16.** Synchronization Point

agram are provided. Each branching points stands for a boolean decision, i.e. the flow of control can proceed along two different paths.

Many modern programming languages provide some notion for pseudo-parallel program execution within a single operating system process. These light-weight processes – usually referred to as "threads" – can be modeled in UML activity diagrams by using two structural elements. A *fork* operation splits a single thread of execution into two or more threads that are subsequently executed in parallel. Thus, a fork bar has one incoming transition and several outgoing transitions. In order to merge several of these parallel threads into a single thread again, UML activity diagrams provide the *join* element. Thus, a join barrier has several incoming transitions and only a single outgoing transition, it can therefore be used to synchronize several parallel threads of execution. Note that a join barrier waits until *all* incoming threads have arrived at the barrier before proceeding with the single master thread.

Because of the fact that activity diagrams tend to become somewhat confusion with growing in size, UML activity diagrams can contain so-called *swimlanes* that are used to partition an activity diagram into several conceptually related parts. Within an activity diagram, each swimlane must have a unique name and each activity must belong to exactly one swimlane.

I will now propose some slight modifications to the basic elements of UML activity diagrams in order to make them usable to describe agent interaction protocols. First of all, we will extend the idea of swimlanes as a means to distinguish between conceptually related parts of an activity diagram. In our interpretation, these swimlanes are interpreted as physically – as opposed to conceptually – separated flows of control which we will refer to as *Control Flow Spaces* in the rest of this section. These control flow spaces are linked with each other via explicit *communication channels* that manage the message exchange between two connected spaces. The message exchange itself is modeled in *synchronization points* that denote the sending and the reception of messages, respectively. The graphical representation of a synchronization point is shown in Figure 5.16 where $CF_S$ and $CF_R$ denote the control flow of the sender and the control flow of the receiver, respectively.

Each synchronization point has several incoming transitions out of which exactly one must be labeled with the keyword **send**. The other transitions are the receivers of the respective message. Whenever the control flow of a receiver enters a synchronization point, the receiver suspends until a message

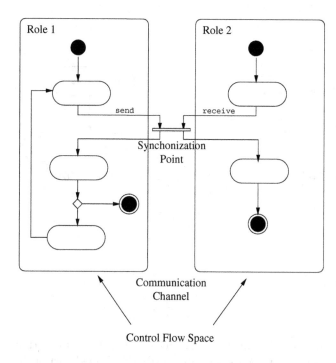

Fig. 5.17. Extended Activity Diagram

has been delivered. This happens whenever the control flow of the sender reaches the synchronization point. After the massage has been delivered, the control flow of the sender and the control flow of the receivers resume after the synchronization point. In order to prevent the receivers from infinite blocking while waiting for a message that never arrives, an additional *timeout* transition for each receiver can be attached to the synchronization. Whenever the timeout is reached and no message has been delivered, the control flow of the respective receiver resumes at the state pointed to by the timeout transition.

A broader view of activity diagrams in conjuction with agent protocol specification is shown in Figure 5.17. The round boxes indicate the control flow spaces that are associated with each role within the agent interaction protocol. The control flow of each of these roles is modeled using the structural elements that are provided by standard UML activity diagrams. However, the self-contained control flow spaces are linked via a communication channel that holds one synchronization point that links the activity diagrams of the different roles.

A very important feature of UML activity diagrams is that they provide a powerful structuring mechanism that can be used to make protocol mode readable. Since activity states can represent complete automata, it is straightforward to use them for macro definitions that can be used in interaction protocols. Figure 5.18 illustrates the idea: 5.18(a) shows an activity diagram for dispatching an incoming message according to the message type.

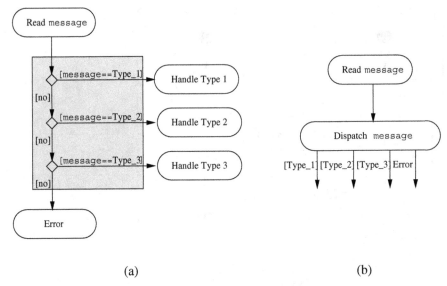

(a)                                                    (b)

**Fig. 5.18.** Defining Macros

Using the UML rule that a state can have several outgoing transitions that
are labeled with conditional statements, we can rewrite the shaded part of the
original automaton that contains three branching points into a single state
as shown in 5.18(b)[2]. Collapsing several states into a single macro state has
not only the advantage to make a diagram more readable, it is also important that the macro state can be given a speaking name that highlights its
purpose. Although the overall gain seems to be pretty small in the above example, the gain soon becomes apparent in more complex protocols where each
decision point or loop construction that is hidden improves the readability of
the protocol. Furthermore, this mechanism can be used to embed protocols
into others, allowing for a hierarchical structuring, flexible combination and
re-use of protocols.

In order to illustrate the use of UML activity diagrams for interaction
protocol specification on a realistic example, recall the English Auction that
was presented earlier in this section. In Figure 5.19, we have depicted an interaction protocol that describes the course of actions and message exchanges
within the auction more formally.

The first step in the interaction design process is to identify the roles
that interact with each other. In the example, we have already identified the
*auctioneer* and the *bidder* as the participating roles. Now, we create a control
flow space that will later hold the finite automaton that describes the behavior
of the agent playing a particular role. It is usually a good idea to develop an
initial version of each automaton without considering the other automata, i.e.

---

[2] Note that conditions on the outgoing transitions are abbreviated in the example.

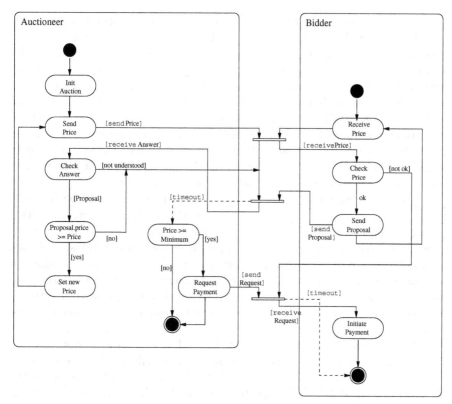

**Fig. 5.19.** English Auction

without switching back and forth between different automata. Thus, for the
auctioneer, the auction starts with an initialization of its internal data, e.g.
with determining the initial price of the product. Then, the auctioneer sends
out a proposal to the bidders and waits for the incoming replies. In order to
make the example more realistic, we assume that a bidder can indicate that
the proposal was not understood, e.g. because the bidder is not familiar with
the ontology used. In that case, the auctioneer simply ignores the message
and continuous to wait for further messages. If, on the other hand, the price
is accepted by the bidder, the auctioneer raises the price according to a fixed
rate and the cycle starts from the beginning. If the offer is not accepted by
the bidder, the auctioneer continuous to wait for incoming replies until a fixed
timeout. When the timeout has expired and no bidder has accepted the offer,
the product is given to the last bidder that has accepted the price (if that
price exceeds a previously defined minimal acceptable price). Please note,
that the *CheckAnswer* state uses the macro mechanism explained earlier to
dispatch the incoming messages.

Now that the behavior of the auctioneer has been fully specified, we can
turn to the bidder role. In the example, the bidder goes into a waiting loop as

soon as the protocol execution is started. It leaves this loop when it receives an offer proposed by the auctioneer and checks whether to offered price is acceptable according to its individual goals. If this is the case, the bidder sends out a positive reply and re-iterates the waiting process. If the actual price is not acceptable, the bidder waits for a message from the auctioneer that indicates if the bidder is given the product or nor. Obviously, this can only happen when the bidder has issued a positive reply during the auction. To avoid an infinite blocking of the bidder, a timeout is applied to terminate the waiting process after a finite time. The bidder that receives the positive acknowledgment from the auctioneer, on the other hand, will immediately initiate the payment process to finally receive the product.

This small example should be sufficient to provide the reader with an impression on how to apply the suggested method to arbitrary agent interaction protocols. The best way to see how the method works in practice is to pick an (preferably easy) protocol from the application domain of interest and then to simply start right away with an iterative modeling process. The value of the diagrams will then quickly become apparent. In order to demonstrate how interaction protocols are actually developed, we will now return to the TCS example and I will explain the three interaction schemes that are used there.

The core interaction scheme of the TCS/MAS system is an optimization process that is executed by the agents in order to reduces their local cost as well as the total cost of the agent society. The key to optimization in the scenario presented is to find agents that use the same location routes and to have these agents share the respective routes by coupling together at the beginning and by splitting up afterwards. This peer matching is achieved by two-step negotiation processes between the agents in the agent society. In our system, we have combined two negotiation protocols to achieve the global optimization of the schedule.

A schedule is generated in the following way: an initial solution for the module schedule is obtained by running the *contract-net* [Smith, 1980] protocol whenever a new task is announced to the system. New tasks are incrementally integrated in the existing scheduling which guarantees, that always a solution for the problem (as far as it is known to the system) exists. However, this solution may be (and usually is) not optimal. In order to improve the quality of the existing solution, the *simulated trading* [Bachem et al., 1992] [Bachem et al., 1993] protocol is run on the set of tasks (or the respective modules) currently known to the system. Unfortunately, executing the simulated trading protocol is a computationally expensive operation and so it is executed only periodically — either after a fixed number of new tasks has been added to the existing solution or explicitly triggered by a user request.

The hierarchical organization of the two negotiation protocols supports the aforementioned properties of incrementality and anytime behavior and also implies a high degree of flexibility because of the possibility to asyn-

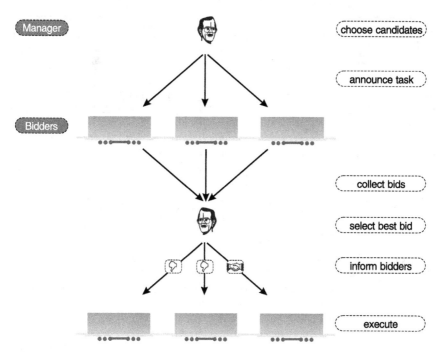

**Fig. 5.20.** Contract-Net Protocol

chronously execute the simulated trading process at any time. A third interaction protocol that is used within TCS/MAS is a *client-server protocol* that is use for the route allocation process. In the following sections, I will present the instantiation of contract-net, simulated trading and client-server protocol in the TCS/MAS system.

The contract-net protocol as depicted in Figure 5.20 features two types of participants: one *manager* and a group of *bidders*. The protocol is initiated by the manager which sends a description of the task under consideration to the bidders. Note, that "task" is not a transportation task mentioned earlier but rather some abstract description of a problem to be solved. We will discuss the instantiation of the general protocol to our scenario later.

After the bidders have received the task description, each of them computes a bid that informs the manager about costs that will be charged if the task is assigned to that particular bidder. After all bidders have submitted their bids to the manager, the manager selects the bid that minimizes his cost and assigns the task to the respective bidder (+) and rejects the offers of the other bidders (-).

In the TCS/MAS system, the contract-net protocol is executed whenever a new (degenerated) union enters the system and after it has computed its local plan. The union then initiates the contract-net protocol as the manager and offers the plan to the other currently active unions. These unions check

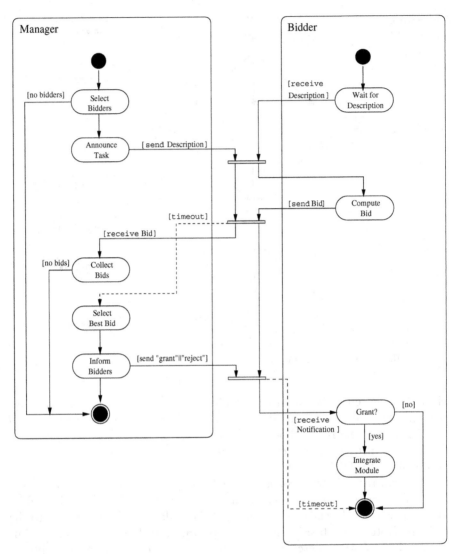

**Fig. 5.21.** Contract-Net Protocol (UML)

if they contain one or more modules that are a potential sharing peers and if this is the case, they offer a sharing commitment to the new union. Appendix B.1 contains a rather detailed explanation of the operator that is capable of finding a maximum degree of overlapping among an arbitrary number of plans. This operator is used by the bidders to compute their internal cost functions. The manager union collects these offers and selects the one that has the largest cost saving potential. To decide which of the potential contractors $U_1, \ldots, U_k$ is best from the point of view of the manager $M$, the manager

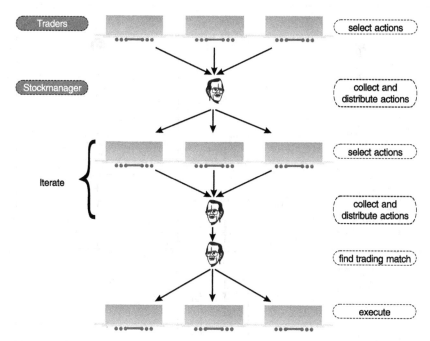

**Fig. 5.22.** Simulated Trading

selects the union $U_i$ where $c^-(M, m) - c^+(U_i, m)$ has a maximum[3]. It then transfers the module to the winning union and ceases to exist because it does not contain other modules. If no union offers a sharing commitment, the new union remains active as degenerated union.

In order to implement the protocol with the TCS/MAS system, the informal notation given in Figure 5.20 must be formalized to derive the necessary design decisions. In Figure 5.21, the Contract-Net protocol is re-written using the UML notation scheme introduced earlier. The graphical representation will be refined into a textual protocol specification later.

The contract net protocol presented in this section is used in the TCS/MAS system to obtain an initial solution for the scheduling task. However, this solution is usually not optimal and can thus be improved further. This improvement process is done with a simulated trading approach as shown in Figure 5.22.

The simulated trading protocol is an algorithm designed to improve existing solutions, not to construct new solutions from scratch. In the TCS/MAS system, the input and the output of the protocol are valid schedules where the cost of the output are always less or equal to the cost of the input. This is trivially true since the output can always be the input if no cheaper schedule exists. However, this property is nonetheless important because it guarantees

---

[3] The definition of the cost function $c$ can be found in Appendix B.1

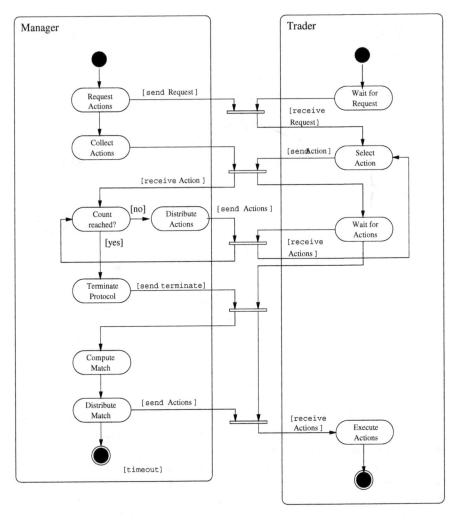

**Fig. 5.23.** Simulated Trading (UML)

that the protocol can be aborted at any time and still yield a valid solution. Furthermore, if the protocol is given enough computation time, it is guaranteed to find the optimal solution in the limit [Bachem et al., 1993]. Now, how does this work?

The protocol shown in Figures 5.22 is initiated by a special agent, the *stock manager*. In the course of protocol execution, the agents (here called *traders*) perform several rounds of hypothetical trading, i.e. the traders either choose to sell some of their goods or to buy something from others. In the context of the TCS/MAS system, a sell operation corresponds to removing a module from a union and a buy operation corresponds to integrating a module in a union. Thus, the unions try to optimize their cost by exchanging unprofitable modules with better ones. The decision which module to sell depends on a probability distribution induced by the potential cost reduction if the module was sold. Vice versa, the decision to buy a module offered by another union depends on the potential cost reduction if the module would be integrated into the union.

Simulated Trading takes place in several rounds where each union decides whether to sell a module or to buy a module offered by another union. After a fixed number of trading rounds, the stock manager has collected the hypothetical sell and buy actions and it must find a valid *trading match* in the set of actions. There a several validity requirements for a trading match e. g. the difference between deletion and insertion costs must be positive, or there must not be two buy actions on the same sell operation, etc. Finding a trading match is NP-complete [Bachem et al., 1992] and accounts for the computational complexity of the simulated trading protocol. Usually, however, the size of the trading graph still allows to find a trading match within a reasonable time[4]. If a trading match is found, the stock manager informs the traders which actions must be executed, i.e. which modules must be exchanged. Figure 5.23 shows the UML specification that will be used to derive the implementation of the simulated trading protocol.

The third and final interaction scheme that is used in the TCS/MAS system is the protocol that coordinates the location route allocation process between the unions and the location route manager. The protocol is a straightforward client-server protocol in which the net manager offers a stateless two-step service for the allocation of location routes:

**check** This message from the union to the location route manager contains a location route identifier, a time window during which the route should be allocated and the minimal speed by which the route should be traveled. Note that the time window is usually larger than the time required by the querying union to travel the location route (the required time is determined by the minimal speed and the length of the route). It is now the task of the net manager to find a time window of the appropriate length that fits in the existing route allocations made by other unions. If it is possible to find such a window, the net manager returns a positive indication to the unions, otherwise a negative indication.

**book** This message type is used by the union to book a particular location route for a given time window. Note that it does not require a prior **check** operation although it is highly unlikely that a union will find a free time window on a route if it omits the prior check. Note also, that multiple **book** operations on the same location route but by different unions are handled in a first-come first-serve manner. This is due to the fact that the net manager is organized as stateless server, i.e. it does not keep track of the order of check operations. The advantages of a stateless organization

---

[4] For a 5000 task problem, the execution of the simulated trading protocol with four rounds takes approximately 40 minutes on a Sun UltraSparc.

are that it limits the memory usage of the net manager agent and that is invulnerable to system failures.

**free** A location route that was allocated by a particular union can be freed by this union if the ongoing planning process makes the use of location route obsolete or when the time window during which the route is needed has changed.

The three interaction protocols that have been discussed in the previous paragraphs are the core part of the TCS/MAS system. The protocols that are used in the system are not specifically developed for the TCS/MAS system but they are adaptation of existing interaction schemes. This reflects a good practice in software engineering: instead of trying to solve every problem alone, existing and tested approaches have been used and adapted for a specific case. Thus, re-using existing protocols that have been tested and found useful usually improves the time to find the solution as well as quality of the solution. Especially in the field of interaction protocols, there is a huge amount of available literature that contains information for almost any situation. A good introductory overview, for example, is provided in [Kendall, 1998a]. More specific aspects of workflow and business processes are discussed in [Kendall, 1998b].

Until now, the interaction protocols of the TCS/MAS system have been developed on a rather high level of abstraction. In the next step of the protocol design process, the graphical representation is transformed into a textual representation that will then be used to construct the final code in terms of the underlying programming language.

**The Protoz Protocol Specification Environment.** Protoz [Philipps, 1998], [Philipps and Lind, 1999] is a protocol specification system that was developed in the Multiagent Systems Group of the DFKI. Protoz was designed to be as simple as possible but still powerful enough to capture the most relevant negotiation protocols currently in use. The specification language is related to Estelle [The International Organization for Standardization, 1997] and uses a similar computational concept. Estelle is a specification language for service description and system behavior in telecommunications that uses extended finite automata to describe the intended behavior. Extended finite state machines are normal finite state machines plus (typed) variables. The state in the finite state machine has a set of associated variables that can be queried and/or manipulated in the transition specifications. In Estelle, a protocol is a collection of several distinct automata where each automaton can have an arbitrary number of interaction points with other automata. These interaction points are called channels and they control the message exchange between different automata. Estelle is a very powerful language that was mainly developed for the specification of low level protocols. It is therefore not directly suitable for the use in multiagent applications.

## Process Model 13 Protoz Protocol Design

1. **Channel definition**
   In the channel definition, the roles are declared that participate in the protocol and also the messages that are allowed for each role.
2. **Role definition**
   a) **Declaration part**
      The declaration part of a role definition declares the number of instances that are allowed to exist within the protocol, the initial parameters of the role and the states that are used within the extended finite state machine. Furthermore the variables and their types (`boolean, integer, string, message, agent` and Lists over the base types) and the names of the application procedures as well as their signatures (parameters, return values) are declared.
   b) **Definition part**
      i. **Transitions**
         For each transition, the entry constraints, the actions on entry and exit transitions to other states are defined. An outgoing transition is described by the name of the destination state, the conditions that must be satisfies for the transition to fire and the actions that are executed when the transition fires. Conditions for transitions can be incoming messages or application procedure calls.
      ii. **Actions**
         The actions that are executed on the entry to or the exit from a particular state can be *messages* that are sent to other agents or to internal procedures, *Variable manipulation* such as value assignment or various operations on lists over those scalar types or *Branches & Iterations* such as (`if-then-else`) statements for branches and a `while` statement for loops.
3. **Error handling**
   a) **Timeouts**
      Timeouts are used to abort the waiting process for incoming messages that do not arrive. Protoz provides two sorts of timeouts:
      - *every*: The timeout is triggered on every entry to the state, the timeout is reset on every subsequent entry to the state.
      - *once*: The first entry to the respective state triggers the timeout mechanism, the timeout is not reset when the state is entered several times.
      
      The difference between these two classes is in their behavior when a state waits for several messages to come in. For example, when a state waits for five incoming messages with a timeout of 20s, the maximum waiting time for timeout type *every* is 100s because the timeout is reset on every incoming message. The maximum waiting time for timeout type *once*, on the other hand, is 20s because the timeout is not reset on every incoming message.
      
      When a timeout fires, a special message is sent to the waiting state that indicates that the timeout was reached. Subsequent actions are defined in the respective state.
   b) **Exceptions**
      Exceptions are used to handle errors or failures during protocol execution (e.g. unexpected messages, premature protocol termination etc.). Protoz provides a single level exception mechanism that activates an application specific procedure whenever an exception is raised.

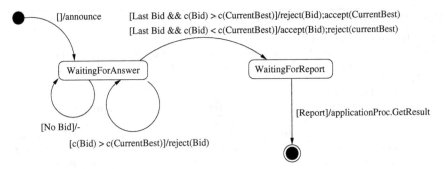

**Fig. 5.24.** Contract-Net Manager

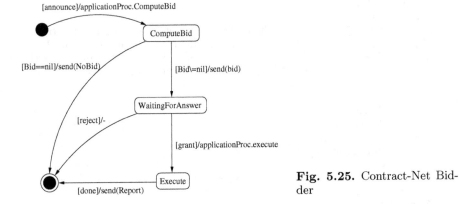

**Fig. 5.25.** Contract-Net Bidder

The **Protoz** environment contains a protocol compiler that generates Oz code [Programming Systems Lab, 1999] from a given protocol specification. A special design focus of the entire system was the clear separation between protocol and application that uses it. Protocols are generic specifications and can be used in many different contexts, the **Protoz** specification language therefore allows to specify the protocols independently of the particular application.

In the **Protoz** system, a protocol is given by a collection of roles where each of these roles is specified as an extended finite state machine. As explained above, extended finite state machines are normal finite state machines plus (typed) variables. The state in the finite state machine has a set of associated variables that can be queried and/or manipulated in the transition specifications.

The state machine transitions fire upon incoming messages; messages may stem from other agents or from internal procedures. These internal procedures implement the connection to the application and allow for a uniform modeling of internal and external communication. The protocol definition follows the process model shown in Process Model 13 on page 163.

In order to demonstrate how an implementation is derived from a protocol specification, recall the contract-net protocol from Figure 5.21. The joint representation from that figure is now split up into two independent finite state machines for each role as shown in Figures 5.24 and 5.25. These finite state machines are then described using the Protoz protocol language and the compiled to directly executable Oz code. The Protoz specification for the Contract-Net is included in Appendix C.

### 5.5.3 Transport Layer

The final step in the interaction design process is to map the abstract messages that have been defined in the protocol specification onto the concepts of a concrete agent framework or operating system. Due to the wast number of different ways that have been proposed as message exchange methods, I will only pick two approaches that are very common in multiagent systems in order to illustrate the typical problems that are dealt with on this level of abstraction.

A straightforward way to implement a message exchange mechanism between two agents is surely to use simple *message passing* between the participating agents. In this approach, each agent has a unique identification tag and an agent that wants to send a message to another agent adds this tag to the message before the message is handed over to the message passing system that is responsible for delivering the message to the addressee. This sort of message passing is usually referred to as one-to-one or point-to-point communication. Often, it is convenient to allow a single message to be delivered to several receivers at the same time, i. e. the sender need not re-send the same message to each receiver one after the other. While this *multicast* option is only a matter of convenience, a *broadcast* message is substantially different. In the case of a broadcast, the message is delivered to all agents that are known to the communication system, i. e. the sender of a broadcast message does not know which other agents will finally receive the message that is sent out as a broadcast message. This is comparable to the situation of a radio or television station that is ultimately unaware who receives the program that is broadcasted.

Another important aspect of direct message passing is whether the messages are sent and received *synchronously* or *asynchronously*. In the first case, a potential receiver must enter an explicit waiting state before it can receive any messages while in the second case, a message can arrive at any time in the addressees control flow. Hence the label asynchronous messages in this respect.

To illustrate this situation, consider the two examples shown in Figure 5.26. In 5.26(a), the information provider asynchronously sends the information to the subscriber without explicit request whereas in 5.26(b), the requester sends an explicit query to the information provider specifying in which information it is interested and enters into the waiting state. The

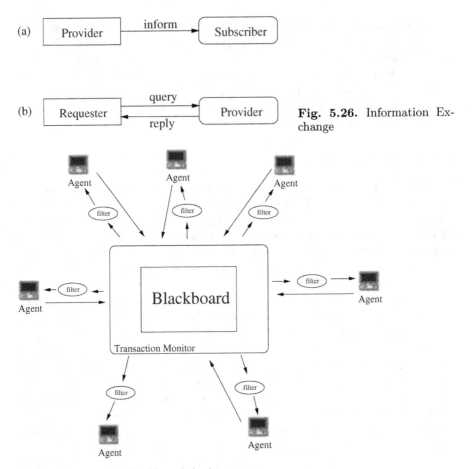

(a) Provider —inform→ Subscriber

(b) Requester —query→ ←reply— Provider

**Fig. 5.26.** Information Exchange

Agent    Agent    Agent

filter    filter    filter

filter — Agent

Blackboard

filter — Agent

Transaction Monitor

filter    filter

Agent    Agent

**Fig. 5.27.** Generic Blackboard Architecture

information providers answers with a reply that contains the requested information given it is accessible to the provider and the requester is authorized to receive the information in question. The first form of interaction is useful when the subscriber needs to be informed about some sort of changes without knowing in advance when a change will take place. Note that the subscription process is not shown in Figure 5.26. The subscription can be either explicit, i.e. the subscriber asks for being informed about new information or implicit in which case the provider broadcasts the information to all reachable receivers regardless of whether they want the information or not.

Besides one-to-one and one-to-many (broadcast) message passing, a second communication architecture is quit common in agent-based systems: *blackboards*. Blackboard architectures [Engelmore and Morgan, 1988] date back to the early days of distributed problem solving and have undergone intensive research since then. In its generic form, a blackboard is organized as shown in Figure 5.27. Several agents are connected to a central authority that encapsulates a particular data structure. The transaction monitor shown in the figure is responsible for controlling the access to the joint data structure and to ensure the validity of each access. Each of the agents connected to the blackboard can read and manipulate the joint data. However, the perception (reading) of the data is not necessarily the same for all agents. Each agent receives only data that has undergone a filtering process that limits the perception of this agent. This individualized scheme enables the designer for example to use blackboard architectures as the basis for distributed virtual worlds (see Appendix A.1).

Blackboards are suitable for a wide range of problem domains that have a non-separable structure. The approach works for either competitive as well as co-operative settings and is not limited to a particular form of interoperation. Furthermore, blackboard architectures usually scale well and are thus suitable for large agent societies. As we have said above, blackboards can be used to implement virtual words and thus simulate a indirect interoperation scheme.

In the TCS/MAS example, the transport layer is implemented as a one-to-one message passing system that allows for asynchronous message exchange. It is thus a proprietary solution that is based on the inter-thread communication features of Oz. I will return to details of implementation in Section 5.7.

## 5.6 Societ   View

This view is concerned with the structure of the agent society that implements the target system. In Section 2.2.2 we have already defined the concepts "structure", "society" and "social system". In this section, we will provide a characterization scheme for agent societies that allows the software developer to describe an existing society or to specify the requirements for the society of the target system. Furthermore, we will also discuss a micro process model for the construction of an agent society according to a given characterization.

### 5.6.1 Characterization of Social Systems

In the field of multiagent systems, the definitions for agent societies and social systems are much simpler then those in sociology as they were given in Section 2.2.2, but this does not necessarily help the system designer to develop the right view on the agent society. In [Werner, 1989], the agent society is defined as the (static or dynamic) assignment of roles to agents. 10 years later, in [Weiss, 1999] not very much has changed: "... a specification and assignment of roles and responsibilities to participants in a cooperative planning and/or problem-solving endeavor. ...". Because of this shortcoming in multiagent

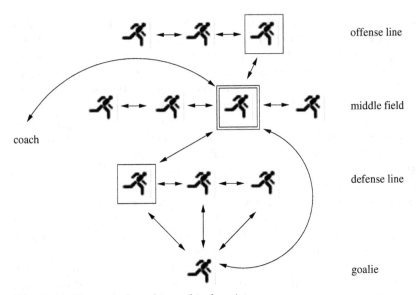

offense line

middle field

coach

defense line

goalie

**Fig. 5.28.** Example for a hierarchical society

research, I will try to give a conceptual framework that allows the designer to characterize or model the agent society according to a unified terminology.

In this scheme, an agent society can be classified along four dimensions: *type, structure, consistency* and *temporal context*.

The type of the society can be either *open*, *semi-open* or *closed*. In an open society, agents can freely enter or leave the society. The entry criteria can be defined by the system designer or they can be defined by the agents themselves. A semi-open society is quite similar except for the fact that any agents can join the society but no agent ever leaves the society again. In a closed society, on the other hand, the members of the society are fixed and no fluctuation either into or out of the society takes place.

The structure of the agent society determines how the agents relate to each other mainly in terms of communication channels. In a *flat* society, the interaction between agents is unlimited, i.e. each agent can interact with any other agent. While this structure provides a maximum degree of flexibility, it also implies a high degree of overhead. For example, in an agent society that uses some sort of explicit communication, a flat society structure requires $n(n-1)$ communication channels.

A *hierarchical* society is not as flexible as a flat society because the interaction channels between the agents are limited. Usually, some agents have special organizational roles and are responsible to filter and/or limit interactions. In Figure 5.28, an example for a hierarchical society in the RoboCup [Noda, 1995] domain is shown. Within each sub-structure (defense line, middle field, offense line), the agents can freely communicate with any other agent of that sub-structure. Each sub-structure also has an agent with the organizational role of a "local captain" (indicated by the single boxed) that is responsible for the communication with the team captain (double box) who in turn manages the communication with the coach. The goalie can communicate with the captain as well as the player of defense line directly.

Instead of 132 connections in the case of a flat society, the resulting structure has only 14 connections and thus less overhead. The drawback of this solution is, however, that in the worst case, messages from an individual player to the coach and vice versa must be forwarded through three intermediate agents.

The consistency of a society refers to the agent classes within the society and differentiates between *homogeneous* and *heterogeneous* societies. In a homogeneous society, all agents have the same external properties such as the underlying architecture or the set of behaviors that they have at their disposal. Even more important is the fact that the agents all have the same knowledge representation which enables the agents to freely exchange messages without complex and error prone translation mechanisms.

In a heterogeneous agent society, the agents can have different architectures, behaviors and knowledge representation. Especially the latter makes the interoperation between agents with different architectures difficult.

The temporal context of an agent society, finally, defines how the structure of the agent society develops during its lifetime. In a *static* society, the structure is fixed from the beginning and does not change during the operation of the system.

In a *dynamic* society, the structure and the interconnections between the agents can change either because of a pre-defined dynamic behavior specified by the system designer or due to a self-adaption process of society in order to achieve a higher performance. Self-adapting agent societies are a promising technology in various application fields [Lind et al., 1999c], [Gerber et al., 1999b] and especially *holonic* approaches [Gerber et al., 1999a] become increasingly interesting.

According to this general classification scheme, we can characterize the society within the TCS/MAS system as *homogeneous* because all agents share the same architecture and the same knowledge formats, *semi-open* because newly created agents enter the agent society but no agent ever leaves the society, *dynamic* because the structure of the society changes according to the holonic union formation process and *flat* because any agent can negotiate with any other. Based on this characterization of the TCS/MAS system, we can now turn to developing a system design according to the above features.

### 5.6.2 Designing Social Systems

I will now give a prescriptive process model on how to develop the optimal social structure for the target system. First, however, we must clarify what the term "optimal" means in this respect as no single organizational design

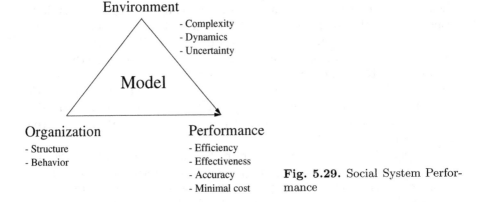

**Fig. 5.29.** Social System Performance

is optimal for all purposes [Rawson, 1992]. According to [Carley, 1999], optimality of a social system depends on the *tasks* to be performed, the *agent capabilities*, the *characteristics of the environment*, *external constraints* (e.g. legal, political) and the *goal* of the optimization process.

The first four aspects in the above list are dealt with in other views within the MASSIVE method leaving the *goal* aspects to be handled in this view. The goal of the optimization process is usually to improve the performance of the society with respect to efficiency, effectiveness, accuracy or minimal cost. According to Figure 5.29 (adapted from [So and Durfee, 1998]), the performance measure of an agent society depends on its structure and the behavior as well as on the requirements that imposed by the environment and quantified in the attributes described above. Thus, the optimal society structure is expressed in terms of some of the characterization developed in the previous section e.g. by specifying maximal communication bandwidth, channel capacity, number of available channels, quality of services or message costs.

The social structure is then constructed according to the six step process shown in Process Model 14. Although the process model describes a very general way for obtaining the optimal society structure, it does not describe the actual means the designer has in order to impose a particular structure onto the system. This aspect is not covered in this section as this is subject of a research field named *Computational Organizational Theory* [Carley, 1999] to which we direct the reader for the solution of a particular problem.

In order to demonstrate how a society structure for a given problem can be derived from a given society characterization, recall the description of the TCS/MAS society from the previous section. There, the society structure was described as flat, i.e. any agent can communicate with any other agent. This means in terms of the TCS approach, that every new degenerated union that handles an incoming transportation task can ask all other agents within the system for location route sharing. This amount of communication, however, can lead to serious performance losses in larger societies. The intended system

| **Process Model 14** MASSIVE Society Design |
| --- |

1. **Identify**
   In the first step, the goals of the optimization process are identified according to the above characterization.
2. **Quantify**
   The goals that have been identified in the prior step are now quantified in order to enable the decision on whether the optimization has led to satisfactory results or not.
3. **Construct**
   Now, the a social structure is set up that is believed to satisfy the goals at the required quality level.
4. **Implement**
   The social structure that was developed in the previous step is implemented.
5. **Evaluate**
   The structure is evaluated with respect to the quality requirements.
6. **Iterate**
   If the social structure fulfills the quality requirements, the process is aborted. If the results are below the previously defined quality standard, the process is iterated from step 3.

of the system are a maximum of 5000 agents and it is easy to imagine what communication overhead results from a flat society structure in a society of this size.

In order to reduce the communication overhead, the TCS/MAS system uses a technique called *clustering* to reduce the amount of communication in the system. The idea of a clustering algorithm is to partition the agent society into several groups that share particular features. The higher the relation between the individuals in a cluster and the higher the differences between the clusters are, the better is the clustering. The idea of clustering is illustrated in Figure 5.30 where we can see twelve unions that are arranged in three clusters. The clustering is not unique because two unions can be assigned to two different clusters each.

However, to find an optimal clustering is an NP-complete problem and thus only feasible in small societies. In the TCS/MAS system with up to 5000 agents, we have to apply heuristics to find a rather good, though usually not optimal clustering. Let's see how it works in TCS/MAS.

In the case of a new task that is announced to the system, any union that is currently active will be contacted by the contract-net manager in order to check whether it has sharing opportunities with the new task or not. Clearly, it is a better idea to limit the class of potential bidders to those who have a potential chance to become a sharing peer. This selection process that is executed whenever a contract-net is initiated is called *dynamic clustering*. The goal of the dynamic clustering algorithm is to select the potential partners for a new degenerated union that wants to find sharing partners. The idea of the following algorithm is to filter out those unions within the society that can never have a chance for route sharing either because the time window of

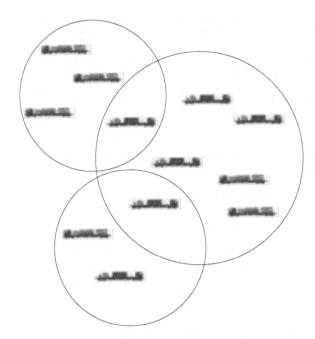

**Fig. 5.30.** Clustering

the union and the time window of the manager union are non overlapping, or because the two unions do not have any location routes in common. Hence, we define the maximum time window of union as the window with the earliest starting time of all modules within the union as the lower bound and the latest arrival time of those modules as the upper bound. Also, we define the em nodelist of a union as the union of all nodes of all modules.

**Definition 5.6.1 (Maximum Time Window).** *The* **maximum time window** *of a union $U_j^{i_0,\dots,i_n}$ is given the lowest lower and the highest upper bound of any module(s) in the union. More formally, let $\underline{t}_i = M_i.TW.\underline{t} \forall i \in \{i_0,\dots,i_n\}$ and $\bar{t}_j = M_j.TW.\bar{t} \forall j \in \{i_0,\dots,i_n\}$. Then $TW(U_j^{i_0,\dots,i_n}) = [\min_{\underline{t}_i}; \max_{\bar{t}_j}]$.*

**Definition 5.6.2 (Nodelist).**
*The nodes the occur within a plan $P$ of a module $M$ are obtained by applying the Nodes function to the plan, i.e. $Nodes(M.P) = \{N_1,\dots,N_n\}$. The Nodes of a union $U_j^{i_0,\dots,i_n}$ then compute to $Nodes(U_j^{i_0,\dots,i_n}) = \bigcup_{i \in \{i_0,\dots,i_n\}} Nodes(M_i.P)$*

Using these definitions, we can then specify the dynamic clustering algorithm for a new union $U$ as shown in Algorithm 1.

During the optimization phase of the existing schedule that uses the Simulated Trading approach, the situation is even worse because Simulated Trading is computationally expensive because the individual unions must execute a lot of plan integration operations in order to decide whether they will want

---

**Algorithm 1** Dynamic Clustering

---

1: $P := 0$
2: **for all** $U' \in \mathcal{U}$ **do**
3:     **if** $TW(U) \cap TW(U') \wedge Nodes(U) \cap Nodes(U') \neq \emptyset$ **then**
4:         $P := P \cup \{U'\}$
5:     **end if**
6: **end for**

---

to buy some offered module or not. In this case, it is important to partition the society into groups of agents that can become potential trading partners in order to limit the number of checks that must be performed by a single unit. This partitioning process that is executed before a trading phase is called *static* clustering.

The idea of the static clustering algorithm shown in Algorithm 2 is to pick arbitrary unions from the set of all unions as long the newly picked unions have no time window or location route (i.e. common nodes) overlapping with previously picked unions. These unions become the core elements of the clusters. If no overlapping-free new union can be found, the remaining unions are assigned to the cores according to some distance measure $d$.

---

**Algorithm 2** Static Clustering

---

1: $C := 0$
2: **while** $\exists U \in \mathcal{U} : \nexists U' \in C : TW(U) \cap TW(U') \neq \emptyset \wedge Nodes(U) \cap Nodes(U') \neq \emptyset$
    **do**
3:     $C := C \cup \{\{U\}\}$
4:     $\mathcal{U} := \mathcal{U} - \{U\}$
5: **end while**
6: **while** $\mathcal{U} \neq \emptyset$ **do**
7:     pick $U \in \mathcal{U}$
8:     find $\{U_{i_0}, \ldots U_{i_n}\} \in C$ such that

$$\forall \{U'_{j_0}, \ldots U'_{j_m}\} \in C : \sum_{i=\{i_0,\ldots,i_n\}} d(U, U_i) \leq \sum_{j=\{j_0,\ldots,j_m\}} d(U, U'_j)$$

9:     $C := C - \{\{U_{i_0}, \ldots U_{i_n}\}\} \cap \{\{U_{i_0}, \ldots U_{i_n}, U\}\}$
10:    $\mathcal{U} := \mathcal{U} - \{U\}$
11: **end while**

---

To improve this algorithm further and to make it more robust, we have implemented some additional features. One of these improvements addresses the fact that the algorithm as presented in Algorithm 2 does not clearly specify how the initial core elements are chosen. The wrong choice however, can endanger the success of the entire clustering idea. If one of the first picks of the algorithm is a large union, i.e. with many modules, that has a low degree of overlapping, i.e. the union has many location routes and thus many nodes, the algorithm will not find many other unions that does not overlap with this large union and consequently, the number of core unions will be small leading to large clusters. To circumvent this difficulty, we have modified the above algorithm in that it prefers small unions over larger ones in the first cycle. The other improvements are only of minor interest and are therefore not discussed here.

In the preceeding sections, we have developed a rather high level model of a multiagent application in general and of the TCS/MAS system in particular. Now, I will explain the main steps in construction the system architecture based on the current system model.

## 5.7 Arc itecture View

The goal of this view is to transform the feature specification of the other views into a system architecture. But what is a system architecture? Because of the fact that there is no widely agreed definition for the term in the Software Engineering community [Shaw and Garlan, 1996], [Saunders et al., 1996], I have to select one of the existing definitions that is most suitable for the ideas presented in this chapter.

**Definition 5.7.1 (Software Architecture).** *The* **software architecture** *describes fundamental structural attributes of a software system.*

Although this definition is rather general and leaves some space for interpretation it is nonetheless expressive enough to clearly define the focus of this view: to model the *components* of the target system and the *connections* between them. The software architecture is therefore a more or less static description of the code of the target system that must, however, account for the dynamic aspects that were defined in some of the other views. Before we start with concrete considerations of how to find the most appropriate system architecture, I will briefly introduce some general properties that should be present in any architecture that is developed.

Two of the most fundamental metrics that have been introduced several years ago are *coupling* and *cohesion*. According to [Conte et al., 1996], coupling measures the number of interconnections among the entities of the system and cohesion measures the internal relationships of these entities. In a good system architecture, the coupling should be low in order to achieve a high degree of modularization and the cohesion of the individual components should be high in order to keep effects of particular operations as local as possible. Furthermore, a good system architecture should try to distribute the complexity of the target system equally over the entire architecture [Rombach, 1994a] as this reduces the complexity of individual components and thus supports the designer's understanding of these components.

Obeying these basic requirements will eventually lead to a system architecture that supports changes because of the reduced complexity of the

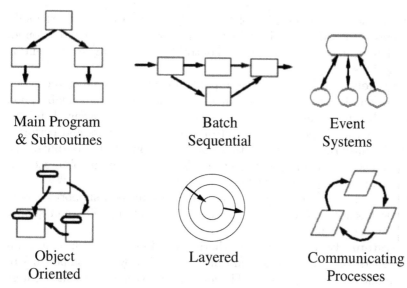

| | | |
|:---:|:---:|:---:|
| Main Program<br>& Subroutines | Batch<br>Sequential | Event<br>Systems |
| Object<br>Oriented | Layered | Communicating<br>Processes |

**Fig. 5.31.** Generic Software Architectures

individual components as well as well as reuse because of the modularization of the architecture.

In the rest of this section, I will address some issues that are characteristic for multiagent systems. Due to the wide range of possible implementations, however, I will not try to suggest a reference architecture [Shaw, 1995], [Kupries and Noseleit, 1999]. The requirements for a particular system can be so specific and individual that it would be highly unnatural to try to fit it into a standard design. However, we strongly believe that some architectural patterns for specific classes of multiagent systems will evolve during the next years when multiagent technology will become more common in industrial systems.

### 5.7.1 System Architecture

In order to find the most appropriate architecture for the target system, it is useful to think first about the overall nature of the system. Then, an appropriate *design idiom*, i.e. a fundamental pattern that is characteristic for the entire design [Shaw, 1995] is chosen according to this classification.

Several of the most common design patterns shown in Figure 5.31 are discussed in [Garlan and Shaw, 1993], [Garlan and Shaw, 1994]:

**Main Program & Subroutines** This is probably one of the oldest design patterns, stemming from the time where procedural programming languages were the only available higher level languages on the market. The characteristic feature of this pattern is the focus on the main program that provides the main control loop and acts as a driver for the subroutines attached to it. This type of architecture is still often found, especially in systems with a simple control flow, for example for scientific calculations.

**Batch Sequential** This architectural pattern is almost as old as the previous one and has its origin in the time when memory was a valuable good and multi-process operating systems had not yet been invented. In this pattern, each component has a set of inputs and outputs and performs a local transformation process that maps the inputs to the outputs. The components are independent of each other and can be invoked sequentially on a single process machine.

However, this architectural pattern may gain some new support because it is well suited for workflow systems [Odgers et al., 1999] and supply chain management.

**Event Systems** Event Systems are characterized by an asynchronous, implicit method invocation mechanism that is used by the components to communicate with each other. The idea is that each component registers with an event dispatching system in order to receive particular events that are issued by other components. This mechanism is called implicit method invocation because the component that issues an event does not explicitly request a service by another component. It may even be the case the issuing component does not know which other components react to the event.

The canonical example for event-driven systems are window systems that contain a large number of and require a flexible, localized control flow.

**Object Oriented** The fundamental abstraction in object oriented systems is the encapsulation of data representations and the associated operations in a single structural entity – the object. Well defined object oriented systems are often easier to understand then systems with a traditional architecture because of the semantic relation of the entities in the system with the entities they are supposed to represent. However, object orientation can easily lead to an over-modularization of the system with fatal consequences to maintenance and runtime behavior. Object-oriented architectures are very common in applications that provide a graphical user interface.

**Layered** In a system with this sort of architecture, several layers are built on top of each other and a each layer uses services from the lower layer and provides some service to the upper layer. Layered architectures are the first choice when the complexity of the task can be hierarchically decomposed. Furthermore, layered architectures support local changes because of the well defined interfaces between the layers. The most prominent examples for layered architectures are the OSI reference model [The International Organization for Standardization, 1998] for protocol system or the TCP [Defense Advanced Research Projects Agency, 1981] architecture.

**Communicating Processes** This design pattern represents a flexible architecture for systems with several independent, interacting entities. These entities can either reside on the same computer or they can be spatially distributed and connected via a communication network. Examples for this architecture include Client-Server systems as well as multiagent systems.

This list of architectural prototypes is not exhaustive but it represents the majority of the common system architectures. However, it is often the case that a particular system is not implemented according to a single idiom, but according to several of them. For example, a multiagent system can be implemented as communicating processes and also have an object oriented architecture at the same time. In fact, we will see in the case study, that this is the case in the TCS/MAS system.

### 5.7.2 The Architectural Feature Space

In the Architecture view, we are concerned with the problem of how to transform the more or less abstract feature specifications of the other views into a coherent system design. Therefore, this view will have to work on a lot of features that are shared with other views and I will therefore first of all characterize the *design space* of the target system. The design space is defined as a three-dimensional space that arranges the features that are addressed within the Architecture view according to three dimensions.

The first dimension describes a particular feature by classifying it according to its *temporal behavior*. Thus, a feature can either be *static* in that it accounts for a structural aspect of the system, or it can be *dynamic* and capture some of the relationships between the static object. Features of the first class will therefore usually relate to components and features of the second class will model the nature of interconnections between components.

The second dimension describes the *level of granularity* of a feature. This can either be the *micro* level that captures properties of individual components or it can describe *macro* aspects, i.e. aspects that influence the architecture of the entire system.

The third dimension, finally, differentiates features according to the *purpose*. The purpose of a feature can be *task specific* or it can be *task independent*. In the first case, the feature will typically represent entities that are characteristic for the domain while in the second case, these features can be found in several domains at the same time.

In the following, I have compiled a non-exhaustive list of selected features that are addressed in this view and classified them according to the three dimensional scheme. Figure 5.32 shows the relations between the listed features. In the following paragraphs, I will discuss the features shown in

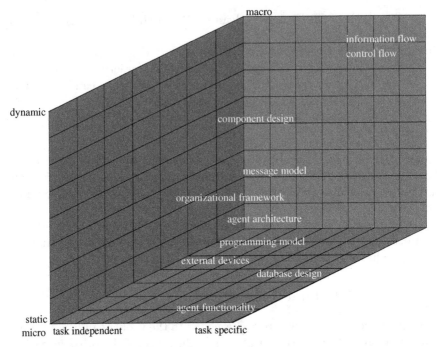

**Fig. 5.32.** Architectural Design Space

the Figure and demonstrate, how they are implemented in the TCS/MAS system.

**Entities** No all entities that are part of the system architecture are necessarily agents although the agents play the major role in the target system. However, it is not always a good idea to encapsulate all relevant entities into agents [Collins and Ndumu, 1998] e.g. when such an entity is frequently used by several agents, it is possibly a better idea to model it as an object that is accessed by the agents because of the communication overhead that would accompany the approach to model the entity as an agent. Therefore, it is the goal of this view to identify and to model the agents and the other major objects within the target system.

The most important entities of the TCS/MAS system and their interconnections are depicted in Figure 5.33 and Figure 5.34.

The agents within the TCS/MAS system are created according to the role deliminations that were discussed in Section 5.4. The *union* agents are the main elements of system as they perform the local planning of transportation routes and the local optimization procedures as discussed in Section 5.5. The *task manager* is responsible for taking incoming transportation requests and forwarding the to a union that serves the respective task. The *net manager* agent, finally, is responsible or controlling the location route allocation process of the unions.

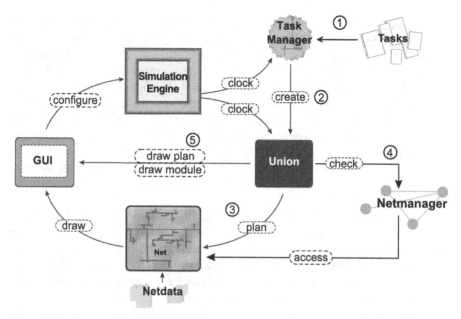

**Fig. 5.33.** System Architecture

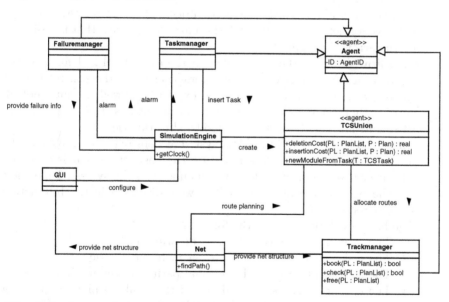

**Fig. 5.34.** System Architecture (UML)

The TCS/MAS system, however, does not only contain agents that accomplish the system functionality; several important activities are encapsulated into objects for the sake of simplicity and efficiency. The *simulation engine* object is the main coordination authority of the TCS/MAS system. It provides the system wide clock that is needed to synchronize the concurrently active agents and it implements an alarm mechanism that allows the agents to suspend their execution until a particular clock cycle. Furthermore, the simulation engine supports system debugging by allowing the designer to run the system in single-step mode.

The *net* object provides a route planning mechanism that can be used by the agents to find an optimal route between any two nodes in the network.

The *graphical user interface (GUI)*, finally, is responsible for the visualization of the system activities and for the configuration of the system behavior. The visualization of the system state is divided in a static component that allows the user to inspect the current status of the agents (e.g. their current plans etc.) and a dynamic component that allows the user to simulate the execution of the agents plans. Additionally, the GUI provides various configuration options that can be used to change the system behavior.

Now that I have introduced the main objects of the TCS/MAS system, I will give a brief description of the data and control flow that is indicated by the arrows in Figure 5.33.

**Control flow** Whereas the control flow at the agent level is defined by the interaction schemes given in the Interaction view, the control flow at the object level must be coordinated explicitly as well. Because not all entities that occur in the target system are agents, the integration of these entities into the system are modeled in this view.

The control flow of the TCS/MAS system is depicted in Figure 5.33. The numbers shown in the figure illustrate the basic cycle that is executed whenever a transportation task is announced to the system. I have left out the plan optimization steps that were discussed in the Interaction view in Section 5.5.

The basic execution cycle is the following:

1. The task manager receives a task description.
2. The task manager creates a new agent to handle the task.
3. The new agent requests the optimal path from the net object.
4. The new agent checks the validity of the resulting plan by querying the net manager for the required location routes according to the previously specified protocol (check). If the routes are not available during the time windows of the plan, an alternative route is considered by backtracking to step 3.; otherwise the location routes are allocated (book). This process iterates until either a valid plan is

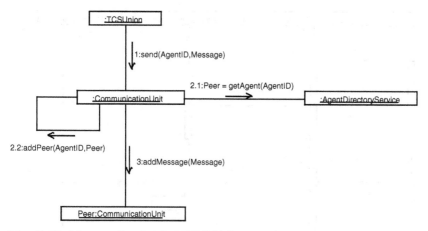

**Fig. 5.35.** Message Passing in TCS/MAS

found or the retry-bound is reached. In the later case, the new agent
is deleted and an error message is raised.

5. The new agent starts to execute its plan when the time is up.

**Information flow** The arguments that hold in the case of the control flow
can be applied to the information flow as well. Again, the information flow
at the agent level is defined in the Interaction view but the information
flow between other entities must be modeled as well.

**Agent management** Agent Management captures all tasks that are concerned with the operational framework of the agents. This framework
includes matters such as the agent identification scheme, available service information or firewall technology. Standards such as described in
[FIPA, 1998] can be a valuable help for the designer in this respect.
The agent management of the TCS/MAS system is quite straightforward
as it does not require a complex set-up or agent initialization procedure
because the agents are modeled as threads within a single Oz process.
Still, the communication system needs some mechanism to manage the
peer identification process in an interaction. Therefore, I have implemented an agent directory service as shown in Figure 5.35. The communication unit of a newly created agent registers itself with the agent
directory service and is assigned a unique identification number that is
used in any message. Whenever an agent wants to send a message to another agent, the communication unit uses the agent directory service to
obtain a handle for the addressee that is used to put the message in the
in-queue of the other agent. For the sake of efficiency, the communication
unit stores this handle in a peer list so that it can avoid to query the
agent directory service twice for the same agent.

**Communication model** The low level communication model of the application must be described and integrated into the system. The range of

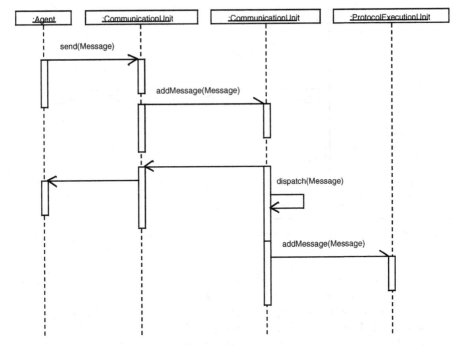

**Fig. 5.36.** Message Passing in TCS/MAS

possible communication techniques for a particular application is very broad and the designer must decide on the need for synchronous or asynchronous messages, one-to-one, multicast or broadcast messages etc. The need for particular communication services can have a huge effect on the entire system as I will illustrate in Chapter 6.

The communication model of the TCS/MAS system is built upon the method invocation process provided by the Oz system. However, since each agent has its own thread of execution, it is necessary to de-couple the sending and the receiving thread. The resulting architecture of the communication sub-system is shown in Figure 5.36. The sending agent passes the message to its communication unit that is responsible for finding the receiving agent within the system. This is achieved by using the agent directory service provided by the agent management system as described above. Then, the communication unit asynchronously adds the message to the input buffer of the receiving agent and resumes the control flow of the local thread of its parent agent. Note that an agent can be engaged in several ongoing interactions at the same time. This is accomplished by spawning a *protocol execution unit* whenever a new interaction process is started. The communication unit that has received the message searches the currently active protocol execution units for the addressee and forwards the message to it. Then, the message is added to the input buffer of the matching protocol execution unit that handles the message within its own thread. If no matching protocol execution unit is found, an exception is raised.

Applying this scheme results in a flexible message passing mechanism that on the one hand de-couples the communicating thread and on the other hand allows an agent to be engaged in several ongoing interactions at the same time.

**Database design** Especially larger systems or systems that are supposed to operate in an industrial context usually need storage facilities and mechanisms that cannot or should not be proprietary. Therefore, the designer must use standard database technology to handle these matters. However, although common database systems provide the necessary software support, it is still up to the designer to develop a database structure that suits the particular needs of the target system. Since database design is a long-known topic in the computer science community, I direct the reader to the widely available literature.

**External components/devices** In order to provide the required functionality to the user, a software system usually relies on external services that are provided either by software or hardware components. It is one of the tasks of the Architecture view to identify these components or devices and to fit them into the overall system design. This integration is achieved by defining the appropriate interfaces and the connections of the external entities to particular entities of the software system.

**Agent architecture** This aspect is one of the most important and also one of the most difficult aspects to deal with. Therefore, I have dedicated Section 5.7.3 to the detailed discussion of this topic.

Each of these features can be characterized according to the three dimensions presented earlier and arranged in a three dimensional space spawned by these dimensions as shown in Figure 5.32.

In some cases, the decision on which of these idioms to apply for a specific target system might be straightforward. In other cases, where the decision is not so obvious, I can only provide as an advice to the system designer to briefly apply the above idioms to the target system in order to develop a feeling for how a system might look that is implemented according to a particular idiom and then to select the most appropriate. Unfortunately, up to now no generally applicable set of guidelines exists that can help the designer in choosing the best architectural idiom. As it was said above, a major aspect in the system architecture is the agent architecture that implements the runtime environment for the role descriptions. In the next section, we will discuss the main aspects of agent architectures and how this topic is treated in the TCS/MAS system.

### 5.7.3 Agent Architecture

One of the most important aspects of multiagent system development is to define the basic entities within the system – the agents. As I have already discussed in Section 5.4.2, an agent is a conceptual abstraction the consists of a set of roles and an architecture that implements these roles. Thus, we define the term "agent architecture" as follows.

**Definition 5.7.2 (Agent Architecture).** *An* **agent architecture** *is a structural model of the components that constitute an agent as well as the interconnections of these components together with a computational model that implements the basic capabilities of the agent.*

To select the best agent architecture for a given set of roles is as least as a big a problem as to find the best architectural idiom as discussed in the previous section. Therefore, I recommend the following two step process to identify the best architecture from the numerous architectures that are currently on the market [Müller, 1996a],[Müller, 1998]. First of all, the system designer should *characterize* the requirements for the architecture according to fixed scheme that covers the most important issues to be addressed. Second, the designer should *evaluate* existing architectures according to the requirements defined in the first step and then select the best matching architecture. I strongly recommend to check existing approaches before trying to define a proprietary architecture. Only if no matching architecture is found, the burden of designing an implementing a new architecture is justified. Even in this worst case, the developer should consult the existing literature (e.g. [Jung, 1999]) in order to avoid sub-optimal results.

To address the first aspect of this two-step process, I have defined the following set of properties that can be used to characterize the requirements for the agent architecture.

**Reasoning capabilities** The reasoning capabilities of the agents define the most important property and often determine the overall complexity of the agent architecture. For example, an agent may be forced to plan its actions if it is not a purely reactive agent, or it may use some utilitarian reasoning mechanisms to chose among several possible actions. Another important issue is the ability for an agent to learn from past experiences or the agent may be used to fulfill special tasks such as theorem proving etc.

The TCS/MAS agents must have a planning unit to find their way through the railroad network and to detect route sharing possibilities with other agents. Furthermore, the agents must encompass some sort of reactivity when it comes to the plan execution simulation and failure handling.

**Resource limitations** This aspect of the characterization describes the resources that are available to a single agent within the multiagent system. If an agent has a very limited amount of processor time or memory space, it is impossible to use an agent architecture that requires, say, the resources of a Unix process. However, this point can also be viewed from a different angle. If the individual agent has to deal with very complex problems, a simple architecture may not be able to cope with the resource requirements of the architecture because it was not designed for heavy weight problems.

An individual agent within the system has only limited computational resources because of the expected size of the target system with approximately 5000 agents running in a single Oz process. Therefore, the agents must not be too complex as efficiency is a crucial factor due to the non-functional requirements given in Section 5.3.

**Control flow** The aim of this requirement is to characterize the control flow that is needed within the agent. First of all, the designer should decide whether a sequential flow of control is sufficient or if the agent is required to do several things at the same time and thus needs some parallel action execution model. In the second case, a concurrent architecture that in most case is much more complex then a sequential architecture must be chosen.

Second, the designer must decide about the required flexibility of the control flow. In a more static setting, the flow of control can be explicitly hard-coded into the architecture while in a dynamic context, the flow of control is likely to undergo changes and must therefore be described implicitly e.g. in plan scripts that are interpreted at run time and that can be changed while the agent is in operation.

The control flow within an agent is fixed over time and there is no need for a flexible, explicit representation of the control flow. However, an agent can potentially engage in several interactions at the same time and will also need to monitor the plan execution process while negotiating with other agents. Therefore, the agent needs a parallel action execution model in its architecture.

**Knowledge handling** The knowledge representation within the target system is defined in the Task view. In the Architecture view, the knowledge structures that are defined there must be characterized in order to decide which architectural features are necessary to effectively handle these structures.

First, it is important if the agents knowledge is stored explicitly in a knowledge base or is it encoded implicitly into the agent code. Second, the knowledge structures may be represented in a symbolic manner using some sort of logical formulae or in a sub-symbolic form e.g. in its simplest form as collection of values or more elaborate in the form of a neural network.

The major knowledge structures of the agents are the plans that hold the nodes, travel times and coupling activities of the agents. These plans are likely to change frequently and they must be interpretable by humans.

Therefore, the plans are explicitly represented and kept in the knowledge base that must be provided by the agent architecture.

**Autonomy** The degree of autonomy that is required by the agent defines how the agent interacts with its environment. A reactive agent simply responds to external stimuli by reproducing a pre-defined behavior when a particular stimulus is given by the environment. A pro-active agent, on the other hand, can become active without external trigger and then perform some action that satisfies the goal. Pro-active agents are usually more complex and their behavior is not always predictable.

The degree of autonomy of the agents varies in the different tasks they perform. In the optimization activities, the degree of autonomy is quite low as the agents only react to a sharing offer by a newly created union. However, things are different in the case of the plan execution facilities. Since failures of location routes must be handled by the agents, the re-planning process offers them the possibility to autonomously adapt their current plan whenever its is needed. Still, the agents do *not* implement pro-active behavior.

**User interaction** The more interaction the agent has with the user, the more elaborate the user interface has to be in order to provide convenient means for input and output data. Furthermore, an advanced user interface agent will perform user profiling and try to learn the users preferences from his or her input/output behavior.

There is very little user interaction between the user and the TCS agents and thus the user interface is limited to presenting the plan and the current coupling state to the user and to allow the user to trigger plan execution.

**Temporal context** This aspect characterizes the agents lifetime. Obviously, an agent with only a limited activation time will need another form of persistence mechanism – if any at all – then a long-running agent. Persistence refers to the ability of the agent to maintain knowledge structures over time and over unavoidable down-times due to service failures such as hardware or software crashes. However, the amount of information that is collected by the agent over its lifetime can become very large and must be handled in an effective manner. Thus, the architecture must provide means to manage the data handling process.

The lifetime of the agents ranges over a few hours and is therefore rather short. However, the system must provide some persistence mechanism to allow the user to store and retrieve schedules generated by the system.

**Decision making** This attribute characterizes the way in which the agent comes to its decisions during its reasoning processes. While some authors claim that rationality is an inherent property of any agent [Russell and Wefald, 1991], [Russell and Norvig, 1995], there are others who consider architectures that support emotional decision making as an alternative [Burt, 1998], [André et al., 1999]. There are two main fields

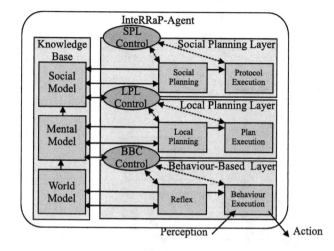

**Fig. 5.37.** InteRRaP

for a potential application of emotional architectures. First, they can become valuable tools to implement lifelike characters and avatars that represent a human user in networked environments. Second, the notion of emotions can be used to express complex heuristics for advanced software agent in a natural way. However, the development of the basic technology is still in its beginnings and does not play a relevant role until now. Still, the developer of a particular application may want to consider these ideas if they are appropriate for the problem in question.

In the TCS/MAS system, I have used the InteRRaP agent architecture [Müller, 1996b] that provides most of the above features and that was also successfully used in the TE ETR K [Bürckert et al., 1998] system which shares some similarities with the TCS/MAS system.

The InteRRaP architecture is a generic agent architecture for situated agents that integrates reactive behavior and deliberation. The architecture was designed for agents that exist within multiagent systems and thus some emphasis is on the communication aspect. As depicted in Figure 5.37, InteR-RaP is a layered architecture that consists of three layers, each consisting of concurrent processes:

**Behavior Based Layer (BBL)** This layer implements the reactive behavior of the agent, i.e. this layer reacts to external requirements without any explicit reasoning, thus it reacts very fast.

**Local Planning Layer (LPL)** This layer performs the planning process of an individual agent, it is also responsible to monitor the plan execution of the agents current plan.

**Social Planning Layer (SPL)** This layer is responsible for the coordination with the other agents within a multiagent system. The coordination with the other agents is achieved with explicit negotiation protocols.

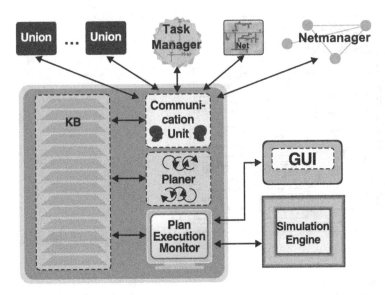

**Fig. 5.38.** Union Agents

All layers run concurrently, the intra-agent coordination between the three layers is achieved via the knowledge-base. The knowledge base is conceptually divided into three layers (world model, mental model, social model), but each computational layer has access to the knowledge on every level of the knowledge base. The conceptual discrimination, however, allows for a clearer design because most of the information stored in the knowledge base can be associated with a particular layer.

The InteRRaP architecture offers a generic framework for agent design that must be instantiated for the particular needs of a concrete scenario. Usually, some aspects of the generic framework are more interesting in a given scenario than others; in the TCS/MAS system, the emphasis of the instantiation is on the local planning layer and the social planning layer, the behavior based layer is not as important right now. However, in a later version of the system with a more realistic plan execution simulation, the BBL will gain more relevance.

A functional decomposition of the relevant parts of the union agents is shown in Figure 5.38.

**Communication Unit (CU)** The communication unit implements the social planning layer of InteRRaP and is thus responsible for executing the negotiation protocols between the agents. These protocols are used for the social planning process of the agent society in order to optimize the global schedule and to handle the location route allocation process.

**Planer** The local planning unit of the TCS unions uses the shortest path service provided by the net object and the route allocation protocol of

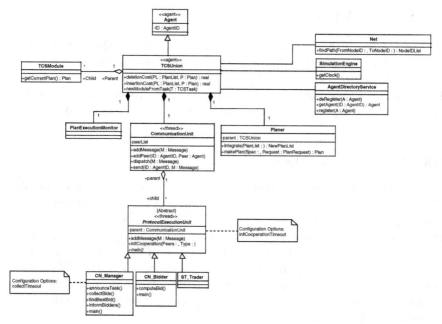

**Fig. 5.39.** Union Agents (UML)

the net manger to find the local plan for an agent. Details of the local planning process are discussed in Appendix B.1.

**Plan Execution Monitor (PEM)** The plan execution monitor resided on the behavior-based layer of the agent architecture and monitors the execution of the current plan of an agent and adapts the plan in the case of external events, e.g. location route failures etc.

The arrows between the agent and the other parts of the system shown in Figure 5.38 indicate the connections of an agent to the outside world. Each arrow between the communication unit and another agent represents a logical connection that is used to execute the negotiation protocols between the agents. The connections to the simulation engine, the graphical user interface and the net object, on the other hand, are achieved by method invocation within the object system. Figure 5.39 show the UML class diagram that corresponds to the InteRRaP implementation within the TCS/MAS system.

In this section, I have outlined the basic objectives of the Architecture view with some emphasis on the overall architectural paradigm underlying a particular application and on the agent architecture because of its complexity and because the agents are the main entities in a multiagent system. In the next section, we will complete our tour through the generic view system of MASSIVE with a view that collects those aspects of a system that usually cannot be assigned to a single view alone.

## 5.8 S stem View

The main idea of the general view system is to structure the features of the target system according to their conceptual and logical links. However, some aspects of the target system are spread all over the system making it difficult to assign them to a particular view. Therefore, I introduce the System view that covers the aspects that affect multiple views or even the system as a whole.

### 5.8.1 User Interface Design

In this section, I will discuss some issues that are related to the user interface of the target system. Today, the main interface between a program and the user is usually a *graphical user interface (GUI)* and so I will limit the scope of this section to GUIs only. The user interface does not only play an important role with respect to the intended use of the system, but it is also important for the designer to know that in most applications, more then 50% of the total system size are dedicated to the UI. However, due to limited space, we can only briefly mention some basic aspects and direct the reader to the literature for more information.

In the case of a multiagent application, the user interface can serve two major purposes. First, it can manage the task-specific user interaction which is to accept inputs from the user and in turn to present the results of processing the input data. Second, the user interface can be used to monitor and manipulate the system activities of the multiagent system, i.e. the designer (and later the user) must be able to trace the systems activities. The concurrent, distributed approach to problem solving makes this a difficult task that must be carefully executed. Monitoring the system activities is also of vital interest for the development phase of the system with respect to debugging. For monolithic systems, debugging features are supported by the programming language or a development environment; in the case of multiagent systems, however, only little or no support is given by existing languages and environments. Thus, either standard agent development frameworks such as ZEUS [Ndumu et al., 1999] must be used to visualize the system activities or the system designer must develop and integrate the facilities to support tracing and debugging into the design.

Despite the requirements of a particular class of applications, however, any user interface should comply with the following principles [Galitz, 1997].

**Clarity** The entities of the GUI should be clearly related to the entities they represent in the real world and they should be given unambiguous names or icons.

**Comprehensibility** The user interface should be intuitive to use and provide an understandable access to the system functions. The key questions that describe this property are *What to look at?*, *What to do?*, *When to do it?*, *Why to do it?* and finally *How to do it?*.

**Consistency** An individual entity should have the same representation even if it occurs in different contexts and actions should always lead to the same results in order to guarantee some sort of predictability to user. Furthermore, the windows, dialogs etc. should have a consistent layout and appearance throughout the entire user interface.

**Directness** The user interface should provide a direct and intuitive access to accomplish the tasks. For example, complicated parameter settings in several menus before a function can be activated should be avoided.

**Control** It is important to design the interface in a way the provides the user with the feeling the he or she controls the behavior of the system and not vice versa.Thus, the system should query the user before taking action and it should keep the user informed about ongoing computations, loading processes etc., for example by showing an hourglass whenever an action is started.

Thus, a good user interface reflects the needs and capabilities of the user, obeys physical constraints of the hardware and conforms with existing standards. Our recommended iterative design process for the user interface consists of seven steps as shown in Process Model 15.

The seven steps of Process Model 15 are independent of a particular programming language or window system and can thus be used to guide the interface design on a very general level of abstraction. In order to speed up the development of the user interface, it is highly recommended to make use of existing software libraries such as Tcl/Tk [Ousterhout, 1994] or Gecco [Knecht, 1996] in order to benefit from off-the-shelf components for standard user interface elements.

The graphical user interface of the TCS/MAS system supports the detailed inspection and monitoring of the ongoing computation as well as the off-line analysis of simulation data obtained in batch-mode of the system. The main elements of the GUI are shown in Figure 5.40 which contains a screen shot of the TCS/MAS system with number of monitoring and statistic elements.

**Map Window** The Map window shows the underlying railroad network and can be used to visualize the plan execution process of the unions. It serves also as the main entry of user interaction as it contains the menu bar that controls all major functions of the system.

**Task Viewer** The Task viewer is used to browse the task file that is currently loaded. For each task, the module identification, the module type, the module length, the source node, the destination node, the earliest possible departure time, the latest allowed arrival time and the time when the task is announced to the system are shown.

**Union Browser** The Unions browser shows the current union structure of the system, i.e. which modules are connected in a particular union. The user can select one or more of these unions to check for the current state

---

**Process Model 15** MASSIVE User Interface Design

1. **Know your user** In this step the user groups are characterized according to their experience, the estimated use frequency, their skills (e.g. typing or other input devices), the available amount of training, their motivation etc. This characterization will help the designer to develop a general idea of the user interface. It is, for example, a completely different task to develop a user interface for a novice that uses the system occasionally or for an expert who is familiar with similar applications and who regularly uses the system.

2. **Relate to the system** The initial idea of the interface must then be related to the system that it is indented to represent towards the user. Therefore, the designer identifies potential points-of-interaction between the GUI and the underlying system. These points-of-interaction are all features that can be visualized or manipulated by the user.

3. **Check standards** Before the real design process of the particular user interface starts, the designer should check its initial idea against existing standards and the constraints they may impose on the interface. This step is important in order to avoid a user interface that is not generally accepted by the user community. However, if the entire target system is a customized application, deviations from the standard may be tolerable.

4. **Define menus** The menus that usually appear on top of the application window define the overall structure of the GUI as they are usually the first entry point for the user. The menus should be related to functional groups within the system and have speaking names in order to enable the user to relate the menu titles and entries to particular functions of the system.

5. **Select windows** In this step, the windows that represent different aspects of the system are being built. First of all, the designer must decide which information should be grouped together in a single window and then the following steps are executed for each window:

   a) **Select presentation techniques** The most appropriate presentation technique, e.g. textual, graphical or audio representation, is chosen for each of these groups and their elements.

   b) **Select the appropriate screen-based controls** The control elements include the entire palette of tools offered by most existing window system interfaces, e.g. text inputs, slide bars, list pickers, etc.

   c) **Create the layout** In this step, the presentation and control elements are arranged within the window.

6. **Create a help system** The help system is an important issue in a user interface when the interface reaches a particular level of complexity. The designer should provide two types of help to the user, the first one is a *general help system* that can be queried for specific topics by the user and the second is *context-specific help* that is activated by the user on-the-fly e.g. by pressing a mouse button while the mouse pointer is over an input field.

7. **Evaluate the interface design** The user interface is ideally checked by selected users if they are available. If the current version of the user interface fails in one of the aspects described above, the entire process is re-iterated from step 1.

---

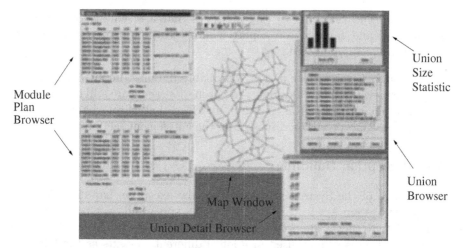

**Fig. 5.40.** Elements of the TCS/MAS GUI

of the unions, e.g. for the current coupling state of the union or the user can trigger the plan execution process for these unions to check the validity of their current plan.

**Plan Browser** The Plan browser is started from the Union browser window and allows for an even closer look at the plans of the modules that make up the union. For each module, the Plan browser shows a sequence of nodes where each of the nodes consists of the node identifier, the earliest possible arrival time in the node, the latest allowed departure time from the node, the scheduled arrival and departure times and the actions that must be executed in the node. For each action, the scheduled time window and the peer modules are also shown.

**Statistics Viewer** The Statistics viewer is a collection of tools that enable the user to examine various properties of the current schedule. The *Union statistic* shows the distribution of the unions in the system over the possible union sizes, the *Coupling Node statistic* uses the Map window to visualize the nodes in the system that are scheduled for coupling activities, the *Source and Sink Node statistic* also uses the Map window to present the nodes where the freight is picked up from or delivered to, and the *Location Route Monitor*, finally, exhibits the usage statistic for every location route that is used in any module plan.

**Trading Monitor** The Trading monitor can be activated by the user to scrutinize the hypothetical trading operations between unions as well as the trading match that is computed by the stock manager. Whenever the Trading monitor is active, the user can interactively decide whether a particular match is accepted or not.

**Communication Monitor** The Communication Monitor, finally, is used to visualize and inspect the messages that are exchanged between the agents. The user can see the messages that are sent by one agent to another and can click on a particular message to inspect the contents that are communicated.

Although user interface design is probably the most important and most extensive view that covers system-wide properties there are still other aspects probably not as exposed as the user interface that affect the system as a whole. These facets will be discussed in the subsequent sections.

### 5.8.2 Exception Handling

This aspect of the System view describes the exception handling policy of the target system – a feature that is usually spread all over the entire system and that effects almost every part of the target system. However, the term exception is usually used in a lot of different contexts as the following definition shows.

**Definition 5.8.1 (Exception [Lang and Stuart, 1998]).** *An* exception *is the union of* error, exceptional case, rare situation *and* unusual event.

In order to provide a structure for the different aspects that are covered by the term, the following categorization was suggested by [Cox and Gehani, 1989]. *Software* or *design errors* are caused by implementation mistakes in the software, e.g. dividing by zero, array index range errors, incorrect loop conditions etc. *Hardware errors* are the result of failures of the underlying hardware such as memory leaks, sensor failures etc. State errors occur if the systems model of the environment is inconsistent with the actual state of the environment; this kind of error is often found in robotic applications. *Timing errors.*finally can occur only in real-time systems and are caused by the violation of timing constraints or resource (processor, memory) overload.

In the System view, however, we are only interested in software and design errors and how to handle them. In order to describe the error handling strategy of the target system, it is often useful to characterize the indented mechanism according to the following scheme.

**Scope** The scope of the error handling mechanism can either be *local* or *global*. A local strategy aims at the individual components of the system and specifies the error handling activities from the individual point-of-view.

A global strategy, on the other hand, introduces a central authority to which all errors are reported and that handles the exceptional situation according to a given plan. Multiagent system seem to naturally suggest a localized exception handling scheme. However this can make it sometimes difficult to cope with temporal information e.g. when the designer needs to detect the exact temporal ordering of exceptions during the debugging phase. In this case, a global scheme can significantly reduce the development cost although the idea of a central authority opposes the basic multiagent idea.

**Purpose** The purpose of the exception handling process can be error detection or error recovery. The first case is easier to handle as it simply requires some sort of notification mechanism to indicate the presence of an exceptional situation to the designer or the user. Error recovery is usually much harder to achieve as it requires a thorough analysis of the current system state and explicit knowledge of how to handle a particular failure. However, in certain types of multiagent system, this type of exception handling will have to be considers as a simple system shut-down may not be an acceptable behavior.

**Technology** The technology aspect of the exception handling mechanism, finally, deals with the concrete implementation of this mechanism. A language-based approach uses the constructs of the underlying programming language to implement the exception handling strategy whereas an operating system-based approach makes use of services provided by the platform on which the target system is running. The choice of the best technology is a difficult matter that requires to weight several factors according to the requirements of the target system. While a language-based approach is usually easier to use and is mostly platform independent, it nonetheless depends on the expressive power of the target language which might be too limited for most multiagent applications. An operating system-based approach, on the other hand, is usually more platform dependent but also usually provides more flexibility to the designer.

Finding the exception handling strategy that is suited best for a particular target system is not easy and may have consequences for the entire system. Thus, it is usually a good idea to consider this aspect quite early in the development process, ideally before the actual implementation is started.

Because of the prototypical nature of the TCS/MAS system, I have refrained from implementing an elaborate exception handling scheme in order to simplify the design of the system at the expense of stability in case of unforeseen events. Thus, the exception handling mechanism that is implemented features only the basic requirements in that it is local, is used only for error detection and is language-based.

Locality means, that each entity performs its own error monitoring process and does not report failures of any kind to a central authority. This is not necessary as the goal of the exception handling process is only error detection and not the recovery from unexpected system states. The TCS/MAS system uses the exception notification mechanisms provided by the runtime system of Oz to detect design errors and to report them to the developer or user. It is then up to him or her to take the appropriate action to prevent the situation that lead to an error in subsequent activations of the system.

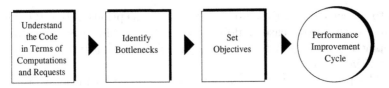

**Fig. 5.41.** The Performance Engineering Process

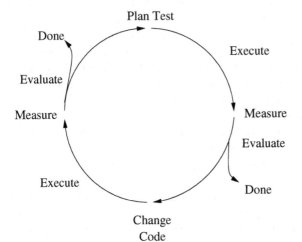

**Fig. 5.42.** The Performance Improvement Cycle

### 5.8.3 Performance Engineering

In this section, I will discuss some ideas that deal with performance aspects of the target system and I will present a micro process model for the Performance Engineering process taken from [Rational Software, 1999b].

**Definition 5.8.2 (Performance Engineering).** **Performance Engineering** *is a method to identify and reduce or eliminate performance problems during the software development cycle after the code has been designed and developed.*

The Performance Engineering process shown in Figure 5.41 is summarized in Process Model 16. The fundamental step in this process is to identify the bottlenecks that are responsible for performance losses in the target system. Some of the major causes for bottlenecks are listed below.

**Useless computation** Useless computation is often the result of program changes that make parts of the original code obsolete without removing the then unnecessary code fragments. Another source of useless computation are default computations that are executed even if they are not required, for example opening connections to remote agents by default can have severe effect on the systems start-up time.

---

**Process Model 16** Performance Engineering

---

1. **Understand** In the first step of the Performance Engineering Process the designer must develop a "feeling" for the runtime behavior of the application. This is best done by dividing the application into several phases (e.g. initialization phase, input passing, etc.). Then the designer can decide, according to the separation of the runtime behavior, which phases are the most time consuming and focus the attention on these phases as improvements in these phases are likely to yield the highest gain in performance.
2. **Identify** The goal of this step in the Performance Engineering Process is the identification of potential bottlenecks in the selected phases of the application. The sources of bottlenecks are manifold but is still possible to identify some prototypical classes that cover most existing bottlenecks.
3. **Set Goals** When the potential bottlenecks are identified, the designer must set quantifiable goals in order to prioritize the bottlenecks according to their relevance. Several criteria for this are possible, the most obvious being the potential performance improvement. However, the cost (effort) to remove a particular bottleneck should always be weighted against any potential gain.
4. **Performance Improvement Cycle** The goal of this, most important step in the entire process, is to isolate and eliminate a particular bottleneck. The Improvement Cycle as shown in Figure 5.42 consists mainly of six activities. First of all, the test for a particular bottleneck must be carefully *planned* in order to enable the designer to focus on the performance aspect under consideration and to exclude any effects that might have influence on the result. Next, the test is *executed* and the performance of the program is *measured*. If the *evaluation* of the test results show, that the performance is already satisfactory according to the previously defined quality standards, the Performance Improvement Cycle can be aborted. If the performance is below the defined measure, the code is *changed* in order to remove the bottleneck and the test is *executed* again. If the next *measurement* shows that the code change has yielded the desired effect, the cycle is aborted. If this is not the case, the cycle starts again and repeats until either the performance goal is met or the effort exceeds a defined amount.

---

**Re-computation** This bottleneck is the result of computing results although the could be cached for later use. The following example shows a very simple case of re-computation

```
if X.getRow() != MAXROW then
    StartRow == X.getRow() + 1;
    . . .
end
```

In the example, the getRow operation on object X is called twice although it could have easily been cached as follows

```
Tmp = X.getRow();
if Tmp != MAXROW then
    StartRow == Tmp + 1;
    . . .
end
```

However, this is a rather trivial example that is often detected and removed by the compiler, but it can nonetheless have some impact on the overall runtime behavior e.g. if the `getRow` function is computationally expensive or when the entire code sequence occurs within a loop.

Generally speaking, the higher the effort to compute a particular result and the more often it is needed, the higher is the performance gain through caching.

**Waiting for service requests to complete** Whenever a program requests a service from the operating system, it is typically blocked until the request is completed. Requests to the operating system are quite frequent in any computer program and consequently, some attention should be paid to these calls and how they can be reduced or transformed such that they are less vulnerable to external effects.

Prominent examples for this kind of bottlenecks are file access and memory management. In the first case, for example, the designer can make sure to be independent from network delays while accessing a file on a file system that is mounted via NFS if the file is read once and then kept in memory for further fast access. Obviously, this does only yield performance gains if the file is accessed more then once. In the case of memory management, it is sometimes useful not to rely on the memory management of the operating system. Allocating a large block of memory and then organizing the memory management locally is often a valuable alternative to the service provided by the operating system [Kernighan and Pike, 1999]. However, even doing so does not prevent the application from being delayed because of page faults and heavy swapping. If this occurs, other mechanisms to speed up memory access must be found.

**Wrong or missing assumptions about the runtime system** This kind of bottleneck can often be found in the use of function parameters or local functions. Whenever a data structures is passed to a function using the call-by-value mechanism, the entire data structure must be copied on the stack and back again when the function is done. In the case of large structures, this copy operation can take a long time and additionally slow down memory access in the function body. Therefore, any call-by-value with a large data structure should be replaced with a call-by-reference even if the data structure is not changed in the function.

Local functions are a similar problem as the are often generated on the heap at runtime. This takes additional time and memory and should be avoided in frequently called function. I will discuss the impact of eliminating local functions in Oz programs in the case study below.

**Non-scalable algorithms or data structures** This is a performance killer that is often found in applications that were developed and tested for small example data and that fail to work with the real operational data. A simple example is the following: assume, an agent has a list in which it stores all its acquaintances and that it looks up by performing a linear search whenever it sends a message and that is updated by appending a new entry whenever it receives a message from a formerly unknown agent. As long as the system is small, the effect of this list search and update mechanism can be neglected. However, if the system is scaled up to several hundred or even thousands of agents, this scheme will lead to performance losses that could be avoided by using a more efficient search strategy and/or a better data representation.

The initial performance of the TCS/MAS showed a promising behavior although the number of agents that were active in the system was quite high with approximately 5000 agents for the largest examples. Nonetheless, however, it was possible to increase the system performance by a factor of six by performing two rather simple nonfunctional optimizations.

Using the profiler that comes with the Oz distribution, I was able to identify several bottlenecks in the actual implementation of the system. The first bottleneck was due to my lack of knowledge of the runtime system of Oz and the second bottleneck was a suboptimal design in a basic data structure.

Let us begin with the runtime behavior of Oz. Whenever a member function of a class contains a local function, the *closure* of this local function is constructed on the heap a runtime, i.e. whenever the member function is called. The following example shows an example for a local function that is used to implement a loop - a method that is quite common in Oz programs.

```
class A
    meth findElem( List Key ?Result )
        FindElem = fun{ $ List Key }
                   ...
                   end
    in
        Result = {FindElem List Key}
    end
end
```

Thus, whenever findElem is executed, the runtime system builds the closure of FindElem on the stack and removes it after findElem is done. This mechanism does not cause any problems as long as findElem is not called frequently in the application.

In the TCS/MAS system, on the other hand, I had a small number of functions that used local functions and that were themselves used millions of times in the course of a system run. These functions were identified using the profiler and their code was re-written as illustrated below.

```
local
    FindElem = fun{ $ List Key }
                    ...
                end

    class A
        meth findElem( List Key ?Result )
            Result = {FindElem List Key}
        end
    end
```

This rather trivial re-arrangement of code fragments brought a performance enhancement by a factor of four and thus by far justified the effort and the break of the principle of locality of computation.

The second bottleneck in the implementation was a combination of the use of a sub-optimal algorithm and re-computation and was caused by the class that encapsulates the network data of the underlying railroad network. The Net class maintains the list of links within the network and provides a member function that takes a link identification number as input and returns the matching link object to the function caller. In the first version of the TCS/MAS system, I used a small network of approximately 25 nodes to develop the basic planning algorithms in a controlled environment of limited size. Therefore, the list of links was relatively small and the member function that mapped link identifications to links was implemented as a sequential search over the link list. As the system was upgraded to the full network, however, the search algorithm was not reviewed with respect to the higher performance demand in a 350 node network and remained in place. Again, the profiler of Oz lead to the this function that was responsible for the performance bottleneck. The search process was replaced by a direct mapping that was held in a dictionary and the performance gain was about a factor of 1.5.

The rather simple nonfunctional optimizations of the TCS/MAS system clearly show, that it pays for the system designer to carefully monitor the systems runtime behavior and that large performance gains are not necessarily hard to achieve.

In this section, I have presented a general-purpose micro process model for Performance Engineering. However, Performance Engineering is not necessarily applied to the entire system, but it can also be applied to specific parts of it [Smith, 1997]. Furthermore, Performance Engineering is closely related to Refactoring [Fowler, 1999] and some of the micro process models that are suggested for the refactoring process can be used for Performance Engineering as well.

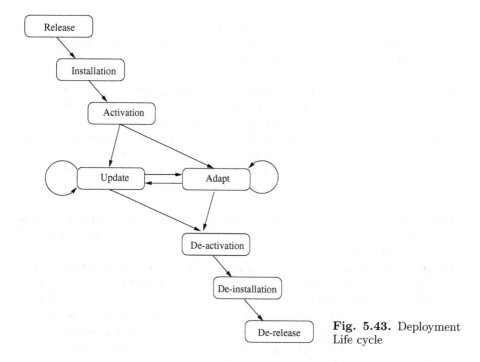

**Fig. 5.43.** Deployment Life cycle

### 5.8.4 Deployment

**Definition 5.8.3 (Software Deployment [Hall, 1999]).** **Software deployment** *is the process that covers all of the activities performed after a software system has been developed.*

The complexity of the deployment process depends on the complexity of the software and the required system environment. Planning of this process is essential for a successful implementation of the target system at the user site.

The deployment life cycle of a software system consists of eight steps as depicted in Figure 5.43.

**Release** This step is the interface between the development and the deployment process and includes all activities that are necessary to package the software system as well as the knowledge to set in operation at a user site.

**Installation** This step is usually the most complex activity because it must find and assemble all necessary resources. In this step the system as well as the external resources such as libraries, software packages etc. are either initially deployed at the user site or updated according to the required versions.

**Activation** The activation of a software system refers to the process of starting the participating components in order to get the system running. For simple software systems, this may require only to push a button or to enter a command line. More complex systems, however, may require more sophisticated, coordinated activities in order to bring all components into operation.

**Update** Updating am already installed software system means to modify it in order to add new functionality or to remove bugs. Updates are issued by the software provider and taken up by the clients.

**Adapt** The adaption of an installed system differs from an update in that the former is limited to local changes only while the latter refers to potentially all installed systems as a whole. Adaption thus refers to changes of the system at a particular site in order to adapt it to changes in the system environment.

**De-activation** De-activation is the inverse process to the activation of the system and refers to a controlled shut-down of all components involved in running the system.

**De-installation** When the system is no longer required at a user site, it must be removed from the site. This it not necessarily a trivial process because attention must be paid to not disturbing the system environment of the user site e.g. by the deletion of shared resources. Thus, this step is not the process of undoing everything that was done upon the installation of system but it requires an analysis of the current state of the user site to detect dependencies of other software systems on resources that were installed with the target system.

**De-release** The final step in the deployment life cycle is reached when a system is regarded obsolete and it is no longer developed or supported by the manufacturer. This step is distinct from the previous one in that it does not mean that the system cannot be used any longer. Rather, the users are free to use the system but they should be aware that no further support will be available.

The deployment of a particular system is usually a highly individualized task and thus hard to capture in a general process model. The following generic deployment process model is thus described at a rather high level of abstraction and will need to be tailored according to characteristics of a specific project. Basically, the deployment process consists of five steps as shown in Process Model 17.

This five-step generic deployment process covers the major parts of the deployment life cycle shown in Figure 5.43: the release of a particular system is described in step 1, the installation in step 4, the activation in step 5 and the update activity of the life cycle is captured in steps 1 and 4. Other activities in the life cycle are not directly covered but the can make use of the gathered information, e.g. the de-installation will certainly use the component characterizations and the dependency information when removing a system from a particular site.

---

**Process Model 17** System Deployment

---

1. **Identify and characterize components**
   The components that are relevant for the planning of the system deployment are for example the executable files, data sources, hardware devices, external (software) components etc. Each of these components is characterized for example by the site characteristics were it should be installed, the deadlines it must hold, its availability or a version specification. The goal of this step in the planning process is to obtain a complete picture of every entity that is related to the target system in one way or another.

2. **Describe dependencies**
   In this step, the dependencies between the components are explicitly modeled. A dependency is for example a "uses" relation between components or temporal precedences in the installation process that must be maintained. Note that dependencies can vary between different user sites.

3. **Define Activities**
   For each component, the activities that are necessary to set a component into the state that is required by a user site are specified. Examples for activities are the steps that must be performed to install a software library or the instructions to set up a particular hardware device.

4. **Execute**
   In this step, the previously defined activities are executed in the order imposed by the dependencies that were modeled in step 2.

5. **Start**
   In the final step of the deployment process, the system is set into operation at the user site.

---

Since the TCS/MAS system was designed as a prototype that was only to be run at the development site to obtain simulation data there was no need for extensive deployment planning.

The only relevant aspects of the system deployment is to ensure the installation of the correct versions of Oz [Programming Systems Lab, 1999] and LEDA [Mehlhorn and Näher, 1999]. For development versions of the TCS/MAS system, Emacs [Stallman and Free Software Foundation, 1999] must be installed as well.

## 5.9 Summ r

In this chapter, I have presented views as the core concept of the MASSIVE development method. Views allow the system designer to break down the target system into several projections that concentrate on particular aspects of the system and abstract away from others. The seven views of the MASSIVE method and some of their content are summarized in Figure 5.44. The Environment view characterizes the environment of the target system from the developers and the systems perspectives. The Task view focuses on what the system should do in terms of functional and nonfunctional requirements and basic problem solving capabilities without thinking in agent-oriented terms.

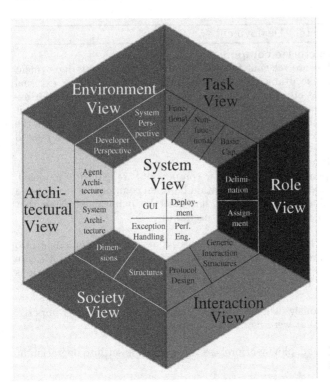

**Fig. 5.44.** The MASSIVE View System

The Role view concentrates on a functional and physical grouping of the problem domain and is used to assemble a set of coherent roles for the agents. It also deals with the assignment of these roles to particular agents. The Interaction View describes the ongoing interactions between agents in terms of interaction protocols and provides a set of generic interaction schemes that can be used by the system developer. The Society view defines the social dimensions of the target system and describes the structure of the agent society. The Architecture view turns the features that have been modeled in the other views into the software design of the system and the agent architecture. The System view, finally, captures all aspects that cannot be assigned to a single view such as the user interface, the global error handling scheme, performance engineering aspects or system deployment.

This product model for multiagent systems represents the current experience with the development of multiagent system. It is meant as an initial model that should be refined and extended in the sense of the institutional framework of an Experience Factory.

The TCS/MAS system was used as a case study throughout this chapter. In order to show the validity of the MASSIVE method in different application areas, I will describe in the next chapter how it was successfully applied in two other problem domains.

# 6. Furt er C se Studies

A development method will never be accepted in an industrial context if it cannot prove its validity in practice. The MASSIVE method is not a method that was developed in the laboratory and then transfered to actual projects. Rather it is derived from projects that were successfully carried out at the DFKI and elsewhere and that were analyzed after completion in order to find similarities in the product and process models. The advantage of this approach is that it provides further case studies that show how the method works and that demonstrate that the method can be used for a broad range of multiagent applications.

## 6.1 T e TEAMWORK LIBRARY

The TEAMWORK LIBRARY [Lind, 1996a], [Denzinger and Lind, 1996] is a framework for the development of distributed search applications according to the Teamwork approach [Avenhaus and Denzinger, 1993], [Denzinger, 1993]. In the following sections, I will present the general idea of the teamwork approach and the design of a library that supports the user in developing teamwork-based applications.

### 6.1.1 Environment View

Since the TEAMWORK LIBRARY is intended as a generic framework for distributed search application in various contexts, it is not possible to describe the environment from the perspective of the agents because this view depends on the particular problem domain. Therefore, we are limited to the developers perspective in the description of then Environment view of the TEAMWORK LIBRARY.

This perspective is dominated by the characteristics of the runtime environment which in turn is determined by the intended initial use of the library in the context of a Solaris environment. Due to efficiency aspects, the goal language was chosen to be C++ [Stroustrup, 1987] and the programming model should be parallel because a pseudo-parallel approach would not adequately exploit the benefits of the teamwork approach. Finally, the communication platform provided by Solaris is TCS/IP. Especially this aspect

J. Lind: The MASSIVE Method, LNAI 1994, pp. 205-241, 2001.
© Springer-Verlag Berlin Heidelberg 2001

has some major impact on the overall structure of the TEAMWORK LIBRARY and will be discussed in Section 6.1.4 in greater detail.

### 6.1.2 Task View

In this section, I present the key ideas of the teamwork approach as they were introduced in [Denzinger, 1993] in the context of equational theorem proving and later extended and generalized in [Denzinger and Lind, 1996].

The teamwork approach is a distributed problem solving algorithm for problems with very large (or infinite) search spaces. Due to the size of the problems of interest, it is impossible to traverse the entire search space, and in some cases (e. g. optimization problems), a rather good, although not the best, solution is usually sufficient. Since there is a large number of possibilities to proceed with the search it is very important to design heuristics or knowledge based algorithms to concentrate on search paths which will lead to the goal quickly.

We can identify two groups of algorithms that have their main difference in the information they need to continue the search process. The first group are search processes that need explicit information about prior search states, i. e. they need to know the history of the search. The processes of the second group do not need any history information to proceed with their search.

The first group of search processes are called *divide and conquer* algorithms and they normally use trees or directed graphs to represent their states. Examples for search processes of this group are the well known Branch and Bound algorithms [Lawler and Woods, 1966]. The way they execute their search is quite straightforward: the problem is divided into several subtasks which are worked on independently, i.e. without any communication between the tasks. The results of the subtasks are assembled at the next higher level and, since the search may lead to dead ends, backtracking is sometimes necessary.

The main problem for this group of search processes is to design good heuristics to identify the subtasks into which the main task will be divided. Load balancing between the physical agents to which the subtasks are assigned and identifying subtasks that can actually be solved by a single agent are key issues for the design of an application that uses these search processes.

In the second group, we have algorithms that perform a *search by extension and focus*. In this group of search processes, the search space is represented by a set of results which is normally unstructured. The search processes do not keep explicit information on how a search state was reached, i. e. no information about the decisions which lead to a particular state are kept. To determine the transitions from one search state to another, the search processes use a set of *extension* rules. Due to the problem size, there are usually a very large number of possible extensions and this is why a *focus* function is needed to limit this number. A characteristic property of problems that can be solved with algorithms of this group is that it is normally not possible to find "natural" partitions of the search space. This is the reason why the teamwork approach was developed for this class of search processes since divide and conquer algorithms are not suitable for these kinds of problems.

The distinction of problems into two classes is not very sharp: There are problems that may be solved by using algorithms from either group, for example to prove the unsatisfiability of a formula of first order predicate logic. This problem can be solved with a semantic tableau [Smullyan, 1968] which belongs to the first group, or by using resolution and factorization [Robinson, 1965] which belongs to the second group. The distinction is, however, precise enough to characterize the problems for which the teamwork approach can be used.

In order to formalize the concepts that have been introduced so far, we have the following definitions.

**Definition 6.1.1 (Search by extension and focus).** Search by extension and focus *is described by a 4-tuple* $(\mathcal{B}, \Omega, \mathcal{I}, \mathcal{S}_{l})$. *Here $\mathcal{B}$ is a set of objects and the subsets $S \in 2^{\mathcal{B}}$ of $\mathcal{B}$ are called* states. *$\Omega$ is a predicate defined on $\mathcal{B}$ and $\mathcal{I}$ consists of* extension *rules of the form $L \cup M \to L \cup N$ with $L,M,N \in 2^{\mathcal{B}}$. $S_0 \in 2^{\mathcal{B}}$ is called the* start state *and for all $s \in S_0$ we require that $\Omega(s)$ holds. We write $S \vdash_{\mathcal{I}} S'$ for states $S$ and $S'$, if there is a rule $L \cup M \to L \cup N$ in $\mathcal{I}$ such that $S = S'' \cup L \cup M$ and $S' = S'' \cup L \cup N$ and $\Omega(s)$ holds for all $s \in S'$. A sequence $(S_0,S_1,...,S_n)$ with $S_{i-1} \vdash_{\mathcal{I}} S_i$ for all $i=1, \ldots ,n$ is called a* search derivation. *We shall call the $S_i$ derivable from $S_0$.*

$\mathcal{B}$ and $\mathcal{I}$ are determined by the (general) problem to be solved and $\mathcal{I}$ is (since it may contain infinitely many elements) usually represented by a finite set of rule schemata. Note that $\Omega$ and $S_0$ are determined by the instance of a problem, i. e. the input of the search process.

**Definition 6.1.2 (Goal of a search by extension and focus).** *Let $(\mathcal{B}, \Omega, \mathcal{I}, \mathcal{S}_{l})$ be a search by extension and focus. Let $>_{\mathcal{B}}$ be a Noetherian partial ordering on $\mathcal{B}$. Then we call an element $g \in \mathcal{B}$ having property $\Omega$ that is minimal with respect to $>_{\mathcal{B}}$ a* goal *of the search. A state containing $g$ is called a* goal state. *The goal is* reachable, *if there is a goal state $S_i$ derivable from $S_0$ by rules from $\mathcal{I}$.*

The definitions given above are not sufficient to completely define a search process because some indeterminism remain unresolved. It is, for example, possible that the goal cannot be reached for a given input or there may be several states containing the goal. These problems are solved by providing a function to select the "best" extension for a given search state. This function is called the *focus* of the search process.

**Definition 6.1.3 (Focus function).** *Let $(\mathcal{B}, \Omega, \mathcal{I}, \mathcal{S}_{l})$ be a search by extension and focus and $g$ a goal. A function $f{:}2^{\mathcal{B}} \times \mathcal{I} \to \mathbb{Z}$ is called a* focus function *and the derivation* $(S_0, S_1, \ldots, S_i, \ldots)$ *is produced by f, if for the extension* $L_i \cup M_i \rightarrow L_i \cup N_i$ *that produced state* $S_i$, $i > 0$, *we have that* $f(S_{i-1}, L_i \cup M_i \rightarrow L_i \cup N_i) \leq f(S_{i-1}, L \cup M \rightarrow L \cup N)$ *for all* $L \cup M \rightarrow L \cup N \in \mathcal{I}$.

The nonfunctional requirements of the TEAMWORK LIBRARY are as follows. First of all, the library should be *easy to use* even for inexperienced users. Thus, the library should provide the necessary structures for a broad range of applications that can be used with little adaptations by the application developer. Second, the library should be *flexible and generic* in a way that it supports different application classes on a high level of abstraction and provide the mechanisms to instantiate the generic base structures for a concrete problem. Finally, the library should be *efficient* in that is has only little administrative overhead and efficient algorithms for aspects such as data transfer etc.

### 6.1.3 Role View

The general idea of the teamwork approach is to work with different algorithms on the same problem and to incorporate the specific benefits of each algorithm into an overall solution that is better than any of the separate solutions alone. This will not work in all cases, but experience shows, that it can – and in most cases will – lead to better results than a single algorithm alone [Pitz, 1993].

The original teamwork approach as presented in [Denzinger, 1993] was inspired by modeling a human project team on a computer network. In bigger companies, it is quite common to have project teams working on a specific problem by using the knowledge and experience of several experts. There is a large number of different ways to organize project teams and the teamwork approach is just one way how to organize it, but since it is not possible and not ingenious to try and cover all possibilities, some assumptions are made to concentrate on one possible realization. In the teamwork view, the composition of a team (i. e. the team members) can be adjusted to a given problem and the composition can change during the problem solving process. The control of the whole process lies within a (team-)supervisor on top of the team hierarchy. It is, however, possible to delegate complete (sub-)tasks to a sub-team, but the main responsibility for the problem solving process stays with the supervisor of the main team. The teamwork approach tries to reflect such a human project team that consists of four types of components: *experts, specialists, referees* and a *supervisor*.

The teamwork approach distinguishes two phases of the problem solving process. During the *working phase*, the problem solving entities generate search states according to their individual specifications. Each of these working phases is followed by a *team meeting* during which the more administrative aspects of the problem solving process are dealt with.

*Experts* and *Specialists* are the only components of a team which work on the problem directly. Each of the different experts must be capable to solve the problem alone, but, because of the different algorithms and heuristics used in the experts, each of the experts has another view on the problem. A very important need for an expert is that it must be able to continue the work started by another expert. This implies, that in contrast to specialists as we will see later, all experts in a team must have the same knowledge representation. Another restriction for the implementation of an expert is the size (the duration) of an atomic step in its computation. This size must not be too large because an expert must be able to stop its computation in a stable state at almost any time to join a team meeting. It is not acceptable for other experts to waste time on waiting for experts to be ready for a team meeting.

Specialist differ from experts mainly in two ways: they may have their own data representation and they may keep knowledge for a longer time (especially for more than one team meeting). This will be explained later when team meetings are discussed. An important requirement for specialists is that they must be able to convert their results (represented in their special knowledge representation) into a format that can be understood by the experts.

The *referees* mentioned above have two major tasks: assessing the work of an expert or a specialist to judge the progress made and choosing "good" results computed by an expert/specialist. The main difference among the referees is their assessment strategy, which, in most cases, are statistical criteria. The assignment of referees to the experts/specialists they assess is not fixed during the entire application. Instead, it is possible that an expert/specialist is assessed by different referees during a system run. This reflects the fact that the problem description evolves during the solution process and that the assessment criteria for what is regarded as a "good" result or a "big" progress may change. Note that a special knowledge representation of the specialists requires special referees to assess the specialists work and to choose the good results. The reports generated by the referees are used to determine the next team supervisor and the results chosen to be good offer the possibility to forget unimportant facts which did not contribute to the solution process. This forgetting of facts is very important in order to avoid blowing up the search space.

The *supervisor* of a team, finally, has the central control over the team activities. Its main tasks are: to build a new, improved problem description before the next working phase starts, to choose the experts to work in the next working phase, and to determine the duration of the next working phase.

These roles (supervisor, expert, specialist and referee) constitute the functional grouping of the teamwork library. The physical grouping of these roles is determined by the complexity of the problem solving capabilities of the agents. In the first application of the teamwork approach [Pitz, 1993], each agent was a full fleshed theorem prover that needed the computational resources comparable to those of a Unix process. The teamwork approach was originally designed for coarse-grained problems that are worked on by resource-intensive inference mechanisms and this fact is reflected in the physical grouping of the agents as well. Thus, as in the very first Teamwork application, we assume that each agent is equipped by the amount of resources mentioned before.

The functional and the physical groupings that were discussed previously map together very well making it easy to define each role according to the functional grouping because the physical grouping is well capable of satisfying the resource requirements of the functional grouping.

Now that the roles within the TEAMWORK LIBRARY have been defined, the next step is to specify the interactions that take place between these roles.

### 6.1.4 Interaction View

The overall control flow of a teamwork application consists of repeated loops of working phases until either a solution is found or the search process is aborted. At the end of each working phase, a team meeting is held to bring together the results of the experts and specialized that have worked on the problem for some time, to evaluate and combine their respective results and to select the next team supervisor and the participants of the next work cycle.

Figure 6.1 shows the information and control flow during a team meeting. During a working phase, the team supervisor acts as a normal expert, its special task starts with the beginning of the meeting. First of all, the supervisor must determine the best expert which will later become the next supervisor. Therefore, the referees start to evaluate the results that were obtained by the experts and specialist during the last working phase (①) and the current supervisor uses short reports (②) (usually containing only a single assessment value) of the referees to select its successor. Control is then instantly passed to the new supervisor (③) that takes over the lead of the team meeting started by the old supervisor.

First, the new supervisor requests the detailed reports from the referees (④). Each report contains the good results and several statistical data, generated on the performance evaluation of the experts or specialists. After receiving all data, the supervisor starts to integrate the results of the experts and specialists into its problem description. Note that this is the problem description of the best expert during the last working phase and thus ideally contains a problem description that is more likely to contain the solution then the descriptions of any other agent. Then, the statistical data of the reports is used to choose the team members for the next working phase by replacing unsuccessful experts by others which are expected to provide better results. This selection of experts and specialists enables the supervisor to adapt the team configuration to the given problem.

In the final step of the team meeting, the supervisor determines the duration of the next working phase and transfers all necessary knowledge (problem

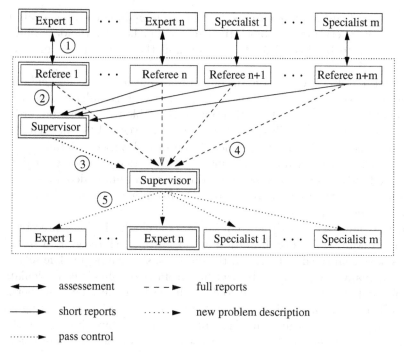

| ←——→ | assessement | – – –► | full reports |
|---|---|---|---|
| ——► | short reports | ······► | new problem description |
| ·······► | pass control | | |

**Fig. 6.1.** Team Meeting

description, team structure and duration of the next working phase) to the experts (⑤). After the transfer is complete, the next working phase starts.

The transfer of the new problem description can easily become a performance bottleneck as it is usually very large. Using standard transfer protocols such as TCP/IP can severely limit the performance of the system when the number of participating agents in a team exceeds a certain threshold because TCP/IP allows only for the sequential transfer of data to several recipients. Clearly, this is not acceptable and so means must be found to speed up the data transfer between the supervisor and the agents at the end of a team meeting. To overcome the performance bottleneck, the TEAMWORK LIBRARY implements a broadcast mechanics on the basis of IP datagrams. The purpose of the broadcast protocol is to provide a transparent, convenient and easy interface to the use of broadcasts. The approach for the use of broadcasts should be the same as for the stream sockets.

During protocol execution, one agent has an outstanding position called the *actual sender*. The actual sender is the only agent that is allowed to send broadcast messages at a certain time, but of course the sender can change over time.

The data transmission from the sender to the receivers is symmetric, i.e. each send operation for a specific amount of data corresponds to a receive operation for exactly the same amount. Furthermore, the data transfer between two agents using broadcasts is done in a buffered manner, i.e. a call to a send/receive operation may block the agent either because the data buffer is full and has to be flushed or it is empty and the new contents must be read.

During the protocol execution, the most important tasks for the agents are order preservation and loss detection of the packets sent. Broadcasts messages are unreliable datagrams and are therefore susceptible to duplication, order confusion or even loss. To illustrate how the TEAMWORK LIBRARY handles these problems, we will now discuss how the protocol works in detail.

Figure 6.2 illustrates how the transfer of a particular amount of data is organized in a *broadcast session* that is in turn subdivided in several *sub-sessions* that themselves consist of a *transmission* and a *acknowledgment/retransmission* phase.

The first thing to do for the current sender is to check whether all receivers are ready by waiting for a confirmation message from each receiver. After all receivers have confirmed to be ready, the data transfer can begin. The sender knows how many bytes have to be sent and from that value it can calculate the total number of packets needed to flush the entire buffer. This number is used to estimate the best number of packets to be sent before requesting an acknowledgment. The estimation will lie between a fixed lower bound and the total number of packets needed and it denotes the size of the next sub-session. The estimation algorithm is based upon prior data about packet duplication or packet losses and thus implements an adaptive protocol.

After selecting the best size for the next sub-session, the sender starts to transfer the proposed number of broadcast datagrams where each of these datagrams has a header and a data field. The header field contains the sub-section and a packet number and an optional operation code to trigger certain actions on the receivers side. The two numbers in the header make it possible to identify every broadcast message during an entire Teamwork application uniquely. The receivers read the datagram messages and the header fields tell them what to do with an incoming packet.

The last packet of every sub-session contains the header opcode `SendAckn` (or, if it is the last packet of the session, the opcode `EndOfTransmission` – which implies a `SendAckn`) that tells the receivers to enter the acknowledgment phase. This packet is protected against loss by the use of a timer, i.e. when the sender realizes that acknowledgments are missing after a certain period of time, it will assume that at least one receiver did not get the packet containing the acknowledgment request. The last packet is then repeated until all receivers have sent their acknowledgment or until a maximum number of retransmissions was performed. In the latter case, the protocol issues an error message and abort because it assumes some irreparable damage at one of the receivers.

The acknowledgment scheme that is used in the TEAMWORK LIBRARY is called a *negative acknowledgment* scheme which means that the receivers

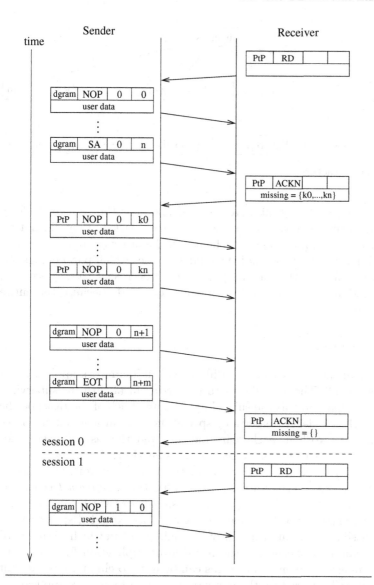

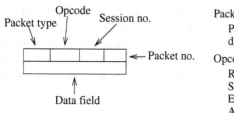

Packet types:
  PtP: point-to-point packet
  dgram: broadcast datagram
Opcodes:
  RD: ready to receive
  SA: SendAckn
  EOT: EndOfTransmission
  ACKN: acknowlegement
  NOP: No operation

**Fig. 6.2.** Broadcast Protocol

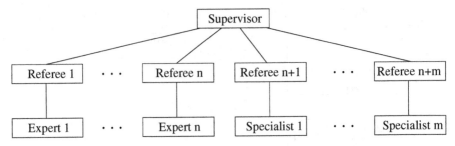

**Fig. 6.3.** Team Structure

keep track of the packets that were received and that the receivers inform the sender in their acknowledgment message which packets they did not receive. In a *positive acknowledgment* scheme, on the other hand, the receivers report which packets they got and the sender decides which packets must be retransmitted. After all the missing packets have been sent to the receivers, a new sub-session begins or the transmission loop ends because the entire buffer was transferred.

### 6.1.5 Society View

The structure of the agent society within a typical Teamwork application is shown in Figure 6.3. The overall structure is hierarchical with the supervisor being the head that controls the subordinate agents. Each of the task specific agents on the lowest level (experts or specialists) has an associated referee that evaluates its work in each team meeting and that is responsible for selecting good results to be forwarded to the supervisor.

In [Kronenburg, 1995], an extension of the basic teamwork approach is presented that focuses on hierarchical team structures. A *team tree* can be built by allowing a team to have one or more *sub-teams* (which can have sub-teams as well). These sub-teams can be regarded as extended specialists as they can be used to solve subproblems of the main problem which are too hard for a single expert or specialist. Another field of application for sub-teams is a more administrative one. Sub-teams can be used to eliminate redundant information in order to reduce the memory usage of a teamwork application. Since the teamwork approach was designed for large search spaces, such a "garbage collection" is often needed to make a problem solution possible.

The sub-team extension, however, is not yet implemented in the teamwork library, but some effort has been taken during the design phase of the library to make the later integration of the sub-team extension as easy as possible.

### 6.1.6 Architecture View

**System Architecture.** In this section, I will characterize the required system architecture according to the scheme given in Section 5.7.

**Entities** The only entities that occur in the Teamwork Library are the agents that play the different roles according to the teamwork paradigm.

**Control flow** The control flow is fully determined by the Interaction view.

**Information flow** dto.

**Agent management** The agent management uses a proprietary mechanism that is executed by the initial team supervisor. Upon start, the initial agent becomes the supervisor and reads a team configuration file. Then, the supervisor launches an ID server that can be accessed by any subsequent supervisor in order to obtain unused unique identification numbers. Next, the supervisor starts new agents on the specified host computers for each teamwork agent. The newly created agents immediately connect to the supervisor and establish the communication network to the other agents.

**Communication model** The communication model of the Teamwork Library is based on proprietary TCP/IP messages that thus do not use any standard agent communication language.

**Agent architecture** The architecture of the Teamwork agents is discussed below.

**Database design** The Teamwork Library itself does not need any central databases, applications specific databases are not subject to this view.

**External components/devices** No external components or devices are used in the Teamwork Library.

**Agent Architecture.**

**Reasoning capabilities** The reasoning capabilities of individual agents must remain unspecified because they are domain specific.

**Resources limitations** Each teamwork agent should be equipped with the computational resources of a Unix process in order to enable it solve demanding tasks in the problem domain.

**Control flow** The control flow within a teamwork agent is sequential because the role activations follow the ordering defined by the teem meeting protocol from Section 6.1.4.

**Knowledge handling** The knowledge representation of the agents depends on task-specific aspects that cannot be covered by a generic framework such as the Teamwork Library.

**Autonomy** The basic idea of the teamwork approach aims at distributed search in a large search space following a rather strict computational model that does not support agent autonomy in any way.

**User interaction** No user interaction is intended for the agent since the teamwork approach is a batch-oriented search scheme.

**Temporal context** The lifetime of the teamwork agents will typically range only over a few hours and will thus not require any persistence mechanisms. However, if persistence is required in a particular application, the necessary mechanisms must be provided by the library user.

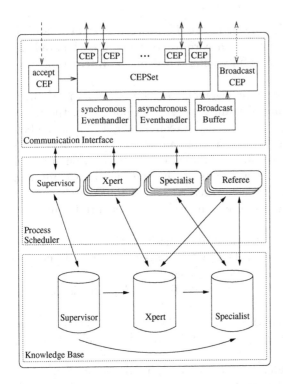

**Fig. 6.4.** Teamwork Agent Architecture

**Rationality** This aspect of the agent architecture is application specific and therefore not covered by the generic agent architecture.

The agent architecture of the TEAMWORK LIBRARY as shown in Figure 6.4 consists of three major parts: The *communication interface* of the agent architecture provides several mechanisms at different levels of abstraction to communicate with other agents of the application. AT the lowest level, normal TCP/IP stream connections are provided. The communication interface implements the standard connection establishing process by offering an accept communication end point (CEP) to which the other agents can connect. A new CEP is then created to handle the messages that are exchanged via the new connection. At a higher level of abstraction, these low level facilities are used to implement more complex forms of message exchange. One of these forms is the broadcast protocol based on IP datagrams that was presented earlier in this section, the two others are synchronous and asynchronous event mechanisms. A synchronous event mechanism assumes that the event subscriber expects an incoming event and dispatches this event according to a pre-defined handler. Asynchronous events differ from this by interrupting the subscribes control flow, dispatching the event and then resuming the control flow from the point where it was interrupted.

The *process scheduler* that is implemented in the teamwork agents activates a particular role during the working phase according to the team structure that is provided by the current team supervisor. It is also responsible for switching between the roles of the working phase and those of the assessment phase and must thus know which expert or specialist is assessed by which referee.

The *knowledge base*, finally, contains the domain knowledge that the agents use during the working phases and the specific knowledge of the supervisor that is needed during the team meeting. The referee roles can access the expert or the specialist part of the knowledge base in order to compute the short report and to select the good results for the long report.

### 6.1.7 System View

**User Interface.** Due to the generic nature of the TEAMWORK LIBRARY, the user interface that is provided together with the library must be limited to task-independent aspects of the final application. Thus, I have included a number of external tools that allow the developer and the user to monitor and analyze the system activities of a typical teamwork application. The tools that are provided with the TEAMWORK LIBRARY are as follows.

The *Agent Monitor* shows the current state of each agent and the incoming and outgoing messages according to the Teamwork protocol described in Section 6.1.4. The second tool that is provided by the TEAMWORK LIBRARY is the *Society Monitor* that is used to visualize the current collection of agents that constitute a Teamwork application. The agent as well as the society monitor that were provided with the first version of TEAMWORK LIBRARY were strictly text based and have been extended in subsequent work [Künzel, 1997]. The extension also includes several tools to manipulate the behavior of individual agents or the agent society and a collection of generic base methods to support the development of a task-specific user interface.

A graphical tool that was provided with the original release of the Teamwork Library is the *Broadcast Analyzer* shown in Figure 6.5. This tools allows the system developer to perform a post-mortem analysis of the broadcast traffic during a teamwork application. The collected information can then be used to optimize the parameter setting for the broadcast protocol that was presented in Section 6.1.4.

**Performance Engineering.** Performance Engineering of the TEAMWORK LIBRARY was mainly focused on the communication subsystem of the agent architecture. To illustrate the performance engineering process, I will now present the estimation algorithm for the size of the next sub-session during a broadcast session. This estimation algorithm uses statistical data that is collected in earlier sub-sessions to estimate the next value.

- The average packet loss $\overline{al}$ during the last *loss history* ($lh$) sub-sessions is the weighted arithmetic mean of the packet losses of these sub-sessions. A weighted mean is used because the losses recorded in earlier sub-sessions

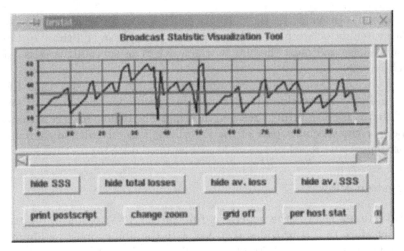

**Fig. 6.5.** Broadcast Statistic Tool

should be taken less into account then more recent data. The weighted average mean is computed according to the following formula.

$$\overline{al} = \frac{\sum_{i=n-lh}^{n-1}\left((\frac{1}{2})^{n-i-1} \cdot \sum_{j=0}^{r}(loss_j(i))\right)}{\sum_{k=0}^{lh-1}(\frac{1}{2})^k} \tag{6.1}$$

In equation 6.1, $n$ denotes the number of the current sub-session, $r$ holds the number of receivers and the function $loss_j(i)$ returns the number of packets lost by receiver $j$ in sub-session $i$. Please note, that the sum is not evaluated if $i$ is less then 0 and note also that if the divisor of equation 6.1 is 0, $\overline{al}$ is assigned a default value ($averageLossDefault($.

- The absolute number $\overline{rl}$ of lost packets containing opcode **SendAckn** or **EndOfTransmission** during the last *acknowledge Request loss history arlh* sub-sessions. This value is critical for broadcast performance because every lost acknowledgment request packet implies a delay (to detect that it was lost) and a retransmission. Therefore, special activities should be taken if this value exceeds a certain bound. The absolute number is computed to

$$\overline{rl} = \sum_{i=n-arlh}^{n-1} \sum_{j=0}^{r} acknReqLoss_j(i) \tag{6.2}$$

Again, $n$ holds the number of the current subsection, $acknReqLoss_j(i)$ returns the number of packets lost by receiver $j$ in sub-session $i$. As in equation 6.1, the sum is not evaluated if $i$ is less then 0.

- The average size $\overline{s}$ of the last *average sub-session size history asssh* sub-sessions. Again, we use a weighted arithmetic mean to reduce the influence of older data.

$$\bar{s} = \frac{\sum_{i=n-asssh}^{n-1} \left( (\frac{1}{2})^{n-i-1} \cdot sss(i) \right)}{\sum_{0}^{asssh-1} (\frac{1}{2})^k} \tag{6.3}$$

In equation 6.3, $sss(i)$ returns the size of sub-session $i$. If $i$ does not denote a valid sub-session number (e. g. if $n - asssh < 0$), the return value is ignored in the computation.

Now I will demonstrate how these values are used to determine the major parameter of the broadcast buffer during the sending phase. The size of the next sub-session is chosen according to

$$nextSSS = \begin{cases} lastSSS + increaseUnitSize & \overline{al} \leq littleLoss \\ \overline{s} & littleLoss < \overline{al} \\ & \leq mediumLoss \\ \overline{s} - \overline{al} & mediumLoss < \overline{al} \\ & \leq highLoss \\ \overline{s} - \overline{al} - decreaseUnitSize & \overline{al} \geq highLoss \end{cases} \tag{6.4}$$

Another parameter that determines the senders behavior is the *send delay*. If a send delay is activated, the last packet of every sub-session which contains the acknowledgment request is sent twice, with a delay of a few microseconds between the two send operations. This helps to reduce the number of acknowledge request losses because the delay enables the receivers to process some datagrams received earlier thus freeing internal buffer space for more incoming packets. The delay option is turned on if the number of acknowledge request packets lost exceeds the value of *absAcknReqLossBound*.

This was only one example of the Performance Engineering activities that have been applied to the TEAMWORK LIBRARY. Further – and more detailed – information about performance aspects of individual parts of the library can be found in [Lind, 1996b].

**Deployment.** Deployment planning was a major concern of the TEAMWORK LIBRARY as it was intended to be usable on a broad variety of hardware platforms that support the basic requirements that were outlined in Section 6.1.1. Therefore, the final release of the Library contained a generic Makefile that was configured by the library user to fit the particular needs of an installation site. The details of the deployment process are beyond the scope of this overview, the interested reader may refer to the reference manual that is shipped with the library [Lind, 1996b].

# 6.2 Person l Tr vel Assist nt: ntermod l Route Pl nning

The Personal Travel Assistant (PTA) [FIPA, 1997] is a scenario described by the FIPA Standardization Organization to evaluate various aspects of the standard. The FIPA Organization is an international consortium of about 50 industrial and academic institutions whose goal is to define standards for communication among agents to ensure interoperability in industrial applications.

The agents in the PTA domain operate on behalf of their users and provide assistance in the pre-trip planning phase as well as during the on-trip execution phase. In order to accomplish this assistance, the PTA interacts with the user and with other agents that represent the available travel services. Besides the core competences such as configuration and delivery of trip planning and guidance services, the PTA also provides added-value services according to personal profiles, e.g. interests in sports, theater, or other attractions and events.

The focus of the services provided by the PTA, however, is on the basic requirements of the trip which is first of all to find the best combination of travel services that take the PTA user from his or her desired starting point to the destination. This route planning service is provided by a special agent, the *Intermodal Route Planner (IMRP)*. The IMRP is responsible for selecting a group of transport carriers that provide the necessary services at the quality required by the user. Figure 6.6 illustrates the basic idea in combining the services of several transportation carriers such as car and plane into a single route plan. Each of the different transportation services is encapsulated by an agent that provides a planning interface to the service. In the example in Figure 6.6, the user agent will query the autoroute planner for the best way from the users starting point to the airport and the air plane agent for a flight to the destination. Obviously, these two plans are not independent of each other as the flight can only be taken after the trip to the airport is complete. Additionally, the person who is traveling will not want to waste too much time because of an early arrival at the airport. Hence, it is the task of the PTA to find partial plans that satisfy the users constraints and to integrate these plans in order to guarantee a smooth trip.

In the following sections, I will describe a solution for the intermodal route planning process that was developed in the MoTiV-PTA project [Bayrische Landesregierung, 1996]. Due to the limited space, however, I will only be able to provide the basic ideas of the design that was used to implement the final system.

## 6.2.1 Environment View

The environment view of the agents within the IMRP domain is determined by the standards that are set by the FIPA. The FIPA97 [FIPA, 1997] specification provides technical standards for *Agent Management* (administration of agent systems, yellow page services, firewall technology etc.), *Agent Communication Language* (FIPA ACL based on speech-act theory, protocol specification etc.) and *Agent Software Integration* (integration of existing SW systems in agent systems (agent wrappers) etc.). This set of standards is extended in

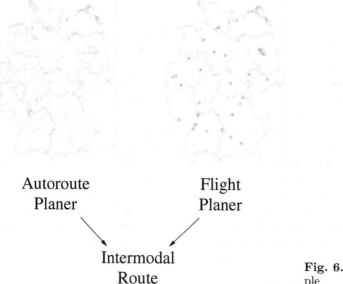

Autoroute
Planer

Flight
Planer

Intermodal
Route

**Fig. 6.6.** IMRP Example

the FIPA98 [FIPA, 1998] specification by defining standards for *Agent Management Support for Mobility* (specification, configuration and handling of mobile agents), *Agent Security Management* (secure communication support, agent authentification, trusted platform specification), *Ontology Service Support* (support for the specification of the semantics of domain-specific message contents) and *Human/Agent Interaction* (interface specification, user profiling, learning about preferences).

Since the PTA domain was created to evaluate the FIPA specifications, it is clear that the resulting application must conform to the standards described in [FIPA, 1997] and [FIPA, 1998].

The FIPA standard requires a minimal framework that provides primitive services for the agent inter-operation based on the following entities. The *Agent Management Service (AMS)* provides the services for the management and administration of agents e.g. by offering a name service, the *Directory Facilitator (DF)* agent contains yellow pages with service descriptions and services and several *Agent Communication Channels (ACCs)* exist for platform-independent communication, secure communication and communication through firewalls. This minimal framework is implemented by the MECCA agent platform [Gerber et al., 1999b] that was used in the IMRP project. The general development environment for the target system is based on three platforms (Solaris, Linux and NT) and uses Java [Sun Microsystems, 1999] as the implementation language. The programming model is parallel because the individual route planer agents are supposed to be physically distributed and the agents will use network communication services to exchange messages.

## 6.2.2 Task View

The Task view describes the task decomposition within the target system and defines the basic concepts that were used to model the problem domain. In the IMRP domain, the overall problem to be solved is to find a trip from a given start point to the destination while preserving additional constraints such as available time windows or preferred transportation means. Before we proceed to the task decomposition of the target sysetem. however, we will first develop a formalization of the IMRP domain in order to obtain a tool for writing precise requirement specifications and solution outlines.

First of all, we define the basic data structures that occur in the problem domain and that must be represented within the target system. The most important data structure for the formalization of the IMRP domain is used to represent the individual travel services. Each of these services operates on a graph structure in which the nodes represent the service access points and the weights of the links represent some abstract cost measure that is associates with traveling a particular link.

**Definition 6.2.1 (Graph).**
   *A **Graph** $G = (V, L, \alpha, \omega, \gamma)$ consists of a set $V$ of vertices, a set $L$ of links, a mapping $\alpha : L \to V, \alpha(l) = v$ where $v \in V$ and $v$ is a starting node of $l$, a mapping $\omega : L \to V, \omega(l) = v$ where $v \in V$ and $v$ is a terminal node of $l$ and a weight function $\gamma : L \to \mathbb{R}$ that assigns a weight to each link.*

   *$l$ is a link between two vertices $v_1$ and $v_2$ iff $\alpha(l) = v_1 \wedge \omega(l) = v_2$. The weight of the link is $\gamma(l)$. In the context of multiple graphs, let $V_G$ and $L_G$ denote the set of vertices and links for a graph $G$, respectively. In the following, we will use the terms vertice and node synonymously.*

Another data structure that is often used in the formalization is a list over a particular set of ground elements. The following definitions describe the basic operations that can be performed on such lists.

**Definition 6.2.2 (List, List Operations).** *Let $L = [e_1, \ldots, e_n]$ be a **List** of elements over a set $E$, i.e. $e_i \in E \quad \forall i \in \{1, \ldots, n\}$. We write $L = [H|T]$ with*

- $H = e_1$
- $T = e_2, \ldots, e_n$

   *Let $LISTS(E)$ be the set of all sets over $E$. The following operations are defined on $LISTS(E)$:*

- *$length : LISTS(E) \to \mathbb{N}$ where $length([e_1, \ldots, e_n]) = n$ returns the **length** of a list.*
- *$head : LISTS(E) \to E$ where $head([H|T]) = H$ returns the **head** element of a list.*
- *$tail : LISTS(E) \to LISTS(E)$ where $tail([H|T]) = [T]$ returns the **tail** element of a list.*

*Furthermore, we define*

- *heads* : $LISTS(LISTS(E)) \rightarrow LISTS(E)$ *where*
  $heads([[H_1|T_1], \ldots, [H_n|T_n]]) = [H_1, \ldots, H_n]$
- *tails* : $LISTS(LISTS(E)) \rightarrow LISTS(LISTS(E))$ *where*
  $tails([[H_1|T_1], \ldots, [H_n|T_n]]) = [[T_1], \ldots, [T_n]]$

After these basic data structure definitions, we can now turn to the actual formalization of the concepts of the IMRP domain. First of all, we formalize the services that are restricted to individual travel services.

### Definition 6.2.3 (Unimodal Map).

*A **unimodal map** is a graph $G$ according to definition 6.2.1, $UMAPS$ is the set of all unimodal maps.*

*We define a predicate valid : $UMAPS \rightarrow \{true, false\}$ on the set of unimodal maps that decides the **validity** of a map in a given context.*

The validity of a route is a personalized function that can be used to express user preferences with respect to a particular travel service. We will not define this function as it is only an interface to higher level functionality of the PTA that is not of interest in the IMRP domain. Next, we define how a particular route is represented such that it can be uniquely identified within a intermodal route.

### Definition 6.2.4 (Unimodal Route).

*A sequence $R = (v_1, \ldots, v_n)$ is a **unimodal route** in a map $M$ iff*

- $v_i \in V_M \quad \forall i \in \{1, \ldots, n\}$ *and*
- $v_i \neq v_j \quad \forall i, j \in \{1, \ldots, n\} : i \neq j$ *and*
- $\exists l \in L_M : \alpha(l) = v_i \wedge \omega(l) = v_{i+1} \quad \forall i \in \{1, \ldots, n-1\}$

*We call a tuple $((v_s, \ldots, v_d), G)$ with $G = \sum_{l \in L(v_s, \ldots, v_d)} \gamma(l)$ a **weighted (unimodal) route** and $U = (M, R, G)$ a **named weighted (unimodal) route** in $M$.*

*Furthermore let $Routes(M)$ denote the Set of all Routes in $M$ and the set of all links of a particular route is $Links : Routes(M) \rightarrow L_M^n$ with*

$$Links(R) = \{l | l \in L_M \wedge \exists v \in V_M : (\alpha(l) = v \vee \omega(l) = v)\}$$

*$\Gamma : Routes(M) \rightarrow \mathbb{R}$ is defined as*

$$\Gamma(R) = \begin{cases} MAXWEIGHT & if \quad v_s = v_d \quad or \quad R = () \\ G & otherwise \end{cases}$$

Note that we have defined the weight of a route to be $MAXWEIGHT$ in the case that the start and the goal node are the same. This trick allows us to simplify the algorithms given below as it automatically rules out empty routes in an intermodal route without an extra check simply because of the high costs that are associated with any intermodal route that contains empty unimodal routes.

Now that the individual travel services have been formalized, we must define how the PTA user can switch from one travel modality to another. Thus, we must define how we describe access points that are shared by several travel services.

**Definition 6.2.5 (Junction Points).**

*The* **junction points** *between two maps $M_1$ and $M_2$ are defined as*

$$J(M_1, M_2) = \{(v_1, v_2)|v_1 \in V_{M_1} \wedge v_2 \in V_{M_2} \wedge samePlace_{M_1 M_2}(v_1, v_2) = true\}$$

*Where the predicate $samePlace_{M_1 M_2} : V_{M_1} \times V_{M_2} \rightarrow \{true, false\}$ decides whether two nodes occupy the same position or not.*

*Furthermore let*

$$J_{M_1 M_2}(v) = \{w|v \in V_{M_1} \wedge w \in V_{M_2} \wedge (v, w) \in J(M_1, M_2)\}$$

*be a function that returns all junction points for a given node and fixed source and destination maps and let $Alias : V \rightarrow V$*

$$Alias(v) = \{w|w \neq v \wedge \exists M_1, M_2 : samePlace_{M_1 M_2}(v, w) = true\}$$

*be a functions that returns all nodes that are equivalent (with respect to the samePlace predicate) to a give node. Note that $v$ itself is contained in this set as well.*

The actual decision whether two nodes of different maps represent a junction point is encapsulated in a specific predicate *samePlace* in order to make it easier to explicitly define junction points. A very straightforward definition of the predicate is to base it on the Euclidean distance of two nodes, but more sophisticated schemes can be implemented as well.

In the next steps in the formalization of the IMRP domain, we will define how several individual travel services can be combined in a single intermodal route. Therefore, we will first of all combine all individual travel services in a joint map in order to ease the reasoning process over several services.

**Definition 6.2.6 (Intermodal Map).**

*A* **intermodal map** *is a set of graphs $(G_1, \ldots, G_n)$ with*

- $L_{G_i} \cap L_{G_j} = \emptyset \quad \forall i, j \in \{1, \ldots, n\} : i \neq j$, *and*
- $V_{G_i} \cap V_{G_j} = \emptyset \quad \forall i, j \in \{1, \ldots, n\} : i \neq j$

*Furthermore let $MAPS$ denote the set of all intermodal maps and let $Map : \bigcup_{G \in \{G_1, \ldots G_n\}} V_{G_i} \rightarrow UMAPS$ be a function that maps a node to the map that contains that node.*

Now, we can express an intermodal route in terms of this underlying data structure.

### Definition 6.2.7 (Intermodal Route).

Let $U = (M, R, G)$ be a named weighted unimodal route in $M$ and define further

- $first(U) = first(M, R, G) = first(M, (v_1, \ldots, v_n), G) = v_1$ and
- $last(U) = last(M, R, G) = last(M, (v_1, \ldots, v_n), G) = v_n$ and
- $V(U) = R$ and
- $M(U) = M$.

A sequence of unimodal routes $MMR = (U_1, \ldots, U_n)$ is called **intermodal route** between $v_1$ and $v_2$ iff

- $v_1 = first(U_1)$
- $(last(U_i), first(U_{i+1})) \in J(M(U_i), M(U_{i+1})) \forall i \in \{1, \ldots, n-1\}$
- $v_2 = last(U_n)$

Let $R(MAPS)$ be the set of all intermodal routes and $\Gamma : R(MAPS) \to \mathbb{R}$ be defined as

$$\Gamma(MMR) = \begin{cases} MAXWEIGHT & if \quad MMR = () \\ \sum_i weight(U_i) & otherwise \end{cases}$$

The **normal form** $\downarrow: R(MAPS) \to R(MAPS)$ of an intermodal route $MMR = ((M, R, G)_1, \ldots (M, R, G)_n)$ is defined as

$$MMR \downarrow = ((M, R, G)_{i_0}, \ldots (M, R, G)_{i_m}))$$

with

- $i_0 < i_1 < \cdots < i_m$
- $G_{i_j} \neq \emptyset \forall j$

In the above definition we require for any intermodal route that junction points exist between any two successive unimodal routes that are combined in the intermodal route. We also define a normal form on intermodal routes in order to able to compare two intermodal routes and to rule out such routes that contain empty unimodal routes.

In the last step of the formalization, we will define how to express a request for an intermodal route in terms of the unimodal maps involved.

### Definition 6.2.8 (Routing Scenario).

A sequence $(M_1, \ldots, M_n)$ of maps is called a **routing scenario** in the set of unimodal maps (UMAPS) if the following conditions hold:

- $v_s \in M_{i1} \land v_d \in M_{in_i}$ for $i = 1, \ldots m$ and
- $\exists v_3, v_4 : (v_3, v_4) \in J(M_{ij}, M_{ij+1}) \ \forall i, j : i \in \{1, \ldots, m\}, j \in \{1, \ldots n_i - 1\}$

*Let RS(UMAPS) denote the set of all possible routing scenarios.*

*The function* $RS$ : $V \times V \rightarrow RS(UMAPS)$ *returns for any two nodes* $v_s$ *and* $v_d$ *a list of possible routing scenarios* $((M_{11}, \ldots, M_{1n_1}), \ldots, (M_{m1}, \ldots, M_{mn_m}))$.

*Furthermore we define filter* : $RS(UMAPS) \rightarrow RS(UMAPS)$ *as follows*

$$filter((M_1, \ldots, M_n)) = \begin{cases} (M_1, \ldots, M_n) & valid(M_i) \quad \forall i \in \{1, \ldots, n\} \\ \emptyset & otherwise \end{cases}$$

*filter is extended on a sequence of routing scenarios by defining filter* : $RS(UMAPS)^n \rightarrow RS(UMAPS)^m$ *as*

$$filter(RS_1, \ldots, RS_n) = (filter(RS_1), \ldots, filter(RS_n))$$

The *RS* function serves as interface to some higher level service that provides all possible routing scenarios between any two nodes of any unimodal travel services and the *filter* function operates as interface to the user preferences just like the *valid* predicate defined above.

The major nonfunctional requirement for the target system is that its architecture and the services provided must be FIPA compliant. Furthermore, the answering time of the target system should lie within a range that allows the user the on-line planning of a trip, thus the answering time will typically range within a few minutes.

Another nonfunctional requirement is to evaluate two different architectural approaches for solving the problem at hand. The first solution should be a central planning approach that features one intermodal route planner that uses the services provided by the unimodal planners. The other solution should apply a distributed scheme where each unimodal planner can become an intermodal planner upon a user request.

In this view, we have formalized the IMRP domain in terms of functional abstractions that can be used by the subsequent views to develop a particular design for the application. We have also defined the nonfunctional requirements of the target system and developed the basic problem solving capabilities that are necessary in the PTA domain. In the next section, we turn to the environment in which the application will be located.

### 6.2.3 Role View

In the IMRP application, we can identify two functional roles. The *Unimodal Route Planner* is responsible for providing access to a particular travel resource and provides a planning service for this resource as defined below.

---

**Algorithm 3** $imrp(v_s, v_d)$

---

1: **for all** $v_1 \in Alias(v_s)$ **do**
2:    **for all** $v_2 \in Alias(v_d)$ **do**
3:        $result := result \cup imrp\_na(v_1, v_2)$
4:    **end for**
5: **end for**
6: **return** $result$

---

### Definition 6.2.9 (Unimodal Route Planer).

*A function* $rp : V_M \times V_M \rightarrow R(M)$ *for a map* $M$ *that returns a weighted route for any two nodes* $v_1, v_2 \in M$, *i.e.* $rp(v_1, v_2) = ((v_1, \ldots, v_2), G)$, *is called a* **(unimodal) route planer** *for* $M$

*Furthermore, the following conditions must hold:*

- $(v_1, \ldots, v_2)$ *is a route from* $v_1$ *to* $v_2$ *and*
- $G$ *is minimal.*

The only atomic problem solving capabilities that is required for this role is the ability to perform unimodal route planning by either planning from first principles or by using an existing service and providing the result to the other agents in the system.

The second roles that occurs in the scenario is the *Intermodal Route Planner* that combines the services of various unimodal route planners in a single plan.

### Definition 6.2.10 (Intermodal Route Planer).

*A function* $imrp : V_M \times V_M \rightarrow R(MAPS)$ *for a given set of maps is a* **intermodal route planer** *iff* $imrp$ *returns a list of unimodal maps* $((M, R, G)_1, \ldots, (M, R, G)_n)$ *for any two nodes* $v_1$ *and* $v_2$, *i.e.* $imrp(v_1, v_2) = ((M, R, G)_1, \ldots, (M, R, G)_n)$.

The process of combining the services of the unimodal route planners into a single plan works as follows: On the first level of the planning process all possible routes between all alias-nodes for the source node and alias-nodes of the destination node are computed according to the following specification.

$$imrp(v_s, v_d) = \bigcup_{v_1 \in Alias(v_s) \times v_2 \in Alias(v_d)} imrp\_na(v_1, v_2)$$

The implementation is shown in Algorithm 3.

Alias nodes exist iff the source or the destination node are junction points with another map. In this case, all routes between all combinations of alias nodes must be computed.

On the second level of the planning process, all routes for all routing scenarios between two alias nodes are computed according to the following formula that is implemented by Algorithm 4.

---

**Algorithm 4** $imrp\_na(v_s, v_d)$

---
1: **for all** $rs \in RS(v_s, v_d)$ **do**
2:    route := $imrp\_sc(v_s, v_d, rs)$
3:    **if** $route \notin result$ **then**
4:       $result := result \cup \{route\}$
5:    **end if**
6: **end for**
7: **return** $result$

---

$$imrp\_na(v_s, v_d) = \bigcup_{rs \in RS(v_s, v_d)} imrp\_sc(v_s, v_d, rs)$$

The final design of the PTA/IMRP application uses two versions of role aggregation in order to evaluate the advantages and disadvantages of one approach or the other.

Broker In this version of the IMRP application, the functional roles are assigned to different agents, i.e. there is one IMRP agent in the scenario that processes the user request and then tries to find UMRP agents that provide services that match the users requirements.

Distributed The distributed version of the application does not assign a fixed functional role to an agent, each agent can play both functional roles depending on the context in which it is incorporated into the joint planning process. If the agent is queried by the user, it acts as the IMRP the tries to integrate services provide by other agents with it own local service in order to generate a route plan. If, on the other hand, it is queried by another agent acting as IMRP, it offers its local service as normal UMRP.

### 6.2.4 Interaction View

The agent interaction that is necessary within the IMRP domain is limited to a rather simple requester-provider protocol. One agent will request a particular service from another agent which will serve the request and return the result to the requester. The application does not feature any market mechanisms or iterative refinements in the agent interaction process and is therefore straightforward to implement.

I have mentioned earlier that the IMRP application uses two different approaches to compute an intermodal route for a given routing scenario. In the following, I will describe how the planning process works for each of these different approaches. The control flow of the broker version is shown in Figure 6.7: the user request the a route planning service from the IMRP agent that in turn forwards partial requests to the UMRP agents and assembles the results according to the user preferences. The computation uses a recursive algorithm based on the following idea:

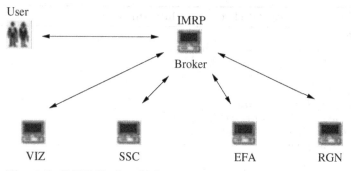

**Fig. 6.7.** IMRP Broker Architecture

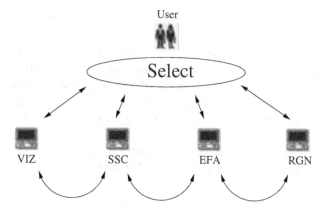

**Fig. 6.8.** Distributed IMRP Architecture

- If the source and the destination node are in the same map or if the routing scenario consist of a single entry, the route can be computed by an individual route planner agent. Note that a routing scenario can be of length 1 only if the destination node is a junction point to the map of the source node.
- If the source and the destination node are in distinct maps, the optimal route (wrt. to a given optimization criterion) is the minimum of all routes between the source node and the intermodal route starting at any possible junction point to the next map.

The formal description of the algorithm is given below. The implementation is shown in Algorithm 5.

$$
imrp\_sc(v_s, v_d, rs) = \begin{cases} rp_{Map(v_s)}(J_{M_{v_s} M_{v_d}}(v_s), v_d) & \begin{array}{c} Map(v_s) = Map(v_d) \\ or \quad |rs| = 1 \end{array} \\[2em] \min_{\substack{(j_1, j_2) \in \\ J(M_1, M_2)}} \begin{array}{l} append(rp_{M_1}(v_s, j_1), \\ imrp\_sc(j_2, v_d, tail(rs))) \end{array} & otherwise \end{cases}
$$

---

**Algorithm 5** $imrp\_sc(v_s, v_d, rs)$ (Broker Architecture)

---

**Require:** $rs \in RS(v_s, v_z)$
1: **if** $Map(v_s) == Map(v_d)||(|rs| == 1)$ **then**
2:     $minroute := rp_{Map(v_s)}(J_{M_{v_s} M_{v_d}}(v_s), v_d)$
3: **else**
4:     $minroute := \emptyset$
5:     **for all** $(j_1, j_2) \in J(M_1, M_2)$ **do**
6:         $route := rp_{M_1}(v_s, j_1) + imrp\_sc(j_2, v_d, tail(rs))$
7:         **if** $\Gamma(route) < \Gamma(minroute)$ **then**
8:             $minroute := route$
9:         **end if**
10:     **end for**
11: **end if**
12: **return** $minroute$

---

In the distributed version of the application, the control flow in the application is as shown in Figure 6.8: The user selects the most appropriate UMRP agent (e.g. the service wrapper for the first service that the user intends to travel with) and places a request. The UMRP will then play the role of the IMRP in subsequent service requests to other UMRP agents and return the result to the user.

The algorithm that implements this flow of control is specified by the following equation. The implementation is shown in Algorithm 6.

$$
imrp\_sc(v_s, v_d, rs) = \begin{cases} rp(v_s, v_d) & Map(v_s) = Map(v_d) \\ \min_{\substack{(j_1, j_2) \in \\ J(M_1, M_2)}} \begin{array}{l} append(rp(v_s, j_1), \\ RP_{M_2}(j_2, v_d, tail(rs))) \end{array} & otherwise \end{cases}
$$

---

**Algorithm 6** $imrp\_sc(v_s, v_d, rs)$ (Distributed Architecture)

---

1: **if** $Map(v_s) == Map(v_d)||(|rs| == 1)$ **then**
2:     $minroute := rp_{Map(v_s)}(J_{M_{v_s} M_{v_d}}(v_s), v_d)$
3: **else**
4:     $minroute := \emptyset$
5:     **for all** $(j_1, j_2) \in J(M_1, M_2)$ **do**
6:         $route := rp_{M_1}(v_s, j_1) + RP_{M_2}(j_2, v_z, tail(RS))$
7:         **if** $\Gamma(route) < \Gamma(minroute)$ **then**
8:             $minroute := route$
9:         **end if**
10:     **end for**
11: **end if**
12: **return** $minroute$

---

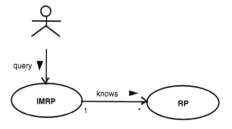

**Fig. 6.9.** Basic Society Structure

## 6.2.5 Society View

The society that operates in the IMRP domain is rather simple and consists of two or three different entities, depending on which of the alternatives (broker or distributed version) is considered. In either case, however, the structure of the society is initially flat as shown in Figure 6.9. The user connects to the IMRP agent which in turn calculates an intermodal route for the user request by connecting the individual travel services and then returns the intermodal travel plan to the user.

This simple form of the society structure is adequate as long as the number of individual travel services is relatively small. However, in a scenario with a large amount of individual travel service, e.g. when each UMRP represents some local public transport facility, this society structure may no longer be adequate. The IMRP agent cannot compute an intermodal travel plan in a one-shot process but it must connect some intermediate IMRP agents that interface to the local travel services. The respective society structure as shown in Figure 6.10 results in a control flow that operates at several hierarchy levels. First of all, the user queries the local IMRP agent that is responsible for the area the user is currently located. Next, this IMRP agent forwards part of the user request to other local IMRP agents that compute a partial intermodal route for their area and return the solution to the first IMRP agent that assembles a full intermodal route for the user request and returns the solution to the user.

In this section, we have modeled the society structure of the IMRP application and outlined some extension to the structure as it will be implemented in a the first version of the system. In the next section, we will see how the various features are transformed into a coherent system architecture.

## 6.2.6 Architecture View

**System Architecture.** In this section, I will characterize the required system architecture according to the scheme given in Section 5.7.

**Entities** The only entities that occur in the target system are agents for unimodal route planning and intermodal route planning, respectively.

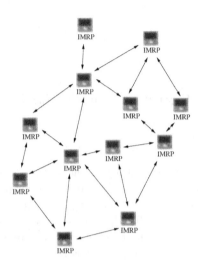

**Fig. 6.10.** Hierarchical IMRP Organization

**Control flow** Because of the fact that the only entities are agents, the control flow within the system is determined by the Interaction view. The same applies for the information flow.

**Agent management** Since the problem domain was chosen as an evaluation domain for FIPA standards, the agent management will be handled according to the requirements specified there.

**Communication model** The system architecture should allow for a geographical distribution of the system components and therefore provide some network based message passing mechanisms. In order to be able to debug the application locally, it is desirable to have local message passing that can be traced within a single debugger.

**Agent architecture** The agent architecture will be discussed in the next section.

**Database design** Since the individual agents within the system do not share data explicitly, it is not necessary to provide a system wide database.

**External components/devices** The external components that must be integrated in the target system are the existing travel services that are run by external providers. These services must be encapsulated in agents in order to achieve the required degree of inter-operability.

Thus, the overall system architecture is determined by the concepts specified in the FIPA standard that is used as the general basis of the application. According to the above requirements, the MECCA agent application framework [Steiner, 1992], [Gerber et al., 1999b] was chosen as the implementation basis for the actual system because MECCA is a FIPA compliant framework that provides libraries of pre-defined agents according to the FIPA standard and includes a generic agent architecture as well as a protocol specification language for the agents.

The target system is implemented in a fully parallel system environment where all agents are running on different host computers. However, the difficult task of debugging a fully distributed system is eased as the MECCA framework offers a transparent scheme for running the agents locally without any changes to the code.

**Agent Architecture.** According to the characterization given in Section 5.7, the agent requirements are as follows.

**Reasoning capabilities** According to their actual role, the agents need some planning facility that enables them to find an unimodal or an intermodal route using the given travel service.

Resources limitations The resource requirements of the agents is low because the planning process mentioned above is not highly complex. However, due to the necessary encapsulation of external services, the agents will be equipped with the computational resources of a complete workstation.

**Control flow** The control flow within the agent is determined by the algorithms described in Section 6.2.4 and is basically a sequential one. It is therefore not necessary for the agent architecture to provide a parallel execution model.

**Knowledge Representation** The major knowledge structures used by the agents are the unimodal and intermodal plans. These plans must be explicitly represented in a knowledge base as they are likely to change in the course of the route planning process and because they must be transfered to a human-readable form.

**Autonomy** The agents in this limited part of the full scenario do not exhibit any pro-active behavior as the only react to a user request or to a request from another agent to provide some well-defined service. In the full scenario, however, the agent are supposed to become active whenever the external state as observed by the agent contains some information that may be useful for their user. Still, this is not subject of this part of the system.

**User interaction** The degree of user interaction is not very high for this part of the system and is limited to the route specification in form of start and destination nodes, travel times, preferred travel modalities and probably a few other things. Therefore, the agents user interface will not need any particular attention.

**Temporal context** The lifetime of an agent in the target system can be quite long as the unimodal route planners are supposed to encapsulate real-world services that are available 24 hours a day. However, the

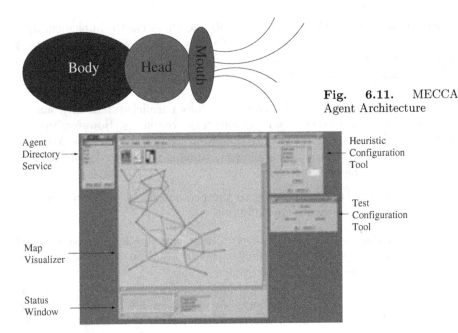

**Fig.    6.11.**    MECCA
Agent Architecture

**Fig. 6.12.** IMRP Graphical User Interface

agents do not need any persistence mechanisms because these are already present in the underlying services.

Because of the above requirements, the MECCA agent architecture was the first choice as agent architecture. MECCA agents are specifically designed to serve as wrapper for proprietary software systems that are to be used in a multiagent systems and are thus well-suited for the encapsulating of the individual travel services. A MECCA agent consists of three parts as shown in Figure 6.11.

The agent *body* encapsulates application specific functionalities e.g. existing SW systems, databases etc., the *head*: contains the goals and plans of the agent and controls the body via the application interface. Furthermore, it also contains the protocol execution unit that can manage several contexts at the same time. The *communicator*, finally, is the physical communication interface that implements low-level communication protocols such as TCP/IP, GSM or IIOP.

### 6.2.7 System View

**Graphical User Interface.** The User interface of the IMRP system as shown in Figure 6.12 consists of five major elements that are briefly described below.

**Map Visualizer** The Map visualizer window contains the graphical representation of the unimodal maps that are managed by the unimodal route planners. The user selects the start and the destination node of the journey and is then queried for the temporal constraints. The system will then calculate an intermodal route according to the provides specification.

**Test Configuration Tool** In order to evaluate the different approaches presented earlier, the user can select between the broker and the distributed variant and between the optimal computation of the intermodal route and the use of a heuristic as is described in Section 6.2.7.

**Heuristic Configuration Tool** This window allows the user to select the heuristic and the parameters of the heuristic. The heuristics that can be used as well as their parameter settings are described in Section 6.2.7.

**Status Window** The Status window informs the user about the result of the computation (e.g. the length or the duration of the intermodal route) and about exceptional situations such as constraint inconsistencies that occur e.g. when the time window is to tight for particular start and destination nodes.

**Agent Directory Service** This window, finally, is provided by the FIPA compliant MECCA agent platform and contains the names of the agents currently known to the system. The user can click on the agent name to obtain additional information about the respective agent.

Since the intermodal route planning facility is only a service that is provided in a larger context, the user interface is only very fragmentary. It is, however, functional enough to enable the user to experiment with the different variants of the system. Experiments that were conducted with early versions of the system showed, that the system performance might become unacceptable if the number of unimodal maps and the size of these maps increases beyond a particular point. Therefore, several attempts were made to obtain rather good – though not optimal – solutions with a reduced effort. The results of these attempts are discussed in the following section.

**Performance Engineering.**

*Suboptimal Solutions.* Until now, the IMRP agent has computed optimal routes for each user request which implied the exploration of the entire search space. In this section, we present some search heuristics that aim at finding sufficiently good solutions with less computational effort. The main idea of the search heuristics discussed below is a flexible steering of the search process by narrowing the set of junction points between two adjacent maps in a routing scenario.

Therefore, we define a selection function for the junction points that should be expanded during the search process as follows.

## Definition 6.2.11 (Selection Function).

*Define select* : $(V, V)^n \rightarrow (V, V)^m, n \leq m$ *as* $select(\{v_i, v_j | (v_i, v_j) \in J(M_k, M_{k+1})\}) = \{v_o, v_p | (v_o, v_p) \in J(M_k, M_{k+1})\}$ *i.e. select chooses an arbitrary subset of the junction points for any two maps.*

Now, by using the *select* function from definition 6.2.11, we extend the search algorithm such that it expands only the selected nodes. In the following, this extension is implemented using the broker architecture discussed earlier, the changes apply in an analogous way to the distributed architecture. The modified broker algorithm is given below, the implementation is shown in Algorithm 7.

$$
imrp\_sc(v_s, v_z, rs) = \begin{cases} rp_{Map(v_s)}(J_{M_{v_s} M_{v_z}}(v_s), v_z) & \begin{aligned} Map(v_s) &= Map(v_z) \\ or \quad |rs| &= 1 \end{aligned} \\[2em] \min_{\substack{(j_1, j_2) \in \\ select(J(M_1, M_2))}} \begin{aligned} &append(rp_{M_1}(v_s, j_1), \\ &imrp\_sc(j_2, v_z, tail(rs))) \end{aligned} & otherwise \end{cases}
$$

---

**Algorithm 7** $imrp\_sc(v_s, v_z, rs)$ with selection function (Broker Architecture)

---

**Require:** $rs \in RS(v_s, v_z)$
1: **if** $Map(v_s) == Map(v_d) || (|rs| == 1)$ **then**
2:  $\quad minroute := rp_{Map(v_s)}(J_{M_{v_s} M_{v_d}}(v_s), v_d)$
3: **else**
4:  $\quad minroute := \emptyset$
5:  $\quad$ **for all** $(j_1, j_2) \in select(J(M_1, M_2))$ **do**
6:  $\quad\quad route := rp_{M_1}(v_s, j_1) + imrp\_sc(j_2, v_d, tail(rs))$
7:  $\quad\quad$ **if** $weight(route) < weight(minroute)$ **then**
8:  $\quad\quad\quad minroute := route$
9:  $\quad\quad$ **end if**
10: $\quad$ **end for**
11: **end if**
12: **return** $minroute$

---

As we have seen, the integration of the selection function is quite straightforward but it is yet unspecified how a particular selection might work to produce satisfactory results. Therefore, we first of all define a *generic selection function* and then instantiate this generic function to obtain specific selection functions.

The generic *select* function operates in three steps:

1. Generate a partial ordering on the set of possible junction points.
2. Sort the junction points according to the partial ordering.
3. Select the best candidates.

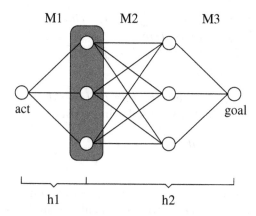

M1          M2          M3

act                              goal

h1                    h2

**Fig. 6.13.** Generic Selection Function

Figure 6.13 illustrates the process. In the first step, we assign a weight to each junction point $x$ with respect to the current search node $act$ and the destination node $gaol$ according to

$$g(x) = h_1(act, x) + h_2(x, goal)$$

where $h_1$ estimates the weight of the route from the current node to the junction point and $h_2$ estimates the weight of the route between the junction point and the goal. Now we can sort the list according to the combined weights and select the best nodes according to a given evaluation depth.

In the following description, we discuss some instantiations of the generic *select* function by specifying the two estimation functions $h_1$ and $h_2$ and the evaluation depth of the final selection step.

Optimal Selection This instantiation realizes the standard case without narrowing the search space. All possible junction points are selected which guarantees, that the optimal solution is found. This instantiation is mainly included for the sake of completeness.

$$h_1(act, x) = weight(rp(act, x))$$
$$h_2(x, goal) = weight(rp(x, goal))$$

Obviously, all junction points must be selected in order to guarantee optimality in the search process.

Greedy Search This variant of the *select* function considers only the locally best alternatives. Therefore, we first define the following concepts.

**Definition 6.2.12 (k-best Search).** k-best search *expands only the first k junction points that have the shortest distance to the source node of the route.*

**Definition 6.2.13 (k-best Junction Points).** *topJPs* : $UMAPS \times UMAPS \times V \times \mathbb{N} \rightarrow (V, V)^n$ *is defined as*

$$topJps(M_1, M_2, v, k) = ((j_{11}, j_{12}), \ldots, (j_{k1}, j_{k2})) \ with$$
$$(\forall i \in \{1, \ldots, k\} : (j_{i1}, j_{i2} \in J(M_1, M_2) \wedge$$
$$(\exists l \in L_M, i \in \{1, \ldots, k\} : \alpha(l) = v \wedge \in \omega(l) = j_{i1}) \wedge$$
$$(\forall j \notin j_{il} \forall i \in \{1, \ldots, k\} : \gamma(v, j) > \gamma(v, j_{i1})))$$

We obtain a greedy algorithm by setting $select(J(M_1, M_2)) = topJPs(M_1, M_2, v_s, 1)$. This corresponds to the following setting

$$h_1(act, x) = weight(rp(act, x))$$
$$h_2(x, goal) = 0$$

In the second step of the selection process, only the first junction point in the ordered set is expanded, an obvious extension of the algorithm is to select not only the best junction point, but the $k$ best junction points by setting $select(J(M_1, M_2)) = topJPs(M_1, M_2, v_s, k)$ for some fixed value of $k$.

Euclidean Distance Measure The Euclidean distance between two points $p = (x_1, y_1)$ and $q = (x_2, y_2)$ is defined as

$$d(p, q) = d((x_1, y_1), (x_2, y_2)) = \sqrt{(x_1 - x_2)^2 + (y_1 - y_2)^2} \qquad (6.5)$$

From this definition, we can derive three different heuristics:

$$h_1(act, x) = weight(rp(act, x))$$
$$h_2(x, goal) = d(x, goal)$$

$$h_1(act, x) = d(act, x)$$
$$h_2(x, goal) = weight(rp(x, goal))$$

$$h_1(act, x) = d(act, x)$$
$$h_2(x, goal) = d(x, goal)$$

The $k$ best junction points are selected from the ordered set of junction points according to the given evaluation depth.

Precedence Ordering on Maps This heuristic uses a partial ordering defined on the set of unimodal maps. We define a weight function $w : UMAPS \rightarrow \mathbb{R}$ that assigns a weight to each unimodal map. We set

$$h_1(act, x) = weight(rp(act, x)) * w(Map(act))$$
$$h_2(x, goal) = weight(rp(x, goal)) * w(Map(x))$$

to obtain the map precedence heuristic.

Figure 6.14 shows an example with two maps indicated by the solid and the dashed line, respectively. The solid line map represents the public

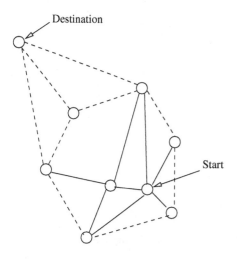

**Fig. 6.14.** Example 1

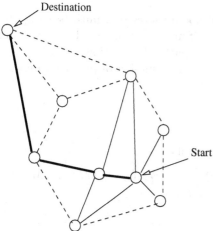

**Fig. 6.15.** Example 2

transport service of a city, whereas the dashed map represents the inter-regional individual traffic.

Using this heuristic, a route query from "source" to "destination" will yield a solution as it is shown in Figure 6.15. This solution reflects the shortest path from the source to the destination node, but it neglects the fact that the public transport is usually much more time consuming then individual traffic. Generally speaking, it is often more efficient to leave the city as fast as possible and to use high speed individual traffic routes around the city.

Using a precedence ordering on maps (and implicitly on means of transport), the higher preference for individual transport towards public transport yields the result presented in Figure 6.16.

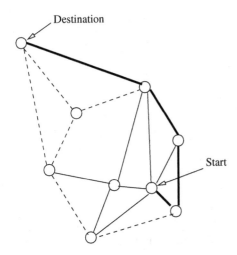

**Fig. 6.16.** Example 3

*Caching.* The maximum number of unimodal routes that must be computed for an intermodal route $(U_1, \ldots, U_n)$ is a function of the number of junction points between the unimodal maps for a particular routing scenario. For a given routing scenario $rs = (M_1, \ldots, M_m)$, the number of possible unimodal routes ($\#_{rs}$) computes as follows:

$$\#_{rs}(v_s, v_z, ()) = 0$$
$$\#_{rs}(v_s, v_z, (M)) = 1$$
$$\#_{rs}(v_s, v_z, (M_1, \ldots, M_m)) = |J(M_1, M_2)| +$$
$$\sum_{(j_1, j_2) \in J(M_1, M_2)} \#_{rs}(j_2, v_z, (M_2, \ldots, M_m))$$

$$(6.6)$$

The recursive formula (6.6) is not optimal for practical purposes and therefore we also give the number of possible unimodal routes in a non-recursive form. Note that we define $|J(M_m, M_{m+1})| = |J(M_{m+1}, M_{m+2})| = 1$ in Formula 6.7.

$$\#_{rs}(v_s, v_z, rs) = \sum_{i=1}^{m+1} \prod_{j=1}^{j \leq i} |J(M_j, M_{j+1})| \qquad (6.7)$$

Comparing this to the number of *unique* unimodal routes which computes to

$$\#_{unique}(v_s, v_z, rs) = \sum_{i=1}^{m-1} |J(M_i, M_{i+1})| * |J(M_{i+1}, M_{i+2})| \qquad (6.8)$$

reveals a high potential for performance gains if the re-computation of unimodal routes can be avoided. For example, given three maps with 10 junctions points between each of them, we obtain a total of 111110 unimodal routes that must be combined according to equation 6.7 out of which only 300 are unique according to equation 6.8. To take profit from this discrepancy, we define a generic cache as follows.

**Definition 6.2.14 (Generic Cache).** *A* **cache** *is a data structure that stores* $(key, value)$ *pairs where* $key \in KEY$ *and value* $\in VALUE$. *We define functions* $store, retrieve$ *and* $flush$ *that operate on these* $(key, value)$ *pairs.*
$$store : KEY \times VALUE \to \{success, failure\}$$

$$store(k, v) = success, C' = (C \setminus \{(k, v') | v' \neq v\}) \cup \{(k, v)\} \tag{6.9}$$

$$retrieve : KEY \to VALUE$$

$$retrieve(k) = \begin{cases} v & falls(k, v) \in C \\ \emptyset & sonst \end{cases} \tag{6.10}$$

$$flush :\to \{success, failure\}$$

$$flush() = success, C' = \emptyset \tag{6.11}$$

Now, whenever the IMRP needs a particular unimodal route, it first checks the cache whether it already contains the route or not. In the first case, the route is used directly whereas in the second case, the IMRP agent issues a request to the UMRP in charge and then stores the result in the cache for potential reuse.

## 6.3 Summ r

In this chapter, we have seen two additional case studies to demonstrated the usefulness of the MASSIVE method in real world applications. The TEAM WORK LIBRARY is a collection of software components that support the development of multiagent applications according to the teamwork distributed search paradigm. The MASSIVE method turned out to be adequate for such a general setting that as well as for more specific domains such as trip planning. The multiagent solution for the intermodal route planning service within the PTA domain has shown how industrial standards such as FIPA can be easily integrated into the design of a multiagent system.

# 7. Conclusion

The basic properties of an ideal software development method for multiagent systems were defined in the introduction: the method should be *flexible, open, simple, scalable, support learning and reuse, have little institutional overhead* and *relate to established software engineering concepts*.

In order to accomplish these goals, I have presented a development method that is built according to these fundamental requirements. The MASSIVE method consists of three major parts: the core of the MASSIVE method is a system of views that form the conceptual basis for a wide range of product models that are developed and refined throughout software projects that are carried out according to the suggested process model. The main idea of the process model is an Iterative View Engineering approach that is itself based on Iterative Enhancement and Round-trip Engineering. The overall process model contains several small micro models that are used for individual tasks within the design process for a particular view. These micro models as well as the overall process model are not fixed for the entire lifetime of the project model, but they are subject to changes and refinements during the course of time. In order to preserve these adaptations and to make them accessible to others, the process model and the product model are both embedded into a larger organizational structure called the Experience Factory. The Experience Factory provides the formal framework for a permanent learning process that takes place over project boundaries and that eventually models the multiagent experience of organization in terms of specific product and process models for various domains.

The MASSIVE method implements the above stated requirements as follows: it is *flexible* because it allows the designer to use and adapt products and processes at various levels of abstraction. The macro development process consists of several micro processes for individual parts of the product model and this macro process as well as the micro processes can be adapted to the needs of a particular project. The product model that has been introduced provides a generic base structure for a wide range of multiagent systems and can also be adapted according to project specific requirements.

The MASSIVE method is *open* in that it does not rely on a particular technology such as a programming language or a specific computational model. It has been demonstrated in the case studies that the method works with

J. Lind: The MASSIVE Method, LNAI 1994, pp. 243-246, 2001.

such different programming languages as Oz, Java or C++. Furthermore, it works for fully distributed applications as well as for threaded applications in a single process.

The method is sufficiently *simple* in that it is straightforward to apply and does not require intensive user training. A lot of the concepts used in the MASSIVE method are common sense and easily understood by a developer. The product model is detailed enough to enable the developer to structure the target system without getting lost in fine grained details that are irrelevant in a particular context.

The MASSIVE method is *scalable* as it can be used by a single developer playing all roles as well as by a larger development team where the roles are assigned to actual persons.

*Learning and reuse* over project boundaries are supported by the concept of the Experience factory that is used to structure and package all sorts of experiences that are made during the course of a project. The resulting knowledge packages are selected for reuse in subsequent projects according to a case-based reasoning mechanism that provides the knowledge structures that are most suitable in a particular situation.

The MASSIVE method has only *little institutional overhead* because it can be introduced into a particular organization in parallel to the ongoing business processes. The Experience factory can be set up over a certain period of time without interfering with the current projects and it can be smoothly integrated step-by-step into the project execution process. The impact on the project organization are minimized as the team members are not forced to contribute to the experience acquisition process because a separate organizational unit is responsible for the analysis and evaluation of a project.

Finally, the method presented in this book is *built upon standard software engineering* techniques and principles that have been developed over many years and demonstrated their validity in practical situations. The macro process of the MASSIVE method combines Iterative Refinement and Round-trip Engineering and puts them in the larger context of the Experience Factory. The suggested view-oriented product model is based on the ideas of aspect-oriented programming and allows the developer to model the system as a whole and viewing it from different angles.

The next step in the advancement of the MASSIVE method is to set up some tool support for the activities that are performed in the course of a project. Interestingly, one of the most recent topics in the design research community is to use multiagent technology to support the design process [Lander, 1997] [Petrie et al., 1998]. Hence, the next step in the development of the MASSIVE method is to use the development method to built a multiagent system that supports the method itself!

But first of all, why are multiagent systems of particular interest to the design research community? According to [Lander, 1997], *multiagent design systems (MADS)* provide the conceptual framework to model systems of flex-

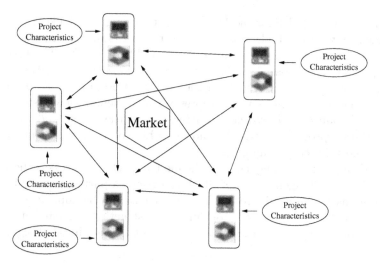

**Fig. 7.1.** MADS View System Selection Process

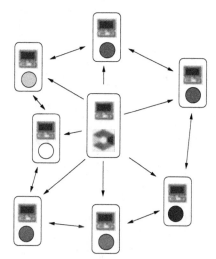

**Fig. 7.2.** MADS Supported View Construction

ible, sophisticated expert agents that collaborate in order to support a human project team in the course of the design process. The individual agents within the system can be personal assistant agents (wizards) that provide the necessary support for humans in the distributed design process.

The well-defined agent boundaries provide separable interfaces to the design process and support the locality of information because the internal specifications of a design element are not communicated over agent boundaries. Thus, each agent represents a particular design element or a design process and is responsible for keeping the other agents up to date about changes that are relevant to them while at the same time hiding changes that have only local effects.

To illustrate how a MADS for the MASSIVE method might look like, I will briefly outline how the model selection process at the beginning of the project and the model construction process can be supported by a MADS. The first step in any project that is based to the MASSIVE development method is to find the most appropriate view system for the project. In Figure 7.1, we have several agents and each of those agents represents a particular view system. Now the user announces the project characteristics to the agents and they begin a negotiation process in order to find out which of them represents a model that is most suited for the project.

In a second step, the winning agent of the model selection process is then split up into several sub-agents each of which represents a particular view in the view system as shown in Figure 7.2. The sub-agents can be implemented as assistance agents that support the user in the construction of a particular view and that informs other sub-agents about relevant changes in the design.

# A. Toolkits for Agent-    sed A    lic  tions

In this chapter, I will review three tool-kits for the development of multia-gent applications. These packages usually offer predefined structures or even tools that can be used by the application developer to build his or her own system using the provided structures that are common to most multiagent applications. All tool-kits discussed in this section are freely available and result from research work in the area, commercial frameworks have not been considered for this section.

## A.1 S F

The Social Interaction Framework (SIF) [Lind, 1998], [Funk et al., 1998], [Schillo et al., 1999] is an open, easy-to-use testbed for multiagent applica-tions. It is intended as a simulation tool for interaction-intensive societies and is – as opposed to most other testbeds – not limited to communication but supports various forms of interaction.

SIF provides an open simulation environment that allows the integra-tion of agents with different architectures in distributed environments. The fine-grained action and perception modeling allow for the design of complex virtual worlds without any predefined semantics on percepts ("The world does not come labeled" [Edelman, 1987]). Furthermore, SIF supports rapid prototyping by providing off-the-shelf components for the simulation of a wide range of interaction environments and also provides flexible human user interaction through the use of avatars. SIF can be used on a number of dif-ferent platforms because of using standard technology whenever possible e.g. Java [Sun Microsystems, 1999], VRML97 [The VRML Consortium, 1997] or CORBA [Object Management Group, 1999].

The interaction model of SIF is based on the Effector-Medium-Sensor (EMS) Model [Lind, 1998] which is a conceptualization of the broad agent definition given in [Russell and Norvig, 1995] that "An *agent* is anything that can be viewed as *perceiving* its environment through *sensors* and *acting* upon that environment through *effectors*." An example for applying this definition to human speech interaction is shown in Figure A.1.

The speech apparatus of the agent on the left hand side of Figure A.1 is the effector that triggers the medium which in turn delivers some perception

J. Lind: The MASSIVE Method, LNAI 1994, pp. 247-254, 2001.

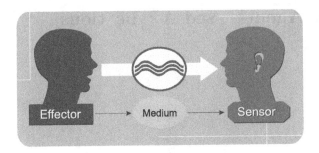

**Fig. A.1.** The EMS Idea

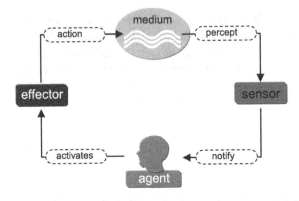

**Fig. A.2.** The EMS Model

to the sensor unit of the agent on the right. Thus, the EMS paradigm captures a very natural model of interaction.

A more technical view onto the EMS model that describes the basic control cycle of an agent is shown in Figure A.2. Whenever several agents are connected to the same medium they can interact with each other by changing the state of the medium. The data-flow within the system is asynchronous due to the independence of the control flow of the agents from the control flow of the medium and the control flow is multi-threaded. Furthermore, the SIF framework implements a subject-oriented point-of-view because the agents locally perceive the world state.

The agents themselves need not have a specific architecture as long as the architecture fulfills a minimal conceptual framework that is shown in Figure A.3. According to the minimal requirements, each agent must have its local thread of execution, the agent must implement a decision function that computes its next action on the basis of the agents current world model and action invocation must be performed asynchronously in order to prevent an agent from blocking the medium and thus the actions of other agents. Note that the action execution is not guaranteed to succeed, i.e. an agent can issue a particular action activation to the medium, however, if the action is not valid in the context that is defined by the medium it will simply be ignored. It is therefore important for the agents to monitor their action execution and

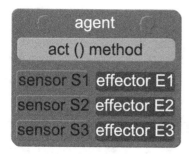

**Fig. A.3.** Conceptual Agent Model of SIF

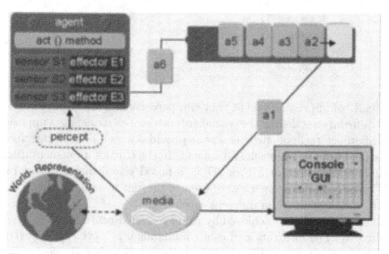

**Fig. A.4.** Information and Control Flow in SIF

not to simply assume that an action will be executed once it is submitted to the medium.

The task of the medium is to model the environment from a static (entities) and dynamic (physics) point-of-view. Thus by designing the medium, the designer defines which entities can be found within a particular world and how the world changes according to action invocations of the agents. The basic control cycle of the medium is shown in Figure A.4.

In each cycle, the medium receives the effector activations of the agents and places them in a queue of pending activations. Then it fetches the first of the pending activation requests and updates the world model according to the effects of the activation. If a particular action is not allowed because of the current state of the world, it is discarded. If, on the other hand, the world state has changed because of a valid action, the medium generates perceptions as the projections of the current world state onto the sensors of each agent.

The visualization of the world state is always modeled from the point-of-view of an agent. However, to enable the user to have a global model of current

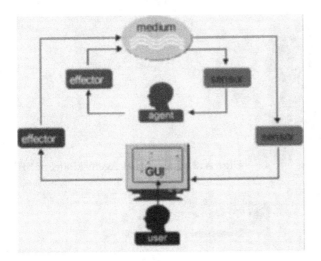

**Fig. A.5.** SIF User Interaction

state, a special "omnipresent" agent that can perceive the full world state is provided. Uniformly modeling the visualization devices as agents supports the use of difference technologies because it provides a well-defined interface between the medium and the visualizing agent. In the current implementation of an example application for SIF, a 2D Java-based visualizing agent and a 3D VRML-based visualizing agent were used to present to same world at the same time to different users on different machines.

In SIF, user interaction is achieved by using so-called *control pads* to steer the agent directly. The integration of user commands is achieved via an extra indirection cycle as shown in Figure A.5: the agent has special effectors to perceive user commands that change its behavior accordingly. The additional indirection de-couples the agent and the user in a way that enables the agent to carry on with its normal operation when no user commands are given and to react to the user inputs whenever this is requested. This scheme provides the necessary flexibility to use the agent as an *avatar* that is autonomous to a certain degree and reliefs the user from having to specify every single behavior activation.

The SIF tool-kit has shown that it is a truly open testbed that can be used to implement applications with SIFAgents, InteRRaP agents or MECCA [Steiner, 1992] agents. The flexible visualization mechanism can be used to generate different views on the same virtual world and the control mechanism that is provided is well-suited for applications with semi-autonomous agents. SIF is platform independent and provides a library of pre-defined off-the-shelf components and algorithms for rapid prototyping and the underlying EMS paradigm allows for the definition of a large variety of different virtual environments. However, developing world models is a work-intensive task because of the fine granularity of the simulations.

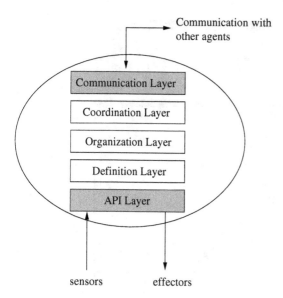

Communication with
other agents

Fig. A.6. ZEUS Agent Architecture

## A.2 ZEUS

The goal of the ZEUS system [Nwana et al., 1999] is to provide a design method and tool support for the engineering of distributed multiagent applications. The provided tools all encompass the direct-manipulation metaphor and allow the designer to use drag-and-drop technology to assemble the application from pre-defined components.

The tool-kit allows the designer to specify models for different types of agents, for the organizational structure of agent societies and for negotiation models. The negotiation models are either pre-defined or the can be build by the designer if no appropriate pre-defined model is available for a particular task.

ZEUS agents all have the same architecture as shown in Figure A.6 that consists of the *definition layer* that implements the reasoning and learning capabilities of the agents, the *organization layer* that manages and maintains the relationships with other agents and the *coordination layer* that is responsible for the inter-agent coordination and that also contains the negotiation knowledge.

Two additional layers are provided that are responsible for the technical framework of the agents. These additional layers are the *communication layer* that provides the communication facilities for the communication with other agents and the *API layer* that serves as the world interface of the agents.

The ZEUS tool-kit is mainly a collection of editors that can be used to develop multiagent applications according to the three models mentioned above. The *Ontology Editor* is used to define the domain ontology, the task within a particular domain are described with the *Task Description Editor*

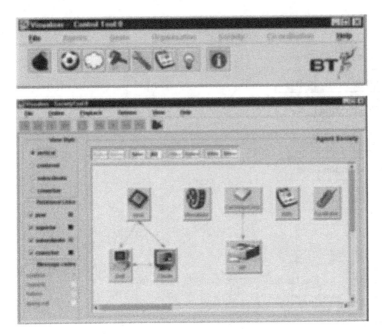

**Fig. A.7.** ZEUS Screen shot

that is supported by the *Summary Task Editor* that is used to define the task compositions of several sub-tasks to a larger task. The *Organization Editor* is used to define the organizational relationships among the agents and their mutual beliefs, the *Agent Definition Editor* is the tool to construct the agents with the architecture described earlier. The *Coordination Editor* is either used to select existing protocols from a protocol library or to define new protocols from scratch. A *Fact/Variable Editor* is provided to describe facts that hold in the problem domain using the ontology defined earlier. Furthermore, a *Constraint Editor* is used to specify the constraints among one or more preconditions of a single tasks, the precondition and effects of different tasks or the effects of a preceding task and the preconditions of a succeeding task in a summary tasks description. The *Code Generation Editor*, finally, is used to specify the code characteristics of the target language.

Besides this extensive collection of editors that allow for the easy definition of various aspects of the target system, the ZEUS tool-kit also provides a large collection of tools for the visualization and debugging of the application. The most important tool is the *visualizer* that is itself implemented as agent. The visualizer requests local information from the other agents and constructs a global view of the system that is presented to the designer or to the user. Additionally, the tool-kit provides a *society tool* that serves as the message monitor for the messages that are exchanged among the agents, a *report tool* that shows the current state of task decomposition and execution, the

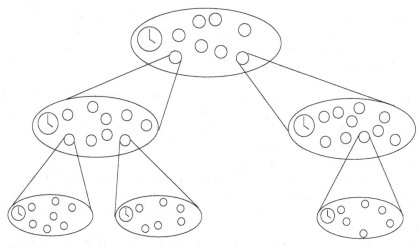

**Fig. A.8.** Swarm Hierarchy

*micro tool* that is used to inspect the internal state of an agent, the *control tool* to remotely modify the internal state of an agent, the *statistics tool* the generates individual and society-wide statistics and, finally, the *video tool* that is used record and replay system runs. A screen shot of the ZEUS system that contains the control tool and the society tool is shown in Figure A.7.

All in all, the freely available ZEUS tool-kit provides a comfortable and flexible framework for the development of multiagent applications. However, ZEUS is limited to task-oriented systems and it restricts the designer to a particular agent architecture that may not be suited for all kinds of applications.

## A.3 Sw rm

Swarm [Hiebeler, 1994], [Minar et al., 1996], [Burkhart, 1997] is a domain-independent simulation toolkit that is based on a discrete event mechanism. The basic units of a Swarm simulation are *agents* that generate *events*, the events that are exchanged among agents is called a *schedule* of events. The structure that is built on top of the basic units consists of a collection of agents and their schedule of events and is referred to as a *swarm*. Swarms represent recursive structures as a swarm can be seen as a single agent within another swarm as shown in Figure A.8. Each of the ellipses represents a swarm that consists of several agents (circles) and a schedule (indicated by the clock symbol). In a swarm, some of the agents are themselves swarms as shown in the figure.

The Swarm toolkit provides several libraries that allow the designer to specify the events that the agents can generate and the (hierarchical) structure of the swarms. The provided libraries are grouped in three classes.

The *simulation library* contains `swarmobject` classes that are used to describe the base objects of the simulations, the `activity` classes that are responsible for the scheduling and execution support and the `simtools` that are used to specify the type of simulations, e.g. interactive or batch mode, etc.

The *software support library* consists of the `defobjs` and `collections` classes that provide general-purpose OO support such as common data-structures etc., the `random` classes that implement the random number support and the `tkobj` classes that hold then Tcl/Tk [Ousterhout, 1994] interface for the visualization of the simulation.

The *model specific library*, finally, embody classes for special purpose applications such as the `space` classes for two-dimensional discrete lattices, the `ga` classes for genetic algorithms or the `neuro` classes for a variety of neural networks.

The major advantage of the Swarm tool-kit is that it is an extremely flexible approach that allows for the hierarchical modeling of multiagent simulations. The holonic approach supports reuse and the assemblance of applications out of already developed components. However, the focus of Swarm simulations is clearly on applications that consist of agents with very little reasoning and communication capabilities. Therefore, it is only of limited use for the analysis of applications with complex individual entities.

## A.4 Summ r

In this chapter, I have presented some tool-kits for multiagent applications that provide development support for multiagent systems with different characteristics. Whereas the Swarm tool-kit focuses on applications with fine grained agents that turn up in large numbers, the SIF library is concerned more with virtual, co-habited worlds that need flexible interaction and visualization mechanisms. The ZEUS tool-kit is probably closest to an industrial tool-box as it provides a vast amount of editors, code generators and predefined interaction and problem-solving mechanisms. Thus, before building their own middle-ware, potential multiagent application developers should consider the tool-support that is available on the market.

# sic Pro lem Solving C    ilities of TCS Agents

## .1 Pl ning Algorit m for    Single T sk

The planning process for a single task completion consists of three steps:

1. Finding the shortest path between the source and the destination node.
2. Forward propagation of arrival times.
3. Backward propagation of departure times.

In the first step a simple Dijkstra-Algorithm is applied to the input nodes in order to find the shortest path between the source and the destination node. In the next step, the *buffer time* for the task is distributed over the intermediate nodes. The buffer time of a task is the fraction of the time window of the task that is not needed by driving operations of the module. Consider, for example, a task that is given by its source and destination nodes and its time window consisting of the Earliest possible Departure Time (EDT) and the Latest allowed Arrival Time (LAT). A module that serves this task will need a particular time to drive from the source node to the destination node. If the size of the time window of the task is bigger then the time needed to drive from the source to the destination node, the module has some additional time it can spent e.g. because it must wait for a location route that is occupied by another module to become free again or if it wants to couple together with another module for location route sharing. The buffer time of the module is equally distributed over the intermediate nodes of the plan such that the module knows exactly for each node when it must arrive at the node and when it must leave from the node such that it can still fulfill the overall time window constraints.

The process of forward and backward propagation is illustrated in Figure B.1. If the module leaves the source node at time EDT then it will arrive (assuming that no route failures occur) at the destination node at time ECP (Earliest Completion Time). If, on the other hand, the module leaves at the Latest allowed Departure Time (LDT), it will not be able to complete its task before the LAT.

J. Lind: The MASSIVE Method, LNAI 1994, pp. 255-260, 2001.
© Springer-Verlag Berlin Heidelberg 2001

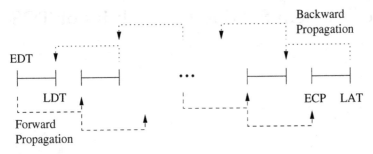

**Fig. B.1.** Time Window Propagation

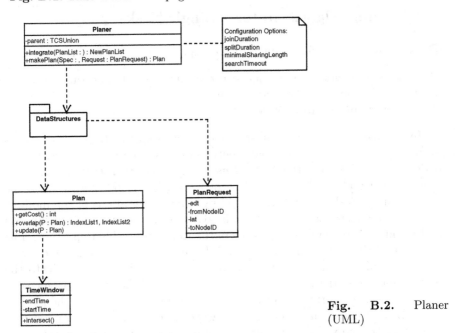

**Fig. B.2.** Planer (UML)

## .2 Pl n ntegr tion O er tor

I will now describe the plan integration operator for the plans of $n$ distinct modules. Plan integration means, that the operator takes the $n$ plans as input and modifies these plans by inserting *join* and *split* actions such that the resulting plans imply a maximum degree of location route sharing. The integration operator is used by the unions to decide whether they can integrate a new module into their set of modules or not.

I will use the following rather simple example to illustrate the basic ideas: two unions $U_1^1$ and $U_2^2$ with modules $M_1$ and $M_2$ serving tasks $T_1\langle A, F, 10, 60, 0\rangle$ and $T_2\langle C, G, 9, 50, 0\rangle$ respectively. Basically, plan integration is achieved in five steps:

1. **Find location route matches**
   The first step in the plan integration operation is to find an overlapping sequence of location routes in the plans. In the example, the path of module $M_1$ is $\overline{ABDEF}$ and the path of module $M_2$ is $\overline{CDEG}$. Thus, the two paths overlap in $\overline{DE}$. If no overlapping is found, the plan integration process is aborted. For $n$ plans, the general overlap condition is $\forall i \exists j :$ $overlap(M_i, M_j) \neq \emptyset$, i.e. for each module, there must exist at least one sharing peer in the union.

2. **Generate joint actions**
   If the overlap condition holds, the next step in the plan integration process is to generate *join* and *split* actions for the respective plans. These actions are referred to as *joint actions* because they require two modules to coordinate their individual actions. In the example, the two modules join in node $D$ and split in node $E$, the actions to be inserted are therefore
   $M_1.\texttt{D.actions} =[(\texttt{type:join peers:}[M_2] \ \ldots)]$
   $M_2.\texttt{D.actions} =[(\texttt{type:join peers:}[M_1] \ \ldots)]$
   $M_1.\texttt{E.actions} = [(\texttt{type:split peers:}[M_2] \ \ldots)]$
   $M_2.\texttt{E.actions} = [(\texttt{type:split peers:}[M_1] \ \ldots)]$

3. **Minimize number of joint actions**
   The number of joint actions generated in the previous step is not optimal because the generation process considers only the local context of the action, i.e. only a single step in the plan. Due to prior actions of a module, however, some actions are obsolete and can be eliminated. To illustrate this situation, assume another Module $M$ with task $T\langle B, G, 10, 60, 0\rangle$. Integrating the three modules $M_1, M_2$ and $M$, yields three overlapping pieces
   
   a) $(M_1, M_2) = \overline{DE}$
   b) $(M_1, M) = \overline{BDE}$
   c) $(M_2, M) = \overline{DEG}$
   
   resulting in three bilateral actions pairs
   
   a) $(M_1, M_2)$: *join at $D$, split at $E$*
   b) $(M_1, M)$: *join at $B$, split at $E$*
   c) $(M_2, M)$: *join at $D$, split at $G$*
   
   This results in a generation of two *join* actions for module $M_2$ at node $D$: one with $M_1$ and one with $M$. These two actions can be reduced to a single action $M_2.D.actions = [(\textit{type:join peers:}[M_1 M] \ ...)]$ because $M_1$ and $M$ are already linked due to their prior *join* operation at node $B$. While this is rather trivial in this example, it is not the case in more complex plans where previous *join* and *split* actions must be recursively traced for a large number of modules.

4. **Specify joint action constraints**
   In this step, the time windows of the newly generated actions are specified. The conditions that must hold are that actions must take place within the time windows of the plan steps of the respective modules and

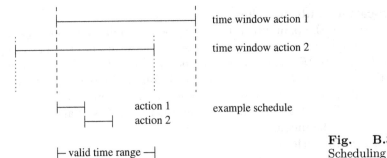

time window action 1

time window action 2

action 1    example schedule
action 2

**Fig.    B.3.**    Action
Scheduling

⊢ valid time range ⊣

that the joint actions must take place simultaneously. In the example, the resulting constraints are

$M_1.D.actions.1.\underline{t} = M_2.D.actions.1.\underline{t} = max(M_1.D.\underline{t}, M_2.D.\underline{t})$

$M_1.D.actions.1.\overline{t} = M_2.D.actions.1.\overline{t} = min(M_1.D.\overline{t}, M_2.D.\overline{t})$

5. **Find action schedule**

In the last step of the plan integration process, the operator must guarantee the existence of a schedule for all actions in each plan step of each module. This means, that all actions occurring in a plan step must be serialized in a way that the action executions do not overlap in time.

For    example    let    $M_i$.N.actions = [(type:join peers:[$M_j$] duration:4 $\underline{t}$:10 $\overline{t}$:30) (type:join peers:[$M_k$] duration:4 $\underline{t}$:14 $\overline{t}$:34)]

be the plan step of module $M_i$ at node $N$. The time windows for the two actions are shown in Figure B.3, the task of this step in the plan integration process is to arrange these actions within their respective time windows such that they do not overlap and that they take place in the time interval given by cutting the action execution time intervals. A valid schedule for the two actions is also shown in Figure B.3.

As one can see in Figure B.3, there are multiple schedules for the actions exist (e.g. action 1 could as well be scheduled after action 2). However, the time windows of the actions are not committed to a particular schedule because this implies an unnecessary restriction imposed at planning time. At planning time, it is sufficient to know that a schedule exists, concrete commitments to a particular schedule are delayed until execution time giving the participating modules a maximum degree of flexibility.

After these steps of the plan integration process have been successfully performed, the output of the plan integration operator is a list of module plans that satisfy the overlap condition mentioned before.

## .3 Decision Functions

In order to decide whether to integrate a new module into an existing union or to exchange a module in the union with an external module, the unions must have decision functions that determine their optimal behavior.

The *insertion cost* $c^+$ of a module $m$ into an existing union $U$ is

$$c^+(U, m) = \sum_{r \in U'.routes \wedge |r.users|=1} \omega(r) \qquad (\text{B.1})$$

where $U'$ is the is the union that emerges when the plan integration operator presented in the previous section is applied to the plans of the modules in $U$ and module $m$. $U'.routes$ denote the location routes used by $U'$ and $|r.users|$ is the number of modules using location route $r$ simultaneously. Thus, the insertion cost are the additional costs that occur because of location routes that are not already used by the union.

The *deletion costs* (or *savings*) $c^-$, on the other hand, occur when a module $m$ is deleted from a union $U$ and compute to

$$c^-(U, m) = \sum_{r \in m.routes \wedge |r.users|=1} \omega(r) \qquad (\text{B.2})$$

i.e. the savings are the costs of the routes of module $m$ that are not shared with other modules.

Thus, it pays to switch a module from an union $U_1$ to another union $U_2$ if the insertion costs for the module in $U_1$ are less than the costs that occur when the module is deleted from union $U_2$, i.e. $c^+(U_2, m) < c^-(U_1, m)$.

## .4 Pl n E ecution Simul tion

The plan execution monitor (PEM) is the link between the planning unit and the real world (or a simulation engine that simulates the real world). The PEM controls the usage of location routes and the coupling activities of the modules. To illustrate how plan execution monitoring works, recall the plan of module $M_2$ from the example in the previous section:   [
(NodeId:C, $\underline{t}$:9, $\overline{t}$:21, actions:nil)
(NodeId:D, $\underline{t}$:20, $\overline{t}$:32, actions:[(type:join peers:[$M_1$] duration:4 $\underline{t}$:11 $\overline{t}$:15)])
(NodeId:E, $\underline{t}$:33, $\overline{t}$:45, actions:[(type:split peers:[$M_1$] duration:3 $\underline{t}$:11 $\overline{t}$:15)])
(NodeId:G, $\underline{t}$:38, $\overline{t}$:50, actions:nil)
]

When the module starts to execute this plan at time $t = 9$, it asks the PEM whether the location route from $C$ to $D$ is available as it should be because it was allocated at planning time. However, the route may not be available at execution time due to external reasons, e.g. route blocking due to mechanical failure of another module while using that particular route and it is the task of the PEM to check whether or not the route is available. If the module is allowed to use the route, it departs from node $C$. When it arrives at node $D$, it issues a coupling request to the PEM, indicating that it is waiting for module $M_1$ to join with it. If module $M_1$ has already arrived at node $D$, the coupling action can start if $M_1$ is not engaged in an ongoing coupling activity with another module. If $M_1$ has not arrived yet or is currently engaged, the coupling action of $M_2$ is stalled. If $M_1$ does not become available within the time interval specified in the *join* action of $M_2$, $M_2$ departs from $D$ without coupling with $M_1$ because otherwise $M_2$ will miss its scheduled latest arrival time at the goal node. If the coupling activity can be completed as it is scheduled, the two modules depart from $D$ after the coupling is finished. When they arrive at node $E$, the two modules inform the PEM that they want to split and after completing the *split* action they depart from node $E$ for their respective goal nodes.

This example is, again, highly simplified. If more than two modules are involved in *join* or *split* actions additional plan integrity constraints must be satisfied. If, for example, three modules $M_1M_2M_3$ are coupled in this order and $M_2$ must split from $M_1$ and $M_3$, an additional *join* action between $M_1$ and $M_3$ must be generated because $M_1$ and $M_3$ are supposed to remain coupled. However, no additional *join* action is necessary if the original module order is $M_2M_1M_3$. The decision of whether to generate additional coupling actions or not must be taken by the PEM upon plan execution time, depending on the actual coupling order of the modules.

# C. Protoz S ecific tion of t e Contr ct-Net Protocol

```
protocol ContractNet

    % channel for messages between manager and bidder

    channel
        Manager(Announce Grant Reject)
        Bidder(Bid NoBid Report)
    end

    % role manager; one instance is allowed within one
    % protocol execution

    role(1) Manager(agentList BidderList,
                    any Task, integer TimeoutValue)

        % channel between the protocol and the applicationProcedures
        % of the agent that has instantiated this role
        %
        % names and parameters of messages to applicationProc correspond
        % with names and parameters of the procedures
        %
        % messages from applicationProc are named as the procedures with
        % the word 'Result' in front

        channel
            protocol(ChooseBid(any Bid1, any Bid2)
                    Inform(string Message)
                    GetResult)

            applicationProc(ResultChooseBid)
        end

        %my states
        states
            WaitingForAnswer
            WaitingForReport
        end

        declare

            %my variables
            message
                BestBid % the currently best bid
                Result
            end

            agent
                Contractor
            end

        end

        timeout
            Timeout1 TimeoutValue startOnEnter in WaitingForAnswer end
            Timeout2 TimeoutValue startOnEnter in WaitingForReport end
        end

        initialize to WaitingForAnswer
        provided (length(BidderList) >= 1)
        begin

            send Announce(Task) to Bidder.BidderList % send the message to all the
                                                      % agents in the list
        end

        initialize to done
        provided (length(BidderList) < 1)

        % to less agents to announce to; there must be 2 or more
```

J. Lind: The MASSIVE Method, LNAI 1994, pp. 261-264, 2001.
© Springer-Verlag Berlin Heidelberg 2001

```
timeout
  Timeout1 TimeoutValue startOnEnter in WaitingForAnswer end
  Timeout2 TimeoutValue startOnEnter in WaitingForReport end
end

initialize to WaitingForAnswer
provided (length(BidderList) >= 1)
begin

  send Announce(Task) to Bidder.BidderList % send the message to all the
                                            % agents in the list
end

initialize to done
provided (length(BidderList) < 1)

% to less agents to announce to; there must be 2 or more
begin
  applicationProc(Inform("bidderList must have at least 2 elements"))
end

trans

  % transition 1

  from WaitingForAnswer to same
  when Bidder.BidderList % one of the agents in the list
  sends Bid
  provided (BestBid == nil)

  % this the first bid
  begin
      remove(sender BidderList)
    BestBid = currentMessage
  end

  % transition 2

  from WaitingForAnswer WaitingForReport to same
  when Bidder.BidderList sends Bid
  provided ((BestBid \= nil)  && (length(BidderList) > 1))

  %there was a bid before
  begin
      remove(sender BidderList)
    insert(CompareBids)    % insert macro
  end

  % transition 3

  from WaitingForAnswer to same
  when Bidder.BidderList sends NoBid
  provided (length(BidderList) > 1)  % not the last reply

  begin
    remove(sender BidderList)
  end

  % transition 4

  from WaitingForAnswer to WaitingForReport
  when Bidder.BidderList sends Bid
  provided (length(BidderList) == 1)
```

```
% last reply
begin
  remove(sender BidderList)
  insert(CompareBids)
  Contractor = getSender(BestBid)
  send Grant() to Bidder.Contractor
end


% transition 5

from WaitingForAnswer to WaitingForReport
when Bidder.BidderList sends NoBid
provided ((length(BidderList) == 1) &&
          (BestBid \= nil))

% last reply
begin
  remove(sender BidderList)
  Contractor = getSender(BestBid)
  send Grant() to Bidder.Contractor
end


% transition 6

from WaitingForAnswer to WaitingForReport
when system sends Timeout1
provided (BestBid \= nil)     % there is a bid
begin
  applicationProc(Inform("timeout in WaitingForAnswer, taking currently
                                                        best bid"))
  Contractor = getSender(BestBid)
  send Grant() to Bidder.Contractor
end


% transition 7

from WaitingForAnswer to done
when system sends Timeout1
provided (BestBid == nil)     % there is no bid
begin
  applicationProc(Inform("timeout in WaitingForAnswer and no bid received"))
end


% transition 8

from WaitingForReport to done
when Bidder.Contractor sends Report
begin
  send GetResult(currentMessage.content) to applicationProc
end


% transition 9

from WaitingForReport to done
when system sends Timeout2
begin
  applicationProc(Inform("timeout in WaitingForReport and no report received"))
end


% transition 10

from WaitingForReport to same
when Bidder.BidderList sends Bid
begin
  send Exception("bid arrived to late") to Bidder.sender
end
```

```
% transition 11

from WaitingForAnswer to done
when Bidder.BidderList sends NoBid
provided ((length(BidderList) == 1) &&
          (BestBid == nil))

% last reply but currently no bid
begin
  applicationProc(Inform("no bid received"))
end

end

macro CompareBids
begin

  Result = applicationProc(ChooseBid(BestBid.content currentMessage.content))

  if (Result.content == BestBid.content)  % the new bid is worse
  then
    send Reject() to Bidder.getSender(currentMessage)

  elseif (Result.content == currentMessage.content) % the new bid is better
  then
    send Reject() to Bidder.getSender(BestBid)
    BestBid = currentMessage

  else    % error
    applicationProc(Inform("wrong result of method chooseBid"))
    exit
  end
end

end

% role bidder; multiple instances are allowed within
% one protocol execution

role(*) Bidder

  %my methods

  channel
    protocol(ComputeBid
             Execute
             Inform(string Message))

    applicationProc(ResultComputeBid ResultExecute)
  end

  %my states
  states
    Start ComputeBid WaitingForAnswer
    Execute
  end

  declare

    %my variables
    any MyTask end
    agent MyManager end

  end
```

# Bibliography

[Adami, 1998] ADAMI, C. (1998). *Introduction to Artificial Life*. California Institute of Technology.

[Adelson et al., 1984] ADELSON, B., LITTMAN, D., EHRLICH, K., BLACK, K., AND SOLOWAY, E. (1984). Novice-expert differences in software design. In SHACKEL, B., editor, *Human-Computer Interaction* INTERACT84, Amsterdam. North-Holland.

[Advanced Software Technologies Inc., 1999] ADVANCED SOFTWARE TECHNOLOGIES INC. (1999). Round trip engineering. http://www.advancedsw.com/round.html.

[Anderson, 1983] ANDERSON, J. R. (1983). *The Architecture of Cognition*. Harvard University Press, Cambridge, MA.

[Anderson, 1996] ANDERSON, J. R. (1996). *Kognitive Psychologie*. Spektrum Akademischer Verlag, 2nd edition.

[André et al., 1999] ANDRÉ, E., M., K., GEBHARD, P., ALLEN, S., AND RIST, T. (1999). Integrating models of personality and emotions into lifelike characters. In *Affect in Interactions Towards a New Generation of Interfaces*.

[Avenhaus and Denzinger, 1993] AVENHAUS, J. AND DENZINGER, J. (1993). Distributing equational theorem proving. In *Proceedings of the RTA'93*, number 690 in LNCS, Montreal.

[Axelrod, 1984] AXELROD, R. (1984). *The Evolution of Cooperation*. Basic Books.

[Bachem et al., 1992] BACHEM, A., HOCHSTÄTTLER, W., AND MALICH, M. (1992). Simulated Trading: A New Approach for Solving Vehicle Routing Problems. Technical Report 92.125, Mathematisches Institut der Universität zu Köln.

[Bachem et al., 1993] BACHEM, A., HOCHSTÄTTLER, W., AND MALICH, M. (1993). The Simulated Trading Heuristic for Solving Vehicle Routing Problems. Technical Report 93.139, Mathematisches Institut der Universität zu Köln.

[Bahrdt, 1994] BAHRDT, H. P. (1994). *Schlüsselbegriffe der Soziologie*. C. H. Beck, München.

[Balzert, 1998a] BALZERT, H. (1998a). *Lehrbuch der Software-Technik*, volume II. Spekrum Akademischer Verlag.

[Balzert, 1998b] BALZERT, H. (1998b). *Lehrbuch der Software-Technik*, volume I. Spekrum Akademischer Verlag.

[Barbucean and Fox, 1995] BARBUCEAN, M. AND FOX, M. S. (1995). The Architecture for an Agent Based Infrastructure for Agile Manufacturing. In *Proceedings of the Fithteenth International Joint Conference on Artificial Intelligence (IJCAI-95)"*,.

[Basili, 1989] BASILI, V. R. (1989). The Experience Factory: Packaging Software Experience. In *Proceedings of the 14th International Conference on Software Engineering*. NASA Goddard Space Flight Center.

[Basili, 1993] BASILI, V. R. (1993). Applying the Goal/Question/Metric Paradigm in the Experience Factory. In *Proceedings of the 10th Annual CSR Workshop*.

[Basili et al., 1994] BASILI, V. R., CALDIERA, G., AND ROMBACH, H. D. (1994). Experience Factory. In MARCINIAK, J. J., editor, *Encyclopedia of Software Engineering*, volume 1, pages 469–476. John Wiley & Sons.

[Basili and Turner, 1975] BASILI, V. R. AND TURNER, A. J. (1975). Iterative Enhacement: A Practical Technique for Software Development. In *Proceedings of the First National Conference on Software Engineering*, pages 56–62. IEEE Computer Society Press.

[Bauer et al., 1999] BAUER, B., MÜLLER, J. P., AND ODELL, J. (1999). An extension of UML by protocols for multiagent interaction. Submission to the ICMAS2000.

[Bayrische Landesregierung, 1996] BAYRISCHE LANDESREGIERUNG (1996). Bayerninfo. http://www.bayerninfo.de.

[Beck, 1999] BECK, K. (1999). *eXtreme Programming eXplained: Embrace Change.* Addison-Wesley.

[Blum, 1992] BLUM, B. I. (1992). *Software Engineering – A Holistic View.* Oxford University Press.

[Boden, 1996] BODEN, M. A., editor (1996). *The Philosophy of Artificial Life.* Oxford readings in philosophy. Oxford University Press, Oxford.

[Boehm, 1988] BOEHM, B. W. (1988). A Spiral Model of Software Development and Enhancement. *IEEE Computer*, 21(5):61–72.

[Booch, 1994] BOOCH, G. (1994). *Object-Oriented Analysis and Design With Applications.* Addison-Wesley.

[Booch, 1996] BOOCH, G. (1996). *Object Solutions: Managing the Object-Oriented Project.* Object-Orieneted Software Engineering. Addison-Wesley.

[Booch et al., 1999] BOOCH, G., RUMBAUGH, J., AND JACOBSON, I. (1999). *The Unified Modeling Language User Guide.* Addison Wesley.

[Bradshaw, 1997] BRADSHAW, J. M., editor (1997). *Software Agents.* MIT Press.

[Brazier et al., 1997] BRAZIER, F., DUNIN-KEPLICZ, B., JENNINGS, N., AND TREUR, J. (1997). Desire: Modelling multi-agent systems in a compositional formal framework. *International Journal of Cooperative Information Systems*, 6. Special Issue on Formal Methods in Cooperative Information Systems: Multi-Agent Systems.

[Brazier et al., 1998] BRAZIER, F., JONKER, C., AND TREUR, J. (1998). Principles of compositional multi-agent system development. In CUENA, J., editor, *Proceedings of the IFIP'98 Conference on Information Technology and Knowledge Systems.* Chapman and Hall.

[Brazier et al., 1996] BRAZIER, F., VAN ECK, P., AND TREUR, J. (1996). Design of a modelling framework for multi-agent systems. In ALBRECHT, R. AND HERRE, H., editors, *Trends in Theoretical Informatics*, Schriftenreihe der Österreichischen Computer Gesellschaft. R. Oldenbourg Verlag.

[Brooks, 1986] BROOKS, JR., F. P. (1986). No silver bullet. In KUGLER, H.-J., editor, *Proceedings of the IFIP Tenth World Computing Conference*, pages 1069–76, Elsevier Science.

[Brooks, 1995] BROOKS, JR, F. P. (1995). *The Mythical Man–Month.* Addison Wesley.

[Brooks, 1991] BROOKS, R. A. (1991). Intelligence without representation. *Artificial Intelligence*, 47:139–159.

[Bürckert et al., 1998] BÜRCKERT, H.-J., FISCHER, K., AND VIERKE, G. (1998). Transportation scheduling with Holonic MAS, the TeleTruck approach. In *Proceedings of the PAAM98.*

[Burkhart, 1997] BURKHART, R. (1997). Schedules of activity in the swarm simulation system. In *roceedings of the 1997 ACM SIGPLAN Conference on Object-Oriented Programming Systems, Languages & Applications (OOPSLA '97).*

[Burmeister, 1996] BURMEISTER, B. (1996). Models and methodology for agent-oriented analysis and design. In FISCHER, K., editor, *Working Notes of the KI'96 Workshop on Agent-Oriented Programming and Distributed Systems*, number D-96-06 in DFKI Documents. DFKI.

[Burmeister et al., 1995] BURMEISTER, B., HADDADI, A., AND SUNDERMEYER, K. (1995). Generic configurable cooperation protocols for multi-agent systems. In CASTELFRANCHI, C. AND MÜLLER, J.-P., editors, *From Reaction to Cognition — 5th European Workshop on Modelling Autonomous Agents in a Multi-Agent World (MAAMAW'93)*, volume 957 of *LNAI*, pages 157–171. Springer-Verlag.

[Burt, 1998] BURT, A. (1998). Emotionally Intelligent Agents: The Outline of a Resource-Oriented Approach. In *Proceedings of the 1998 AAAI Fall Symposium Emotional and Intelligent: The Tangled Knot of Cognition*.

[Bussmann and Müller, 1993] BUSSMANN, S. AND MÜLLER, H. J. (1993). A Communication Structure for Cooperating Agents. *Computers and AI*, I.

[Cammarata et al., 1983] CAMMARATA, S., MCARTHUR, D., AND STEEB, R. (1983). Strategies of cooperation in distributed problem solving. In *Proceedings of the Eighth International Joint Conference on Artificial Intelligence (IJCAI-83)*.

[Carley, 1999] CARLEY, K. M. (1999). Computational organizational theory. In *Multiagent Systems - A Modern Approach to Distributed Artificial Intelligence*. MIT Press.

[Carroll and Rosson, 1985] CARROLL, J. M. AND ROSSON, M. B. (1985). Usability specifications as a tool in iterative development. In HARTSON, H. R., editor, *Advances in Human-Computer Interaction*, volume 1. Norwwod.

[Carroué, 1997] CARROUÉ, L. (1997). La ruinease maladie du ≪ tout-routier ≫ — une europe des transports menacée d'embolie. *Le Monde Diplomatique*, pages 18–19.

[Chase and Simon, 1973] CHASE, G. W. AND SIMON, H. A. (1973). The minds eye in chess. In CHASE, W. G., editor, *Visual Information Processing*. Academic Press, New York.

[Ciancarini and Wooldridge, 2000] CIANCARINI, P. AND WOOLDRIDGE, M., editors (2000). *Proceedings of the First International Workshop on "Agent-Oriented Software Engineering" held at the International Conference on Software Engineering (ICSE2000)*, Limerick, Ireland. Springer.

[Clocksin and Mellish, 1994] CLOCKSIN, W. F. AND MELLISH, C. S. (1994). *Programming in Prolog*. Springer Verlag.

[Collins and Ndumu, 1998] COLLINS, J. AND NDUMU, D. (1998). The ZEUS Role Modelling Guide. Technical report, BT, Adastral Park, Martlesham Heath.

[Conte et al., 1996] CONTE, S. D., DUNSMORE, H. E., AND CHEN, V. Y. (1996). *Software Engineering Metrics and Models*. The Benjamin/Cummings Publishing Company.

[Cook, 1979] COOK, W. A. (1979). *Case Grammar: Development of the Matrix Model*. PhD thesis, Georgetown University, Washington.

[Cox and Gehani, 1989] COX, I. J. AND GEHANI, N. H. (1989). Exception Handling in Robotics. *IEEE Computing*, 22(3).

[Curtis, 1989] CURTIS, B. (1989). Five paradigms in the psychology of programming. In HELANDER, M., editor, *Handbook of Human-Computer Interaction*. Elsevier (North-Holland), Amsterdam.

[Dahl et al., 1972] DAHL, O.-J., DIJKSTRA, E. W., AND HOARE, C. A. R. (1972). *Strcutured Programming*. Academic Press, London.

[Defense Advanced Research Projects Agency, 1981] DEFENSE ADVANCED RESEARCH PROJECTS AGENCY (1981). Transmission Control Protocol.

[DeMarco, 1978] DeMarco, T. (1978). *Structured Analysis and System Design.* Englewood Cliffs:Yourdon Press.

[Denzinger, 1993] Denzinger, J. (1993). *Teamwork: Eine Methode zum Entwurf verteilter, wissensbasierter Theorembeweiser.* PhD thesis, Universität Kaiserslautern.

[Denzinger, 1994] Denzinger, J. (1994). The teamwork approach to distributed search. Technical report, University of Kaiserslautern.

[Denzinger and Lind, 1996] Denzinger, J. and Lind, J. (1996). TWlib - a library for distributed search applications. In *Proceedings of the ICS96-AI*, pages 101–108, Kaohsiung.

[Desmond and Moore, 1994] Desmond, A. and Moore, J. (1994). *Darwin.* Rowolt.

[Détienne, 1990] Détienne, F. (1990). Expert programmers and programming languages. In *Psychology of Programming.* Academic Press Ltd., London.

[Doke and Hardgrave, 1998] Doke, E. R. and Hardgrave, B. C. (1998). *An Introduction to Object Cobol.* John Wiley & Sons.

[Dröschel and Wiemers, 1999] Dröschel, W. and Wiemers, M. (1999). *Das V-Modell 97.* Oldenbourg, München.

[Dyer, 1992] Dyer, M. (1992). *The Cleanroom Approach to Quality Software Development.* Wiley and Sons.

[Edelman, 1987] Edelman, G. M. (1987). *Neural Darwinism : the Theory of Neuronal Group Selection.* Basic Books.

[Engelmore and Morgan, 1988] Engelmore, R. and Morgan, T., editors (1988). *Blackboard Systems.* Addison-Wesley.

[Epstein and Axtell, 1996] Epstein, J. M. and Axtell, R. (1996). *Growing Artificial Societies : Social Science from the Bottom Up (Complex Adaptive Systems).* Brookings Institution Press.

[EURESCOM, 1999] EURESCOM (1999). MESSAGE: Methodology for Engineering Systems of Software AGEnts. EURESCOM – European Institute for Research and Strategic Studies in Telecommunications. http://www.eurescom.de/Public/Projects/p900-series/P907/P907.htm.

[Fabel, 1996] Fabel, P. (1996). Increasing the flexibility of freight traffic - using modular train units as an example. In *Proceedings of the World Congress of Railway Research (WCRR)*, Colorado Springs, USA.

[Finin and Fritzson, 1994] Finin, T. and Fritzson, R. (1994). KQML — a language and protocol for knowledge and information exchange. In *Proceedings of the 13th International Distributed Artificial Intelligence Workshop*, pages 127–136, Seattle, WA, USA.

[Finkelstein and Fuks, 1989] Finkelstein, A. and Fuks, S. (1989). Multi-party specification. In *Proceedings of the 5th International Workshop on Software Specifications and Design.*

[FIPA, 1996] FIPA (1996). *AgenTalk Reference Manual.* NTT Communication Science Laboratories and Ishida Laboratory, Department of Information Science, Kyoto University.

[FIPA, 1997] FIPA (1997). Fipa '97 specification parts 1–7, version 1.0. The Foundation for Intelligent Physical Agents.

[FIPA, 1998] FIPA (1998). Fipa '98 specification parts 1–13, version 1.0. The Foundation for Intelligent Physical Agents.

[Fischer, 1993] Fischer, K. (1993). Rollenverteilung unter gleichberechtigten agenten. In *Verteilte Künstliche Intelligenz.* BI Wissenschaftsverlag.

[Fischer et al., 1993] Fischer, K., Kuhn, N., Müller, H. J., Müller, J. P., and Pischel, M. (1993). Sophisticated and Distributed: The Transportation Domain. In *Proceedings of MAAMAW-93*, Neuchatel, CH.

[Fischer et al., 1994] FISCHER, K., KUHN, N., AND MÜLLER, J. P. (1994). Distributed, knowledge-based, reactive scheduling in the transportation domain. In *Proceedings of the Tenth IEEE Conference on Artificial Intelligence and Applications*, pages 47–53, San Antonio, Texas.

[Fischer and Müller, 1995] FISCHER, K. AND MÜLLER, H. J. (1995). Cooperative problem solving in the transportation domain. In DERIGS, U., editor, *Proceedings of the International Conference on Operations Research (OR'94)*. Springer-Verlag.

[Floyd, 1983] FLOYD, C. (1983). A Systematic Look at Prototyping. In BUDDE, R., KUHLENKAMP, K., MATHIASSEN, L., AND ZÜLLINGHOVEN, H., editors, *Approaches to Prototyping*.

[Foner, 1993] FONER, L. N. (1993). What's an Agent, Anyway? A Sociological Case Study. Agents Group, MIT Media Lab. Agents Memo 93-01.

[Fowler, 1999] FOWLER, M. (1999). *Refactoring – Improving the Design of Existing Code*. Object Technology Series. Addison-Wesley.

[Fox, 1981] FOX, M. (1981). An organizational view of distributed systems. *IEEE Trans. on Man, Systems and Cybernetics*, 11(1):70–80.

[France and Rumpe, 1999] FRANCE, R. AND RUMPE, B., editors (1999). *UML99 - The Unified Modelling Language - Beyond The Standard*, number 1723 in LNCS. Springer.

[Franklin, 1997] FRANKLIN, S. (1997). *Artificial Minds*. MIT Press.

[Franklin and Graesser, 1997] FRANKLIN, S. AND GRAESSER, A. (1997). Is it an agent, or just a program?: A taxonomy for autonomous agents. In *Proceedings of the Third International Workshop on Agent Theories, Architectures, and Languages*.

[Fulbright and Stephens, 1994] FULBRIGHT, R. D. AND STEPHENS, L. M. (1994). Classification of multiagent systems. Technical Report ECE-LMS-94-06, University of South Carolina, Columbia, SC 29208.

[Funk et al., 1998] FUNK, P., GERBER, C., LIND, J., AND SCHILLO, M. (1998). SIF: An agent-based simulation toolbox using the EMS paradigm. In *Proceedings of the 3rd International Congress of the Federation of EUROpean SIMulation Societies (EuroSim)*.

[Funk and Lind, 1997] FUNK, P. AND LIND, J. (1997). What is a friendly agent? In *Workshop Notes of the AAAI Fall Symposium 1997 on Socially Intelligent Agents*.

[Galitz, 1997] GALITZ, W. O. (1997). *The Essential Guide to User Interface Design*. Wiley Computer Publishing.

[Gamma et al., 1994] GAMMA, E., HELM, R., JOHNSON, R., AND VLISSIDES, J. (1994). *Design Patterns: Elements of Reusable Object-Oriented Software*. Addison-Wesley.

[Garlan and Shaw, 1993] GARLAN, D. AND SHAW, M. (1993). An introduction to software architecture. In AMBRIOLA, V. AND TORTORA, G., editors, *Advances in Software Engineering and Knowledge Engineering*, volume I. World Scientific Publishing.

[Garlan and Shaw, 1994] GARLAN, D. AND SHAW, M. (1994). An introduction to software architecture. Technical Report CMU-CS-94-166, Software Engineering Institute, Carnegie Mellon University.

[Gasser, 1995] GASSER, L. (1995). Introduction to multi-agent systems. In *Working Notes of Tutorial A at ICMAS95*, San Francisco, CA.

[Genesereth and Nilsson, 1987] GENESERETH, M. AND NILSSON, N. (1987). *Logical Foundations of Artificial Intelligence*. Morgan Kaufman Publishers, Inc.

[Genesereth and Fikes, 1992] GENESERETH, M. R. AND FIKES, R. E. (1992). Knowlege interchange format, version 3.0, reference manual. Technical Report

Logic-92-1, Logic Group, Computer Science Department, University of Stanford.

[Georgeff, 1983] GEORGEFF, M. P. (1983). Communication and interaction in multi-agent planning. In *Proceedings of the Third National Conference on Artificial Intelligence (AAAI-83)*, pages 125 – 129.

[Gerber, 1997] GERBER, C. (1997). An agent society is more then a collection of agents. In *Workshop Notes of the AAAI Fall Symposium 1997 on Socially Intelligent Agents*.

[Gerber, 2000] GERBER, C. (2000). *Self-Adaptation and Scalability in Multi-Agent Societies*. PhD thesis, University of the Saarland.

[Gerber et al., 1999a] GERBER, C., SIEKMANN, J., AND VIERKE, G. (1999a). Holonic multi-agent systems. Technical Report TR-99-01, DFKI.

[Gerber et al., 1999b] GERBER, C., STEINER, D., AND BAUER, B. (1999b). Resource adaptation for a scalable agent society in the MECCA domain. In *Intelligent Software Agents for Communication Networks*. Springer.

[Goodwin, 1993] GOODWIN, R. (1993). Formalizing properties of agents. Technical Report CMU–CS–93–159, School of Computer Science, Carnegie-Mellon Universit, Pittsburgh, PA.

[Graham, 1995] GRAHAM, P. (1995). *ANSI Common LISP*. Prentice Hall.

[Green, 1990] GREEN, T. R. G. (1990). Programming languages as information structures. In *Psychology of Programming*. Academic Press Ltd., London.

[Grenno and Simon, 1988] GRENNO, J. G. AND SIMON, H. A. (1988). Problem solving and reasoning. In ATKINSON, R. C., HERRNSTEIN, R. J., LINDZEY, G., AND LUCE, R. D., editors, *Stevens Handbook of Experimental Psychology*, volume 2. Wiley.

[Guindon et al., 1987] GUINDON, R., KRASNER, H., AND CURTIS, B. (1987). Breakdowns and processes during the early activities of software design by professionals. In OLSON, G., S.SHEPPARD, AND SOLOWAY, E., editors, *Empirical Studies of Programmers: Second Workshop*, Norwood, NJ. Ablex.

[Hall, 1999] HALL, R. (1999). *Agent-based Software Configuration and Deployment*. PhD thesis, University of Colorado.

[Hayes-Roth and Hayes-Roth, 1979] HAYES-ROTH, B. AND HAYES-ROTH, F. (1979). A cognitive model of planning. *Cognitive Science*, 3:275–310.

[Heise, 1992] HEISE, D. (1992). Computer assistance in qualitative sociology. *Social Science Computer Review*, 10:531–543.

[Hennessy and Patterson, 1990] HENNESSY, J. L. AND PATTERSON, D. A. (1990). *Computer Architecture: A Quantitative Approach*. Morgan Kaufmann Publishers Inc.

[Hiebeler, 1994] HIEBELER, D. (1994). The swarm simulation system and individual-based modeling. In *Proceedings of the Intenational Conference on Advanced Technology for Natural Resource Management*.

[Hoc, 1988] HOC, J.-M. (1988). Towards effective computer aids to planning in computer programming. theoretical concern and empirical evidence drawn from assessement of a prototype. In VAN DE VEER, G. C., GREEN, T. R. G., HOC, J.-M., AND MURRAY, D., editors, *Working with Computers: Theory versus Outcomes*. Academic Press, London.

[Holzmann, 1991] HOLZMANN, G. J. (1991). *Design and Validation of Computer Protocols*. Prentice Hall.

[Horn and Reinke, 1999] HORN, E. AND REINKE, T. (1999). Musterarchitekturen und entwicklungsmethoden für Multiagentsysteme. *KI*.

[Houdek et al., 1998] HOUDEK, F., SCHNEIDER, K., AND WIESER, E. (1998). Establishing Experience Factories at Daimler-Benz: An Experience Report. In *Proceedings of the 20th International Conference on Software Engineering*.

[Huhns and Singh, 1998] HUHNS, M. N. AND SINGH, M. P., editors (1998). *Readings in Agents*. Morgan Kaufmann, San Francisco, California.

[Iglesias et al., 1998] IGLESIAS, C., GARRIJO, M., AND GONZALEZ, J. (1998). A Survey of Agent-Oriented Methodologies. In MÜLLER, J. P., SINGH, M. P., AND RAO, A. S., editors, *Intelligent Agents V — Proceedings of the 1998 Workshop on Agent Theories, Architectures, and Languages (ATAL-98)*, volume 1555 of *LNAI*.

[Iglesias et al., 1997] IGLESIAS, C., GARRIJO, M., GONZALEZ, J., AND VELASCO, J. R. (1997). Analysis and design of multiagent systems using MAS-CommonKADS. In SINGH, M. P., RAO, A., AND WOOLDRIDGE, M. J., editors, *Intelligent Agents IV: Agent Theories, Architectures and Languages*, number 1365 in LNAI.

[Intelligent Reasoning Systems, 2000] INTELLIGENT REASONING SYSTEMS (2000). Jam agent architecture. http://members.home.net/marcush/IRS/.

[Ishikawa, 1985] ISHIKAWA, K. (1985). *What is Total Quality Control? The Japanese Way*. Englewood/Cliffs, New York.

[Jacobson, 1992] JACOBSON, I. (1992). *Object-oriented software engineering : a use case driven approach*. ACM Press/Addison-Wesley.

[Jalote, 1997] JALOTE, P. (1997). *An Integrated Approach to Software Engineering*. Spinger, 2nd edition.

[Jennings, 1999] JENNINGS, N. R. (1999). Agent-Oriented Software Engineering. In IMAN, I., KODRATOFF, Y., EL-DESSOUKI, A., AND ALI, M., editors, *Proceedings of the 12th International Conference on Industrial and Engineering Applications of Artificial Intelligence and Expert Systems*, number 1611 in LNAI. Springer.

[Jennings et al., 1998] JENNINGS, N. R., SYCARA, K. P., AND WOOLDRIDGE, M. (1998). A roadmap of agent research and development. *Journal of Autonomous Agents and Multi-Agent Systems*, 1(1):7–36.

[Jennings and Wooldridge, 1998] JENNINGS, N. R. AND WOOLDRIDGE, M. J., editors (1998). *Agent Technology : Foundations, Applications, and Markets*. Springer, Berlin.

[Johnson-Laird, 1983] JOHNSON-LAIRD, P. N. (1983). *Mental Models*. Cmabridge University Press, London.

[Jung, 1999] JUNG, C. G. (1999). *Theory and Pratice of Hybrid Agents*. PhD thesis, Universität des Saarlandes.

[Jung et al., 1999] JUNG, C. G., LIND, J., GERBER, C., SCHILLO, M., FUNK, P., AND BURT, A. (1999). An architecture for co-habited virtual worlds. In LANDAUER, C. AND BELLMAN, K. L., editors, *Virtual Worlds and and Simulation Conference (VWSIM'99)*, Simulation Series. The Society for Computer Simulation International.

[Kant and Newell, 1984] KANT, E. AND NEWELL, A. (1984). Problem solving techniques for the design of algorithms. *Human-Computer Interactions*, 28:97–118.

[Kendall, 1998a] KENDALL, E. A. (1998a). Agent Analysis and Design with Role Models. Technical report, British Telecom. Volume I: Overview.

[Kendall, 1998b] KENDALL, E. A. (1998b). Agent Analysis and Design with Role Models. Technical report, British Telecom. Volume II: Role Models for Agent Enhanced Workflow and Business Process Management.

[Kenworthy, 1997] KENWORTHY, E. (1997). Use case modelling. http://www.zoo.co.uk/~z0001039/PracGuides/pg_use_cases.htm.

[Kephart et al., 1989] KEPHART, J. O., HOGG, T., AND HUBERMAN, B. A. (1989). Dynamics of Computational Ecosystems: Implications for DAI. In GASSER, L. AND HUHNS, H. M., editors, *Distributed Artificial Intelligence, Volume II*. Morgan Kaufmann Publishers, Inc., San Mateo, CA.

[Kernighan and Pike, 1999] KERNIGHAN, B. W. AND PIKE, R. (1999). *The Practice of Programming*. Addison Wesley Publishing Company.

[Kernighan and Plauger, 1974] KERNIGHAN, B. W. AND PLAUGER, P. J. (1974). *The Elements of Programming Style*. McGraw-Hill, London.

[Kiczales et al., 1997] KICZALES, G., LAMPING, J., MENDHEKAR, A., MAEDA, C., LOPES, C. V., LOINGTIER, J.-M., AND IRVIN, J. (1997). Aspect-Oriented Programming. In *Proceddings of the European Conference on Object-Oriented Programming (ECOOP)*, number 1241 in LNCS. Springer-Verlag.

[Kinny and Georgeff, 1996] KINNY, D. AND GEORGEFF, M. (1996). Modelling and design of multi-agent systems. In J. P. MÜLLER, M. J. W. AND JENNINGS, N. R., editors, *Intelligent Agents III — Proceedings of the Third International Workshop on Agent Theories, Architectures, and Languages (ATAL-96)*, number 1193 in LNCS, pages 1–20. Springer-Verlag.

[Knecht, 1996] KNECHT, A. (1996). Gecco - Toolkit zur direkten Manipulation grafischer Objekte. Master's thesis, University of Kaiserslautern.

[Knuth, 1992] KNUTH, D. E. (1992). *Literate Programming*. Chicago of University Press.

[Kögl, 1995] KÖGL, C. (1995). Verteilte Berechnung von Gröbnerbasen unter Verwendung des Teamwork-Paradigmas. Master's thesis, Universität Kaiserslautern.

[Kolb, 1995] KOLB, M. (1995). A cooperation language. In *Proceedings of the First International Conference on Multi-Agent Systems (ICMAS'95)*, pages 233–238.

[Kolodner, 1993] KOLODNER, J. (1993). *Case Based Reasoning*. Morgan Kaufmann.

[Kotonya and Sommerville, 1992] KOTONYA, G. AND SOMMERVILLE, I. (1992). Viewpoints for requirements definition. *BCS/IEE Software Engineering Journal*, 7(6).

[Kowalski, 1979] KOWALSKI, R. (1979). *Logic for Problem Solving*. North Holland, Amsterdam.

[Kracke et al., 1995] KRACKE, R., SIEGMANN, J., VOGES, W., BOECKER, J., AND ZIRKLER, B. (1995). Systemgestaltung des Schienengüterverkehrs unter Einsatz der Strategie des Train-Coupling and -Sharing. Technical report, Universität Hannover. Studie im Auftrag der DB AG.

[Kronenburg, 1995] KRONENBURG, M. (1995). Hierarchisierung der Teamwork-Methode mittels Zerlegungsplanung. Master's thesis, Universität Kaiserslautern.

[Kuhn et al., 1994] KUHN, N., MÜLLER, H. J., AND MÜLLER, J. P. (1994). Simulating cooperative transportation companies. In BIETHAHN, J., HUMMELTENBERG, W., SCHMIDT, B., AND WITTE, T., editors, *Simulation als betriebliche Entscheidungshilfe*, chapter 18, pages 263–264. Vieweg Verlag, Braunschweig/Wiesbaden.

[Kuhn, 1975] KUHN, T. S. (1975). *The structure of scientific revolutions*. Univ. of Chicago Press, 2nd edition.

[Kulak and Guiney, 2000] KULAK, D. AND GUINEY, E. (2000). *Use Cases – Requirements in Context*. Addison-Wesley.

[Künzel, 1997] KÜNZEL, K. (1997). Eine graphische Benutzerschnittstelle und Analyseumgebung für Systeme basierend auf dem Teamwork-Konzept. Master's thesis, Universität Kaiserslautern.

[Kupries and Noseleit, 1999] KUPRIES, M. AND NOSELEIT, C. (1999). Software architecture type-based interagent connections. In *Autonomous Agents '99*, Seattle.

[Lander, 1997] LANDER, S. E. (1997). Issues in Multiagent Design Systems. *IEEE Expert*.

[Lang and Stuart, 1998] LANG, J. AND STUART, D. B. (1998). A study of the applicability of existing exception-handling techniques to component-based real-time software technology. *ACM Transactions on Programming Languages and Systems*, 20(2).

[Langton, 1989] LANGTON, C., editor (1989). *Artificial Life*, Redwood City, Calif. Addison-Wesley.

[Lawler and Woods, 1966] LAWLER, E. L. AND WOODS, D. E. (1966). Branch-and-Bound Methods: A survey. *Operations Research*, 14(4):699–719.

[Lee et al., 1998] LEE, L., NWANA, H., NDUMU, D., AND DE WILDE, P. (1998). The stability, scalability and performance of multi-agent systems. *BT Technology Journal*, 16(3).

[Leopold, 1995] LEOPOLD, T. (1995). Verteilte Lösung des Travelling-Salesman-Problems durch TEAMWORK. Master's thesis, Universität Kaiserslautern.

[Lichter et al., 1994] LICHTER, H., SCHNEIDER-HUFSCHMIDT, M., AND ZÜLLIGHOVEN, H. (1994). Prototyping in industrial software projects – bridging the gap between theory and practice. *IEEE Transactions on Software Engineering*, 20(11):825–832.

[Lind, 1992] LIND, J. (1992). Sicheres Broadcasting für DISCOUNT. Projektarbeit, Universität Kaiserslautern.

[Lind, 1996a] LIND, J. (1996a). TWLib – A Generic Library for TEAMWORK Applications. Master's thesis, University of Kaiserslautern.

[Lind, 1996b] LIND, J. (1996b). *TWLib – Reference Manual*. University of Kaiserslautern.

[Lind, 1998] LIND, J. (1998). The EMS Model. Technical Report TM-98-09, DFKI, Stuhlsatzenhausweg 3, D-66123 Saarbrücken.

[Lind, 1999a] LIND, J. (1999a). A Process Model for the Design of Multi-Agent Systems. Technical Report TM-99-03, DFKI, Stuhlsatzenhausweg 3, D-66123 Saarbrücken.

[Lind, 1999b] LIND, J. (1999b). A Review of Multiagent Systems Development Methods. Technical report, British Telecom, Adastral Park Labs, Martlesham Heath, Suffolk.

[Lind, 2000a] LIND, J. (2000a). A development method for multiagent systems. In *Cybernetics and Systems: Proceedings of the 15th European Meeting on Cybernetics and Systems Research, Symposium "From Agent Theory to Agent Implementation"*.

[Lind, 2000b] LIND, J. (2000b). Issues in agent-oriented software engineering. In *Proceeedings of the First International Workshop on Agent-Oriented Software Engineering (AOSE-2000) held at the 22nd International Conference on Software Engineering*, Limerick, Ireland.

[Lind, 2000c] LIND, J. (2000c). The MASSIVE development method for multiagent systems. In *Proceedings of the Fifth International Conference on the Practical Application of Intelligent Agents and Multi-Agents*, Manchester, UK.

[Lind, 2000d] LIND, J. (2000d). MASSIVE: *Software Engineering for Multiagent Systems*. PhD thesis, University of the Saarland.

[Lind, 2000e] LIND, J. (2000e). Specifying Agent Interaction Protocols with UML Activity Diagrams. Technical Report TM-00-01, DFKI.

[Lind and Böcker, 1999] LIND, J. AND BÖCKER, J. (1999). Optimising the Train Coupling and -Sharing system with a multi-agent approach. In *Proceedings of the 11th Mini-EURO Conference on AI in Transportation Systems and Science*, Helsinki.

[Lind et al., 1999a] LIND, J., BÖCKER, J., AND ZIRKLER, B. (1999a). Optimising the Operation Management with a Multi-Agent Approach - Using TCS as an

Example. In *Proceedings of the World Congress on Railway Research (WCRR)*, Tokyo.

[Lind and Fischer, 1998] LIND, J. AND FISCHER, K. (1998). Transportation Scheduling and Simulation in a Railroad Scenario: A Multi-Agent Approach. Technical Report TM-98-05, DFKI, Stuhlsatzenhausweg 3, D-66123 Saarbrücken.

[Lind and Fischer, 1999] LIND, J. AND FISCHER, K. (1999). Transportation Scheduling and Simulation in a Railroad Scenario: A Multi-Agent Approach. In KOPFER, H. AND BIERWIRTH, C., editors, *Logistik Management*. Spinger.

[Lind et al., 1999b] LIND, J., FISCHER, K., BÖCKER, J., AND ZIRKLER, B. (1999b). Transportation Scheduling and Simulation in a Railroad Scenario: A Multi-Agent Approach. In *Proceedings of the Fourth International Conference on the Practical Application of Intelligent Agents and Multi-Agents (PAAM99)*, London.

[Lind et al., 2000] LIND, J., GERBER, C., FUNK, P., SCHILLO, M., BURT, A., AND JUNG, C. (2000). SIF-VW: Eine integrierte Systemarchitektur für Agenten und Benutzer in virtuellen Welten. *KI – Zeitschrift Künstliche Intelligenz*, 2. Schwerpunktthema "Intelligente Virtuelle Umgebungen".

[Lind et al., 1999c] LIND, J., JUNG, C. G., AND GERBER, C. (1999c). Learning and Adaptivity in Intelligent Real-Time Systems. In *Proceedings of the Third International Conference on Autonomous Agents (Agents'99)*.

[Linger and Trammell, 1996] LINGER, R. C. AND TRAMMELL, C. J. (1996). Cleanroom software engineering reference model version 1.0. Technical Report CMU/SEI-96-TR-022, Carnegie Mellon University.

[MacGregor and Bates, 1987] MACGREGOR, R. AND BATES, R. (1987). The LOOM Knowledge Representation Language. Technical Report ISI/RS-87-188, University of Southern California.

[Mayfield et al., 1995] MAYFIELD, J., LABROU, Y., AND FININ, T. (1995). Evaluating KQML as an agent communication language. In WOOLDRIDGE, M., MÜLLER, J. P., AND TAMBE, M., editors, *Intelligent Agents — Proceedings of the 1995 Workshop on Agent Theories, Architectures, and Languages (ATAL-95)*, volume 1037 of *LNAI*, pages 347–360. Springer-Verlag.

[McCarthy, 1979] McCARTHY, J. (1979). Ascribing mental qualities to machines. In RINGLE, M., editor, *Philosophical Aspects in Artificial Intelligence*. Harvester Press.

[McConnell, 1993] McCONNELL, S. (1993). *Code Complete: A Practical Handbook of Software Construction*. Microsoft Press.

[McKeithen et al., 1987] McKEITHEN, K. B., REITMAN, J. S., RUETER, H. H., AND HIRTLE, S. C. (1987). Knowledge organization and skill differences in computer programmers. *Canadian Journal of Psychology*, 13.

[McNealy, 1996] McNEALY, S. (1996). Scott says... kick butt and have fun". *Sun Microsystems*. http://www.sun.com/960601/cover/.

[Mehlhorn and Näher, 1999] MEHLHORN, K. AND NÄHER, S. (1999). *The LEDA Platform of Combinatorial and Geometric Computing*. Cambridge University Press.

[Merriam-Webster, 2000] MERRIAM-WEBSTER (2000). Wwwebster dictionary. http://www.m-w.com.

[Microsoft Corporation, 2000] MICROSOFT CORPORATION (2000). Visual c++. http://msdn.microsoft.com/visualc/.

[Miller, 1956] MILLER, G. A. (1956). The magical number seven, plus or minus two: some limits on our capacity of information processing. *Psychological Review*, 63:237–260.

[Mills et al., 1987] MILLS, H., DYER, M., AND LINGER, R. (1987). Cleanroom software engineering. *IEEE Software*, pages 19–24.

[Minar et al., 1996] MINAR, N., BURKHART, R., LANGTON, C., AND ASKENAZI, M. (1996). The swarm simulation system: A toolkit for building multi-agent simulations. Technical Report 96-06-042, Santa Fe Institute.

[Mullender, 1993] MULLENDER, S. (1993). *Distributed Systems*. ACM Press.

[Müller, 1996a] MÜLLER, J. P. (1996a). Control Architectures for Autonomous and Interactin Agents: A Survey. In CAVEDON, L., RAO, A., AND WOBCKE, W., editors, *Intelligent Agent Systems: Theoratical and Practical Issues*, number 1209 in LNAI.

[Müller, 1996b] MÜLLER, J. P. (1996b). *The Design of Intelligent Agents: A Layered Approach*, volume 1177 of *Lecture Notes in Artificial Intelligence*. Springer-Verlag.

[Müller, 1998] MÜLLER, J. P. (1998). The Right Agent (Architecture) to do the Right Thing. In MÜLLER, J. P., SINGH, M. P., AND RAO, A. S., editors, *Intelligent Agents V — Proceedings of the 1998 Workshop on Agent Theories, Architectures, and Languages (ATAL-98)*, volume 1555 of *LNAI*.

[Naur and Randell, 1969] NAUR, P. AND RANDELL, B., editors (1969). *Software Engineering. Report on a Conference sponsored by the NATO Science Commitee*, Garmisch, Germany, 7th to 11th October 1968. NATO, Scientific Affairs Division.

[Ndumu et al., 1999] NDUMU, D. T., NWANA, H. S., LEE, L. C., AND COLLINS, J. C. (1999). Visualising and debugging distributed multi-agent systems. In *Proceedings of the 3rd International Conference on Autonomous Agents*.

[Neches et al., 1991] NECHES, R., FIKES, R., FININ, T., GRUBER, R., PATIL, R., SENATOR, T., AND SWARTOUT, W. (1991). Eanbling Technology for Knowledge Sharing. *Ai magazine*, 12(3):36–56.

[Noda, 1995] NODA, I. (1995). Soccer Server: A Simulator of Robocup. In *Proc. of AI symposium 1995*. JAPANESE SOCIETY FOR ARTIFICIAL INTELLIGENCE.

[Nwana et al., 1999] NWANA, H. S., NDUMU, D. T., LEE, L. C., AND COLLINS, J. C. (1999). ZEUS: A tool-kit for building distributed multi-agent systems. *Applied Artifical Intelligence Journal*, 13(1):129–186.

[Object Management Group, 1999] OBJECT MANAGEMENT GROUP (1999). CORBA: Common Object Request Broker Architecture and Specification, revision 2.3.

[Odgers et al., 1999] ODGERS, B., SHEPHERDSON, J., AND THOMPSON, S. (1999). Distributed workflow co-ordination by proactive software agents. In *Proceedings of the IJCAI-99 Workshop on Intelligent Workflow and Process Management*.

[O'Hare and Jennings, 1996] O'HARE, G. M. P. AND JENNINGS, N. R., editors (1996). *Foundations of Distributed Artificial Intelligence*. Wiley & Sons, New York.

[OMG and FIPA, 1999] OMG AND FIPA (1999). Agent working group. http://www.objs.com/isig/wg-agents06-minutes.html.

[Opdyke, 1992] OPDYKE, W. F. (1992). *Refactoring Object-Oriented Frameworks*. PhD thesis, University of Illinois, Urbana-Champaign.

[Ormerod, 1990] ORMEROD, T. (1990). Human cognition and programming. In *Psychology of Programming*. Academic Press Ltd., London.

[Ousterhout, 1994] OUSTERHOUT, J. K. (1994). *Tcl and the Tk Toolkit*. Addison-Wesley Professional Computing.

[Parnas, 1996] PARNAS, D. (1996). Why Software Jewels are Rare. *IEEE Computer*, 29(2).

[Parnas and Clements, 1986] PARNAS, D. AND CLEMENTS, P. (1986). A Rational Design Process: How and Why to Fake It. *IEEE Transactions on Software Engineering*, SE-12(2).

[Parunak, 1995] PARUNAK, H. V. (1995). Case Grammar: A Linguistic Tool for Engineering Agent-Based Systems. Technical report, Industrial Technology Institute.

[Parunak, 1997] PARUNAK, H. V. (1997). 'Go to the Ant': Engineering Principles from Natural Agent Systems. *Annals of Operations Research*, 75:69–101.

[Parunak, 1999a] PARUNAK, H. V. (1999a). Blue-Collar Agents: Keynote of the PAAM99 conference. http://www.erim.org/~van/Presentations.

[Parunak, 1999b] PARUNAK, H. V. (1999b). *Multiagent Systems - A Modern Approach to Distributed Artificial Intelligence*, chapter 9. MIT Press.

[Parunak et al., 1997] PARUNAK, H. V., SAUTER, J., AND CLARKE, S. (1997). Towards the specification and design of industrial synthetic ecosystems. In *Proceedings of the 1997 Workshop on Agent Theories, Architectures, and Languages*.

[Pennington and Grabowski, 1990] PENNINGTON, N. AND GRABOWSKI, B. (1990). The tasks of programming. In *Psychology of Programming*. Academic Press Ltd., London.

[Pernici, 1990] PERNICI, B. (1990). Object with Roles. In *Proceedings of the ACM/IEEE International Conference on Office Information Systems*, Boston.

[Petre, 1990] PETRE, M. (1990). Expert programmers and programming languages. In *Psychology of Programming*. Academic Press Ltd., London.

[Petre and Winder, 1988] PETRE, M. AND WINDER, R. L. (1988). Issues governing the suitability of programming languages for programming tasks. In *People and Computers IV: Proceedings of HCI'88*, Cambridge. Cambrdige University Press.

[Petrie et al., 1998] PETRIE, C., GOLDMANN, S., AND RAQUET, A. (1998). Agent-Based Project Management. In *Artificial Intelligence Today*, number 1500 in LNAI. Springer.

[Philipps, 1998] PHILIPPS, S. (1998). Entwurf und Implementierung eines Systems zur Definition und Ausführung von Protokollen für Multi-Agentensystemen. Master's thesis, Fachhochschule Trier.

[Philipps and Lind, 1999] PHILIPPS, S. AND LIND, J. (1999). Ein System zur Definition und Ausführung von Protokollen für Multi-Agentensystemen. Technical Report RR-99-01, DFKI.

[Pitz, 1993] PITZ, W. (1993). Realisierung eines Systems zum verteilten, wissensbasierten Gleichheitsbeweisen mit Hilfe der Teamwork-Methode (in german). Master's thesis, Universität Kaiserslautern.

[Poore and Trammell, 1996] POORE, J. H. AND TRAMMELL, C. J. (1996). *Cleanroom Software Engineering: A Reader*. NCC Blackwell, Oxford.

[Programming Systems Lab, 1999] PROGRAMMING SYSTEMS LAB (1999). The mozart programming system. University of the Saarland. http://www.mozart-oz.org.

[Rao and Georgeff, 1995] RAO, A. S. AND GEORGEFF, M. (1995). BDI Agents: from theory to practice. In *Proceedings of the First International Conference on Multi-Agent Systems (ICMAS-95)*, pages 312–319, San Francisco, CA.

[Ratcliffe and Siddiqi, 1985] RATCLIFFE, B. AND SIDDIQI, J. A. (1985). An empirical investigation into problem decomposition strategies used in program design. *International Journal of Man-Machine Studies*, 22:77–90.

[Rational Software, 1999a] RATIONAL SOFTWARE (1999a). Goals of the UML. http://www.rational.com.

[Rational Software, 1999b] RATIONAL SOFTWARE (1999b).    Performace Engineering: A Practical Approach to Performance Improvement.  Whitepaper.
http://www.rational.com.

[Rawson, 1992] RAWSON, S. (1992).  *Analysing Organisations.*  The Macmillon
press.

[Robinson, 1965] ROBINSON, J. (1965).  A machine oriented logic based on the
resolution principle. *Journal of ACM 12,* 1:23–41.

[Rombach, 1994a] ROMBACH, H. D. (1994a). Vorlesungsscript Software Engineering I.

[Rombach, 1994b] ROMBACH, H. D. (1994b). Vorlesungsscript Software Engineering II.

[Rovatsos and Lind, 1999] ROVATSOS, M. AND LIND, J. (1999). Learning cooperation in repeated games. In *Proceedings of the IJCAI-99 Workshop on Agents
Learning About, From and With other Agents.*

[Rovatsos and Lind, 2000] ROVATSOS, M. AND LIND, J. (2000).    Hierarchical
common-sense interaction learning. In *Proceedings of the Fourth International
Conference on MultiAgent Systems,* Boston, MA, USA.

[Royce, 1970] ROYCE, W. W. (1970). Managing the development of large soft-
ware systems: Concepts and techniques. In *WESCON Technical Papers, v. 14,*
Los Angeles. WESCON. Reprinted in Proceedings of the Ninth International
Conference on Software Engineering, 1987, pp. 328–338.

[Rumbaugh et al., 1999] RUMBAUGH, J., JACOBSON, I., AND BOOCH, G. (1999).
*The Unified Modeling Language Reference Manual.* Addision-Wesley.

[Russell and Norvig, 1995] RUSSELL, S. AND NORVIG, P. (1995). *Artificial Intelligence: A Modern Approach.* Prentice Hall.

[Russell and Wefald, 1991] RUSSELL, S. J. AND WEFALD, E. H. (1991).  *Do the
Right Thing : Studies in Limited Rationality.* MIT Press.

[Saunders et al., 1996] SAUNDERS, T. F., HOROWITZ, B. M., AND MLEZIV, M. L.
(1996). A New Process for Acquiring Software Architecture. Mitre Corporation.

[Schillo et al., 1999] SCHILLO, M., LIND, J., FUNK, P., GERBER, C., AND JUNG,
C. (1999).  SIF - The Social Interaction Framework System Description and
User's Guide to a Multi-Agent System Testbed. Technical Report TR-99-02,
DFKI GmbH.

[Searle, 1969] SEARLE, J. R. (1969). *Speech Acts.* Cambridge University Press.

[Shaw, 1995] SHAW, M. (1995). Patterns for Software Architectures. In COPLIEN,
J. AND SCHMIDT, D., editors, *Pattern Languages of Program Design,* volume I.

[Shaw and Garlan, 1996] SHAW, M. AND GARLAN, D. (1996). *Software Architecture : Perspectives on an Emerging Discipline.* Prentice Hall.

[Shiffrin, 1973] SHIFFRIN, R. M. (1973).  Information persistence in short-term
memory. *Journal of Eperimental Psychology,* (100).

[Shoham, 1993] SHOHAM, Y. (1993). Agent-oriented programming. *Artificial Intelligence,* 60(1):51–92.

[Siemens AG, 1997] SIEMENS AG (1997). Verfahren und Anordnung zur Ermit-
tlung einer Route von einem Startpunkt zu einem Zielpunkt. Deutsche Paten-
tanmeldung 197 46 417.3.  Donald Steiner, Jürgen Lind, Alastair Burt and
Hartmut Dieterich.

[Sloman, 1996] SLOMAN, A. (1996).  What sort of architecture is required for a
human-like agent? In *Cognitive Modeling Workshop, AAAI96.* Invited Talk.

[Smith, 1997] SMITH, C. U. (1997). Performance Engineering for Software Architectures. In *Proceedings of the Twenty-First Annual International Computer
Software and Applications Conference (COMPSAC'97).* IEEE COMPUT. SOC.

[Smith, 1980] SMITH, R. (1980). The contract net protocol: High-level communication and control in a distributed problem solver. *IEEE Transactions on Computers.*

[Smolka, 1995] SMOLKA, G. (1995). The Oz programming model. In VAN LEEUWEN, J., editor, *Computer Science Today*, Lecture Notes in Computer Science, vol. 1000, pages 324–343. Springer-Verlag, Berlin.

[Smullyan, 1968] SMULLYAN, R. (1968). *First-Order Logic.* Springer.

[Sneed, 2000] SNEED, H. (2000). Source animation as a means of program comprehension for object-oriented systems. In *Proceedings of the 8th International Workshop on Program Comprehension (IWPC2000)*. IEEE Computer Society Press.

[So and Durfee, 1998] SO, Y. AND DURFEE, E. H. (1998). Designing Organizations for Computational Agents. In *Simulating Organizations*. MIT Press.

[Sommerville, 1995] SOMMERVILLE, I. (1995). *Software Engineering.* Addison-Wesley, 5th edition.

[Spada, 1990] SPADA, H., editor (1990). *Allgemeine Psychologie.* Verlag Hans Huber, Bern.

[Stallman and Free Software Foundation, 1999] STALLMAN, R. M. AND FREE SOFTWARE FOUNDATION (1999). Emacs. http://www.gnu.org.

[Steiner, 1992] STEINER, D. (1992). MEKKA: Eine Entwicklungsumgebung zur Konstruktion kooperativer Anwendungen. In MÜLLER, J. AND STEINER, D., editors, *Kooperierende Agenten*, number D-92-24 in DFKi Document Series, pages 17–21. DFKI, Saarbrücken.

[Stroustrup, 1987] STROUSTRUP, B. (1987). *The C++ Programming Language.* Addison-Wesley, Massachusetts.

[Sun Microsystems, 1999] SUN MICROSYSTEMS (1999). The Java Programming System. http://java.sun.com.

[Sun Microsystems, 2000] SUN MICROSYSTEMS (2000). Java Beans. http://java.sun.com/beans.

[Sundermeyer, 1993] SUNDERMEYER, K. (1993). Modellierung von agentensystemen. In *Verteilte Künstliche Intelligenz*. BI Wissenschaftsverlag.

[Tanenbaum, 1988] TANENBAUM, A. S., editor (1988). *Computer Networks.* Prentice Hall, 2nd edition.

[Tel, 1994] TEL, G. (1994). *Introduction to Distributed Algorithms.* Cambridge University Press.

[The DSDM Consortium, 1998] THE DSDM CONSORTIUM (1998). DSDM method overview. http://www.dsdm.org/.

[The International Organization for Standardization, 1997] THE INTERNATIONAL ORGANIZATION FOR STANDARDIZATION (1997). IS-9074 (Information processing systems/Open systems interconnection): Estelle — a formal description technique based on an extended state transition model.

[The International Organization for Standardization, 1998] THE INTERNATIONAL ORGANIZATION FOR STANDARDIZATION (1998). Iso-35.100.05 multilayer application.

[The VRML Consortium, 1997] THE VRML CONSORTIUM (1997). *The Virtual Reality Modeling Language, ISO/IEC DIS 14772-1.* unknown.

[Turing, 1937] TURING, A. M. (1937). On computable numbers, with an application to the entscheidungsproblem. *Proceedings of the London Mathematical Society*, 2(42).

[Visser, 1987] VISSER, W. (1987). Strategies in programming programmable controllers: a field study on a professional programmer. In OLSON, G., S.SHEPPARD, AND SOLOWAY, E., editors, *Empirical Studies of Programmers: Second Workshop*, Norwood, NJ. Ablex.

[Visser, 1990] VISSER, W. (1990). More or less following a plan during design: Opportunistic deviations in specification. *International Journal of Man-machine studies.*

[Voges and Mierau, 1997] VOGES, W. AND MIERAU, U. (1997). Train Coupling & -Sharing. In *Proceedings of the World Congress of Railway Research (WCRR),* Florence; Italy.

[Wall et al., 1996] WALL, L., SCHWARTZ, R. L., AND CHRISTIANSEN, T. (1996). *Programming Perl.* O'Reilly & Associates Inc., 2nd edition.

[Weiss, 1999] WEISS, G., editor (1999). *Multiagent Systems - A Modern Approach to Distributed Artificial Intelligence.* MIT Press.

[Wellman, 1996] WELLMAN, M. P. (1996). Market-Oriented Programming: Some Early Lessons. In CLEARWATER, S. H., editor, *Market-based Control.* World Scientific.

[Werner, 1988] WERNER, E. (1988). A formal computational semantics and pragmatics of speech acts. In *Proceedings COLING-88,* pages 744–749.

[Werner, 1989] WERNER, E. (1989). Cooperating agents: A unified theory of communication and social structure. In GASSER, L. AND HUHNS, M. N., editors, *Distributed Artificial Intelligence,* volume II.

[Windhoff AG, 1996] WINDHOFF     AG     (1996).             CargoSprinter. http://www.windhoff.de.

[Wirth, 1995] WIRTH, N. (1995). A plea for lean software. *IEEE Computer,* 28(2):64–68.

[Wisser and Hoc, 1990] WISSER, W. AND HOC, J.-M. (1990). Expert software design strategies. In *Psychology of Programming.* Academic Press Ltd., London.

[Wooldridge, 1997] WOOLDRIDGE, M. (1997). Agent-based software engineering. *IEE Proceedings on Software Engineering,* 144(1):26–37.

[Wooldridge and Jennings, 1995] WOOLDRIDGE, M. AND JENNINGS, N. R. (1995). Intelligent agents: Theory and practice. *The Knowledge Engineering Review,* 10(2):115–152.

[Wooldridge et al., 2000] WOOLDRIDGE, M., JENNINGS, N. R., AND KINNY, D. (2000). The gaia methodology for agent-oriented analysis and design. *Journal of Autonomous Agents and Multi-Agent Systems.* to appear.

[Wooldridge and Jennings, 1998] WOOLDRIDGE, M. J. AND JENNINGS, N. R. (1998). Pitfalls of agent-oriented development. In *Proceedings 2nd International Conference on Autonomous Agents (Agents-98),* pages 385–391, Minneapolis.

[Zappa, 1979] ZAPPA, F. (1979). Joe's garage. Munchkin Music.

[Zemanek, 1985] ZEMANEK, H. (1985). Formal definition the hard way. In NEUHOLD, E. J. AND CHROUST, G., editors, *Formal Models in Programming.* Elsevier, Amsterdam.

# Glossary

**Agent** An autonomous, pro-active, reactive entity with social abilities to interact with other entities.

**Agent Architecture** A structural model of the components that constitute an agent as well as the interconnections of these components together with a computational model that implements the basic capabilities of the agent.

**Aspect-Oriented Programming** A design technique that conceptualizes the idea of collecting several cross-cutting aspects of the software design in a single abstraction.

**Deployment** The process that covers all activities that are performed after a software system has been developed.

**Environment** Either the organizational or the runtime context of the target system.

**Experience Factory** A conceptual framework that supports systematic learning within an organization.

**Knowbble** A conceptual abstraction that can represent design entities such as design decisions or physical entities such as components, devices or code fragments.

**Knowbble aggregation** The process of grouping several knwobbles into a single abstraction that represents the entire group.

**Knowbble family** The transitive refinement closure of a collection of knowbbles.

**Knowbble Map** A visualization of knowbble families and/or views.

**Knowbble Refinement** The process of decomposing a single knowbble into several other knowbbles and therewith increasing the degree of detail of the model.

**Implementation** The manifestation of a design into the code of a particular programming language.

**Interaction** The mutual adaption of the behavior of agents.

**Iterative View Engineering** A software development model that combines Round-trip Engineering and Iterative Refinement.

**Multiagent System** Systems with a variable number of interacting, autonomous entities that communicate with each other using flexible, complex protocols.

**Notation** Is a language for communicating decisions that are not obvious or cannot be inferred from the code itself, that provides rich enough semantics sufficient to capture all important strategic and tactical decisions and offers a concrete form for humans to reason about decisions.

**Performance Engineering** A method to identify and reduce or eliminate performance problems during the software development cycle and the code has been designed and developed.

**Process Model** A formalization of the software design and implementation activities and of the products that are connected with these activities.

**Product Model** A representation of the characteristic features of a class of documents that constitute the description of a software system.

**PTA** A test domain for the FIPA agent standard and for multiagent system design in general.

**Role** A logical grouping of functions that obeys the physical constraints of the operational environment of the target system.

**Round-trip Engineering** A software engineering process model that combines constructive code generation with analytic model refinement.

**Shared Knowbble** A knowbble that belongs to several views at the same time and that represents a dependency between these views.

**Society** A structured set of agents that agree on a minimal set of acceptable behaviors.

**Social system** A society that implements a closed functional context with respect to a common goal.

**Software Development Method** A combination of a notation, whose purpose is to provide a common means of expressing strategic and tactical decisions, ultimately manifesting themselves in a variety of artifacts and a process, responsible for specifying how and when certain artifacts should be produced.

**System Architecture** The fundamental structural attributes of a software system.

**TCS** A novel approach in freight transport scheduling on the railway.

**Teamwork Approach** A programming scheme for distributed search in large, unstructured search spaces.

**UML** A general purpose description language for software blueprints.

**View** A set of conceptually linked knowbbles that forms a projection of the complete model onto a particular aspect.

# Index

# ecture Notes in Artificial Intelligence (LNAI)

# Lecture Notes in Computer Science